STUDIES IN ENGLISH LITERATURE

Volume VI

SYMBOL AND MEANING
IN THE FICTION OF
JOSEPH CONRAD

by

TED E. BOYLE

1965

MOUTON & CO.

LONDON THE HAGUE PARIS

Printed in the Netherlands.

To Mary

TABLE OF CONTENTS

I. INTRODUCTION

Conrad's theory of art, which rested on the truth of his own sensations, had much in common with impressionistic theory. But to call Conrad an impressionist is to saddle him with "one of the temporary formulas of his craft" (XXIII, xiv). [1] In an 1894 letter to Mme. Poradowska, Conrad commented on her novel *Le Mariage du Fils Grandsire* and indicated a distrust of his own impressionistic response to literature:

Mon appréciation de Votre livre – du tout livre – est purement émotionale. – De l'ouvrage, du travail, de la ciselure – si je puis m'exprimer ainsi – je ne peux guère juger; et comme l'émotion est une affaire personnelle mon jugement ne peut qu'être incomplet et bien souvent incorrect. [2]

He is not speaking as a novelist but as a judge of literature; however, it is obvious that the subjective approach which he rejects as a critic he would also reject as an artist.

Eleven years later, in an essay entitled "Books", Conrad discusses the novelist's craft and, while recognizing that the genesis of the creative process is inseparable from the artist's initial perception, he cautions the artist not to restrict himself to the experiences of his own imagination in violation of the actuality of human experience:

---

[1] Numbers following all quotations from Joseph Conrad not otherwise indicated refer to volume and page in the *Complete Works of Joseph Conrad*, 1926 Doubleday Edition.

[2] John D. Gordon, *Joseph Conrad: The Making of a Novelist* (Cambridge, Mass., 1940), p. 108.

In truth every novelist must begin by creating for himself a world, great or little, in which he can honestly believe. This world cannot be made otherwise than in his own image: it is fated to remain individual and a little mysterious, and yet it must resemble something already familiar to the experience, the thoughts and the sensations of his readers. (III, 6)

The artist, while creating his own world, must be cautious, lest he force his own sensations into some too-convenient pattern:

Let him mature the strength of his imagination amongst the things of this earth, which it is his business to cherish and know, and refrain from calling down his inspiration ready-made from some heaven of perfections of which he knows nothing. And I would not grudge him the proud illusion that will come sometimes to a writer: the illusion that his achievement has almost equalled the greatness of his dream. (III, 10)

Conrad also rejected the realistic approach to literature. In a 1902 letter to Bennett, Conrad discussed Bennett's *Man from the North*:

Here's a piece of pure metal scrupulously shaped, with a true – and more – a beautiful ring: but the die has not been struck hard enough. I admit that the outlines of the design are sharp enough. What it wants is a more emphatic modelling; more relief.... You stop just short of being absolutely real because you are faithful to your dogmas of realism. Now realism in art will never approach reality. And your art, your gift, should be put to the service of a larger and freer faith.[3]

Conrad recognized a reality beyond the mere phenomenal world, a reality which the artist could imagine and capture by giving a consistent form to the shapeless facts of actual human existence. Conrad was neither a Quixotic idealist who searched for some private epiphany nor a scientific realist who examined human specimens under a sterile microscope. He started with actuality and proceeded to the dream – the ideal which he felt only a disciplined art could attain. In describing Conrad's conception of the novel, one might well borrow the language of S. H. Butcher's famous summary of the Aristotelian conception of fine art:

[3]   G. Jean-Aubry, ed., *Joseph Conrad, Life and Letters* (Garden City, N. Y., 1927), I, 303.

The work of art was not a semblance opposed to reality, but the image of a reality which is penetrated by the idea, and through which the idea shows more apparent than in the actual world. Whereas Plato had laid it down that "the greatest and fairest things are done by nature, and the lesser by art, which receives from nature all the greater and primeval creations and fashions them in detail", Aristotle saw in fine art a rational faculty which divines nature's unfulfilled intentions, and reveals her ideal to sense. The illusions which fine art employs do not cheat the mind; they image forth the immanent idea which cannot find adequate expression under the forms of material existence.[4]

As is evidenced by the Author's Notes of the collected edition of his works and by the recollections which he makes in *A Personal Record* and *The Mirror of the Sea,* the source of many of Conrad's novels and tales is actual experience. Conrad the artist, however, was not content merely to restate experience in a coldly scientific manner. He felt a need to shape it, a need to discover the reality which lay hidden in the actuality of his own life. Thus, the merely incompetent Almayer of *A Personal Record* becomes to Conrad a symbol of all those men who are kept from entering into the spectacle of the universe by their own flabby illusions. Thus, the experiences of Conrad's Congo diary, when touched by the magic of his art, become a sort of mythic descent into the underworld.

In a letter to Cunninghame Graham in 1899 Conrad wrote:

I am simply in the seventh heaven to find you like the "H. of D." so far. You bless me indeed. Mind you don't curse me by and bye for the very same thing. There are two more instalments in which the idea is so wrapped up in secondary notions that you – even you! – may miss it. And also you must remember that I don't start with an abstract notion. I start with definite images and as their rendering is true some little effect is produced.[5]

Nineteen years later, in a letter to Barrett Clark he wrote:

Coming now to the subject of your inquiry, I wish at first to put

---

[4] S. H. Butcher, *Aristotle's Theory of Poetry and Fine Art* (New York, 1951), p. 160.
[5] Jean-Aubry, I, 268.

before you a general proposition: that a work of art is very seldom limited to one exclusive meaning and not necessarily tending to a definite conclusion. And this for the reason that the nearer it approaches art, the more it acquires a symbolic character. This statement may surprise you, who may imagine that I am alluding to the Symbolist School of poets or prose writers. Theirs, however, is only a literary proceeding against which I have nothing to say. I am concerned here with something much larger.[6]

In both of these letters, one written relatively early in his literary career, one relatively later, Conrad indicates that symbolism is an integral part of both the genesis and the substance of his art. Also in both letters there is a recognition of the multiplicity of meaning to which the symbolic method leads in its most artfully handled forms. Conrad was not an admirer of Melville, but had he commented on Melville's most famous symbol, the great white whale, he would have undoubtedly praised the ambiguity which surrounds Moby Dick as evidence of the vitality of Melville's symbolic design.

The best place to look for evidence of Conrad's symbolic mode of expression is, of course, not in his autobiographical writings, in his letters, or even in his author's notes, but in his novels and stories. The preceding brief view, indicative of the emphasis which Conrad placed upon the symbolic element in literature, is presented as a partial justification for an analysis of the symbolism in several of Conrad's novels and stories. Of course, such an analysis would be justified had Conrad never uttered a single word concerning the literary symbol. The rich symbolism of his work speaks for itself. But if it is an "intentional fallacy" to measure a work of literature against its author's design, is it not some other kind of fallacy to pretend that literature exists in a vacuum or that the artist is merely some kind of inferior brood animal?

It is the purpose of this book to demonstrate by an examination of the symbols in various of Conrad's novels and stories – those written early in his writing career, and those written relatively late – that Conrad's use of symbolism comprises one of the major

[6] Jean-Aubry, II, 204–205.

facets of his art. It is also hoped that this book shall serve to uncover the meaning of some of Conrad's more complex novels and tales through an explication of their symbolism. Heretofore, though the symbolic aspect of Conrad's art has by no means escaped notice, most critical attention has been directed toward investigation of Conrad's philosophical system. Few full-scale investigations of Conrad's symbolism have been done, and Conrad criticism is now entering a phase in which detailed studies of the text are most valuable. Conrad was somewhat neglected until after World War II, and those critics who inspired the post-war renaissance of Conrad studies necessarily had to content themselves with more general critiques than they would have perhaps wished. Theirs was the task of familiarizing the literate community with the body of Conrad's work; thus, they could devote only limited attention to close analysis of the text. Only one full-scale analysis of Conrad's symbolic system has been published to date, Paul Wiley's *Conrad's Measure of Man,* but even Professor Wiley is perhaps more interested in a study of Conrad's philosophic attitudes than in his symbolic and archetypal modes of presentation.

A detailed examination of Conrad's use of image, symbol and myth reveals a pattern so rich and complex that no amount of analysis can ever exhaust its full meaning. Such an analysis, however, serves to indicate yet another facet of Conrad's genius, and at the same time may indicate that the basic meaning of many of Conrad's more controversial works is a direct function of the symbols which the works contain.

II. ALMAYER'S FOLLY

" . . . a sigh which is not a sob, a
smile which is not a grin"

A. CRITICAL OPINION OF *ALMAYER'S FOLLY*

Almayer's Folly occupies a peculiar position in the body of
Conrad's work. It cannot be ranked with Conrad's great novels,
yet perhaps it is not really so inferior as some critics indicate. In
any case, the novel deserves a detailed analysis both because it
is Conrad's first novel and because it contains the embryonic
forms of many of the themes and character types with which
Conrad dealt in his later work.

In Almayer, with his dream of recovering a buried treasure,
is seen the same self-destroying romantic vision which Conrad
was to present so memorably in *Lord Jim.* In Almayer's disintegrative tragedy is prefigured the terrible decay of Kurtz of
"Heart of Darkness". Almayer, though he is surrounded by half-
savage Arabs and Malayans, is an isolated man having much in
common with Conrad's most famous hermit, Heyst. And, an
analysis of the significance of two of the most important and
fascinating characters in *Almayer's Folly,* Almayer's half-caste
daughter Nina and her savage mother, aids in interpreting the
role of many of the women characters in Conrad's later work.
Also present in *Almayer's Folly* is the subtle irony which was
to be an ever-present element in Conrad's fiction.

This is not to say that *Almayer's Folly* contains all the elements of Conrad's later fiction. There is no stolid, unimaginative
man of duty in *Almayer's Folly,* such as old Singleton of *The
Nigger of the "Narcissus",* Captain MacWhirr of "Typhoon" or
Captain Mitchell of *Nostromo.* And, certain elements of Con-

rad's first novel are unique – the ingenious Malay statesman Babalatchi is a character type which does not appear in Conrad's later works.

A good deal of critical misapprehension surrounds *Almayer's Folly*. A year before Conrad's death, Ernest Bendz described with admiration Conrad's ability to make real "the intricate and subtle workings of the Malay mind".[1] Vernon Young, some thirty years later, disagrees. Young states that at the time Conrad wrote *Almayer's Folly* he "had not yet mastered the portrayal of Malay psychology".[2] What both Bendz and Young seemingly do not notice is that the Far Eastern setting and the native characters of Conrad's first novel are only incidental to its real meaning. Babalatchi and Lakamba are indeed Malayan, but more important, they are human. White and dressed in Western clothes, they could handle the affairs of any Western nation with as much skill as they handle the affairs of the island kingdom of Sambir. Morton Zabel, while noting that *Almayer's Folly* is a work of promise, also emphasizes the locale of the novel to what seems an undue degree. Zabel writes: "*Almayer's Folly*, which combined exotic material with a passionate emotion unlike anything else then perceptible in English storytelling, announced an arresting talent. Men concerned with watching the weather of art were soon conscious of a new force in the air."[3]

If the Malay archipelago is an "exotic setting", it is certain that Conrad thought of this exotic quality as only a secondary matter. The fact that certain of his characters have brown skins and live in the jungle enables Conrad to employ some rather sharp irony. Babalatchi says that since Nina Almayer is half white, she of course has no decency, and Karain, waiting with his friend to ambush a white man, has trouble distinguishing just which white man to attack, for "those Dutchmen are all alike". But the characters in Conrad's Far Eastern tales are not

---

[1] Ernst Bendz, *Joseph Conrad: An Appreciation* (Gothenburg, 1923), p. 20.
[2] Vernon Young, "Lingard's Folly: The Lost Subject", *Kenyon Review*, XV (Autumn, 1953), 528.
[3] Morton D. Zabel, *The Portable Conrad* (New York, 1952), p. 6.

so much Arab, Malay or Dutch as they are human. They are not so much citizens of Sambir or Patusan as they are citizens of the world.

When Sir Hugh Clifford charged Conrad with knowing nothing of things Malayan, Conrad acquiesced readily. Conrad never claimed to have an expert's knowledge of the Malayan islands. He only hoped to reveal a small knowledge of the human heart. The Malay Karain confesses his crime to the narrator of one of Conrad's most "exotic" tales, but the fact that the sinner is brown and lives in the jungle and his confessor is white and lives on a ship is of no importance:

... words are spoken by the camp-fires, in the shared solitude of the sea, in riverside villages, in resting-places surrounded by forests – words are spoken that take no account of race or colour. One heart speaks – another one listens; and the earth, the sea, the sky, the passing wind and the stirring leaf, hear also the futile tale of the burden of life. (VIII, 26)

Unfortunately, many Conrad critics would, with Robert Haugh, dismiss *Almayer's Folly* as "for the sophisticated reader in Conrad".[4] However, Walter Wright, in his comprehensive book on Conrad, sees the indirect method of presentation in *Almayer's Folly* as "one of Conrad's major contributions for the artistic exploration of the mind".[5] Wright also recognizes that Conrad's presentation of Almayer's disintegration does not constitute an unqualified statement of pessimism. Almayer has, at the end of the novel, "discovered one great and bitter truth which he persisted in trying to deny – the meaninglessness of life as an assertion of one's ego".[6]

Paul Wiley in *Conrad's Measure of Man* also pays more than cursory attention to *Almayer's Folly*. Though his analysis of the novel is by no means detailed, he does note that allegorical and mythical undertones are present. Wiley adds credence to

---

[4] Robert Haugh, *Joseph Conrad: Discovery in Design* (Norman, Okla., 1957), p. vi.
[5] Walter F. Wright, *Romance and Tragedy in Joseph Conrad* (Lincoln, Neb., 1949), p. 126.
[6] Wright, p. 128.

Wright's earlier judgment of the qualified nobility of Almayer's tragedy, for as Professor Wiley asserts, "Almayer, for all his absurdity and weakness, acquires at the end a measure of tragic dignity which imparts a strong note of ambivalence to the conclusion of the tale with its reflections of the Schopenhauerian doctrine of life's cruelty".[7]

In view, then, of the fact that the perceptive, yet brief, analyses of Wright and Wiley constitute the most detailed criticisms which *Almayer's Folly* has received, a longer study of the novel, with attention to the essential symbolic elements of Conrad's art, would seem to be justified.

Perhaps there is a general lack of critical agreement concerning *Almayer's Folly* because it is presupposed to be an exotic tale and thus worthy of only one cursory reading. Indeed, on the first reading *Almayer's Folly* yields little but the impression of a confused mass of overdrawn symbolism created by an author with a naively pessimistic view of life. Subsequent readings, however, reveal that though many of the symbolic elements simply do not mesh with the plot, and though many of the descriptive passages are overwritten to the point of sentimentalism, Conrad at times demonstrates the unrestrained power of his genius as he evokes with the skillful employment of a symbolic or mythic referent that reality more beautiful than actuality.

B. THE FOUR GENERAL TYPES OF IMAGERY IN *ALMAYER'S FOLLY* AND THEIR SYMBOLIC FUNCTION

The images of *Almayer's Folly* are of four general types: imagery having to do with Almayer's materialistic imagination; that having to do with the half-caste Nina, her savage mother, and the slave Taminah; that concerning the sometimes sympathetic, sometimes indifferent moods of the natural world; and that reflecting Almayer's spiritual decay. As these images build to a cumulative effect they function as symbols, and the symbols thus

[7] Paul Wiley, *Conrad's Measure of Man* (Madison, Wis., 1954), p. 38.

created take their place in the general mythic structure of the story.

When *Almayer's Folly* opens, Almayer is already a defeated man, but he refuses to accept his defeat. He is dreaming of old Lingard's treasure and will not face the reality of his sordid existence:

He absorbed himself in his dream of wealth and power away from this coast where he had dwelt for so many years, forgetting the bitterness of toil and strife in the vision of a great and splendid reward. They would live in Europe, he and his daughter. They would be rich and respected. Nobody would think of her mixed blood in the presence of her great beauty and of his immense wealth. Witnessing her triumphs he would grow young again, he would forget the twenty-five years of heart-breaking struggle on this coast where he felt like a prisoner. All this was nearly within his reach. (XI, 3–4)

Almayer's dream is comparable to Jim's, in that it prevents him from immersing himself in the real world. It is different from Jim's dream, however, in that it is markedly less noble. As Jim's dream is one of heroic triumph, Almayer's is of material wealth. In fact, it is the dream of the immense wealth to be gained through trade with the natives that has lured Almayer to the decaying jungles of Sambir.

Before he began his term as Lingard's agent on Sambir, Almayer was employed in old Hudig's counting house at Macassar. While he dreams of conquering the world, he is intoxicated by the material wealth of the place, the "long and straight avenues of gin cases and bales of Manchester goods" (XI, 5), the "long table loaded with bottles of various shapes and tall water pitchers" (XI, 6) which occupy Hudig's inner office. Above all, Almayer is charmed by the discreet and continuous clink of the silver guilders being counted by the Chinese clerks.

In Hudig's counting house Almayer meets Tom Lingard, the soldier of fortune who roams the Malay seas in search of treasure and adventure. Lingard, in one of his fights with the Sulu pirates, has overwhelmed a pirate craft and there found a young Malay girl. He has adopted the girl and educated her in a convent, and at the time Almayer comes to work for Hudig, Lingard is looking for a husband for his adopted daughter.

After taking an inexplicable fancy to Almayer, Lingard proposes that the young clerk marry the girl. Anticipating Almayer's objections Lingard says:

"And don't you kick because you're white!" he shouted, suddenly, not giving the surprised young man the time to say a word. "None of that with me! Nobody will see the colour of your wife's skin. The dollars are too thick for that, I tell you! And mind you, they will be thicker yet before I die. There will be millions, Kaspar! Millions I say! And all for her – and for you, if you do what you are told." (XI, 10)

Just as Gentleman Brown intuitively senses the weakness in Lord Jim's character, Lingard perceives Almayer's weakness. Almayer is seduced by the vision of "great piles of shining guilders" (XI, 10), a palatial mansion in Amsterdam, and days of opulent leisure. As for the Malay girl, he knows that he will be untrue to the shallow white man's code by marrying her. He does not even vaguely realize, however, that he will initiate the destruction of his spirit by accepting her as a liability in a business contract.

Hudig's firm fails. Lingard, in an attempt to recoup his fortunes, travels to Europe and dies there, an evil, sentimental pirate to the end. But the silver guilders never cease to clink in Almayer's imagination. Anticipating that the British will press a territorial claim to Sambir, Almayer builds a new and larger house designed to accommodate the great flow of Englishmen who are sure to come. But the British abandon their claim. The Englishmen never come, and the Dutch name Almayer's new house Almayer's Folly.

Almayer's "strong and active imagination" (XI, 10) will not, however, allow him to recognize his miserable situation. While poring over a notebook which Lingard has left behind, Almayer decides that certain vague indications that the old man has left in his notebook point to a hidden treasure buried someplace deep in the inlands of Sambir. The silver guilders still clink in Almayer's imagination, and he transfers his dreams of material wealth from Almayer's Folly to Lingard's buried treasure. He is not to make a success of treasure hunting either;

but the distant imagined gleam of the buried treasure, the tepid breeze blowing through the empty rooms of Almayer's Folly, and the clink of silver guilders dominate Almayer's imagination and, thus, his entire life.

The deserted house, Almayer's Folly, is a symbol of the failure of Almayer's materialistic hopes. The pathetic nature of Almayer's failure and the congenital weakness which has led to this failure is further emphasized by Almayer's savage wife. The imagery which surrounds Mrs. Almayer clearly indicates that Conrad intends her to function as a symbol of savage woman incarnate. Soon after her marriage to Almayer, Mrs. Almayer begins to treat him with undisguised contempt. She is unfaithful to him with the Malay Lakamba and, in her hatred, she burns his furniture and rips the curtains from the walls of his house.

A daughter is born to Almayer and his wife, and when the daughter is still very young Tom Lingard returns and proposes that he take the young girl, Nina, to Singapore to be educated. Almayer dreads the separation from Nina, but also fears the reaction of his wife, "the tigress deprived of her young":

She will poison me, thought the poor wretch, well aware of that easy and final manner of solving the social, political, or family problems in Malay life.

To his great surprise she took the news very quietly, giving only him and Lingard a furtive glance, and saying not a word. This, however, did not prevent her the next day from jumping into the river and swimming after the boat in which Lingard was carrying away the nurse with the screaming child. Almayer had to give chase with his whale-boat and drag her in by the hair in the midst of cries and curses enough to make heaven fall. Yet after two days spent in wailing, she returned to her former mode of life, chewing betel-nut, and sitting all day amongst her women in stupefied idleness. (XI, 27)

Such extremes of emotion are clearly characteristic of the uncivilized mind. Mrs. Almayer has no spirit to be grieved at the loss of her daughter. Her reaction is purely physical, and, animal-like, she forgets quickly.

The convent education which Mrs. Almayer received, though it did not convert her to Christianity, made a formidable impression on her savage mind. Even after her marriage to Almayer, she continues to wear about her neck the little brass cross which the sisters at the convent gave to her. She is impressed by its "vague talismanic properties" (XI, 41), but has no notion of its Christian significance. In her hands it becomes a travesty of Christianity and civilization.

Mrs. Almayer is the priestess of the corrupt savage jungle from which she has sprung. Both Almayer and Babalatchi frequently refer to her as a witch. Fulfilling her function as savage priestess, before Nina escapes with Dain Maroola, Mrs. Almayer instructs her daughter in the lore of the barbaric woman:

"I was a slave, and you shall be a queen", went on Mrs. Almayer, looking straight before her; "but remember men's strength and their weakness. Tremble before his anger, so that he may see your fear in the light of day; but in your heart you may laugh, for after sunset he is your slave." (XI, 149)

She calls the white man's God a "woman god" (XI, 149) and combines threats and her occult influence to keep Nina from seeing Almayer one final time before she escapes with Maroola. She thus functions as a witch who appeals to Nina's half-savage nature and lures her daughter back to the barbaric code of the jungle.

Mrs. Almayer also reflects Almayer's absurd materialism. After serving dinner to her father one evening, Nina surprises her mother worshipping her treasure:

Entering, she saw that Mrs. Almayer had deserted the pile of mats serving her as bed in one corner of the room, and was now bending over the opened lid of her large wooden chest. Half a shell of cocoanut filled with oil, where a cotton rag floated for a wick, stood on the floor, surrounding her with a ruddy halo of light shining through the black and odorous smoke. Mrs. Almayer's back was bent, and her head and shoulders hidden in the deep box. Her hands rummaged in the interior, where a soft clink as of silver money could be heard. She did not notice at first her daughter's approach, and Nina, standing silently by her, looked down on many little canvas bags ranged in the bottom of the chest, wherefrom her mother extracted handfuls of shining guilders and Mexican dollars, letting them stream slowly back again through her claw-like fingers. The music of tinkling silver seemed to delight her, and her eyes sparkled with the reflected gleam of freshly-minted coins. She was muttering to

herself. "And this, and this, and yet this! Soon he will give more
– as much more as I ask. He is a great Rajah – a Son of Heaven!
And she will be a Ranee – he gave all this for her!" (XI, 66)

The tinkle of Mrs. Almayer's silver counterpoints the tinkle of
Hudig's great heap of silver guilders which Almayer has eter-
nalized in his imagination. Almayer, his illusions keeping him
from any decisive action, will never find his treasure horde.
Mrs. Almayer, who also dreams of great wealth and influence,
ironically achieves her goal through the barbaric expedient of
selling her daughter to Dain Maroola.

Almayer is not strong enough to overcome his wife. She makes
his existence almost unbearable, but more important, she wins
the contest for the daughter, Nina. Nina, whose "education
ended in an outburst of contempt from white people for her
mixed blood" (XI, 42), is torn between a sincere affection for
her father and a fascination for the savage ravings of her mother.
Though she preaches a creed of primitive avarice, Mrs. Almayer
wins, for in her mother's scheme Nina sees the promise of life.
In the sterile dreams of her father's imagination she sees captiv-
ity and death.

Nina seldom speaks to the natives of Sambir. She moves
among them "calm and white-robed, a being from another
world" (XI, 38). Neither of the white man's world nor of the
savage world of her mother, she awaits a prince to free her from
her enchanted state. Her liberator is indeed a prince, Dain
Maroola, the son of a Malay chieftain. Nina, to whom Maroola
is "the master of life" (XI, 149), flees from the decaying world
of her father to seek life as a Malay princess. In one of the last
conversations she has with her father, Nina says:

". . . both our voices, that man's and mine, spoke together in a sweetness
that was intelligible to our ears only. You were speaking of gold
then, but our ears were filled with the song of our love, and we did
not hear you. Then I found that we could see through each other's
eyes: that he saw things that nobody but myself and he could see.
We entered a land where no one could follow us, and least of all you.
Than I began to live." (XI, 179)

Instead of maintaining his civilized heritage Almayer has babbled of gold and has been defeated by his wife and the jungle. But to help Nina, to defeat his wife, would have necessitated the destruction of his flimsy dreams. Almayer loves his dream more than his daughter and, thus, loses her. She becomes, then, yet another symbol of Almayer's failure.

Besides Mrs. Almayer and Nina, there is yet another important female character in *Almayer's Folly*, Taminah, the slave girl. Each character in *Almayer's Folly* is to some degree deceived by an illusion, but Almayer and Taminah are the only ones whose illusions are so far removed from reality that they become destructive. Taminah desires Dain Maroola, but though she knows that love between a Malay prince and an Arab slave girl is impossible, with her dreams she nourishes her love. Almayer dreams of a mansion in Amsterdam; Taminah dreams of Dain Maroola.

After Maroola carries Nina off, Taminah is sold by her Arab master to the grotesquely ugly Babalatchi, the one-eyed prime-minister of Sambir. In a conversation with Captain Ford shortly before Almayer's death, Babalatchi reports her fate:

"Tuan", he said, "you remember the girl that man Bulangi had? Her that caused all the trouble?"

"Yes", said Ford. "What of her?"

"She grew thin and could not work. Then Bulangi, who is a thief and a pig-eater, gave her to me for fifty dollars. I sent her amongst my women to grow fat. I wanted to hear the sound of her laughter, but she must have been bewitched, and ... she died two days ago." (XI, 206–207)

Taminah, like Almayer, is bewitched by an impossible vision, and her death forms a part of the frame which surrounds Almayer's death.

The three women of Almayer's story, a Malayan savage, an Arab slave, and a beautiful half-caste girl are symbols of Almayer's failure. Mrs. Almayer stands as a symbol of his inability to overcome the savage necessities of his existence. Taminah's wretched death reflects Almayer's decay. Nina is a symbol of all that Almayer has lost through his shallowly romantic inaction.

An awareness of the symbolic relationship of each of these

three women to Almayer and his tragedy makes such criticisms as that of Vernon Young seem a bit misguided. Young sees Conrad's treatment of his female characters in *Almayer's Folly* as evidence of a deep-seated misogyny.[8] But one must give Conrad his "donnée". The female characters function as Conrad intended – to make Almayer's decay the more pathetic. They are consistent with the fictional world which Conrad created, and to accuse him of misogyny in fitting them into his story is only to wish that he had created a different fictional world.

The third general type of imagery in *Almayer's Folly* has to do with nature, and it is in the handling of this natural imagery that the major defect of this novel lies. Walter Wright justly criticizes Conrad for reading in nature "expressions of sentiment which would have caused Ruskin acute pain".[9] The natural imagery of *Almayer's Folly* is simply overdrawn. Just before Almayer loses Nina there is a terrible thunderstorm, obviously intended to prefigure Almayer's loss. When Dain Maroola and Nina sigh, the breeze sighs. They meet and "all the seething life and movements of tropical nature seemed concentrated in the ardent eyes, in the tumultuously beating hearts of the two beings drifting in the canoe, under the white canopy of mist, over the smooth surface of the river" (XI, 69–70). When in the forest Nina approaches Dain, Conrad cannot keep from making a brushwood fire their accomplice:

As he stood still, fighting with his breath, as if bereft of his senses by the intensity of his delight, she walked up to him with quick, resolute steps, and, with the appearance of one about to leap from a dangerous height, threw both her arms round his neck with a sudden gesture. A small blue gleam crept amongst the dry branches, and the crackling of reviving fire was the only sound as they faced each other in the speechless emotion of that meeting; then the dry fuel caught at once, and a bright hot flame shot upwards in a blaze as high as their heads, and in its light they saw each other's eyes. (XI, 171)

But strained as much of the natural imagery is, a good deal of it is so well presented that it enables the reader to have a more

8   Young, p. 529.
9   Wright, p. 55.

real sense of Almayer's folly. To catalogue the well-handled natural imagery in *Almayer's Folly* would indeed be a tedious process. It is sufficient to note that if all the natural imagery were poorly handled, the symbolic effect of the savage jungle would be either laughable or inconsequential. It is neither.

One aspect of the natural imagery in *Almayer's Folly,* the water imagery, does, however, deserve close attention, for it bears a direct symbolic relationship to Almayer's story. As the novel opens, Almayer, engrossed in his dreams of wealth and power, looks at the river which flows past his house:

There was no tinge of gold on it this evening, for it had been swollen by the rains, and rolled an angry and muddy flood under his inattentive eyes, carrying small drift-wood and big dead logs, and whole uprooted trees with branches and foliage, amongst which the water swirled and roared angrily.

One of those drifting trees grounded on the shelving shore, just by the house, and Almayer, neglecting his dream, watched it with languid interest. The tree swung around slowly, amid the hiss and foam of the water, and soon getting free of the obstruction began to move down stream again, rolling slowly over, raising upwards a long, denuded branch, like a hand lifted in mute appeal to heaven against the river's brutal and unnecessary violence. Almayer's interest in the fate of that tree increased rapidly. He leaned over to see if it would clear the low point below. It did; then he drew back, thinking that now its course was free down to the sea, and he envied the lot of that inanimate thing now growing small and indistinct in the deepening darkness. As he lost sight of it altogether he began to wonder how far out to sea it would drift. Would the current carry it north or south? South, probably, till it drifted in sight of Celebes, as far as Macassar, perhaps! (XI, 4)

Here Conrad lets his description of nature speak for itself. The flood does not splash sympathetic drops on Almayer's forehead; it merely does its job of carrying uprooted trees out to sea. Conrad's description of Almayer observing the river is the first step in a subtle and complex system of imagery which equates the river and the ocean with life, and the forest with death.

The river rushes headlong past Almayer's house to the ocean, but never until he pursues Nina does Almayer travel on the river. Lakamba, the fat Malay chieftain, makes his visits to the young

Mrs. Almayer by means of the river. Dain uses the river to carry him from his brig to Almayer's clearing where he woos Nina, and Dain and Nina consummate their love on the river. Later they escape on the river to the ocean which promises them life. As Dain waits for Nina to come to him he contemplates "the great blue sea that was like life" and "the forests that were like death" (XI, 169).

The river is clearly a symbol of the active, realistic life – sometimes cruel, sometimes gentle, but always dynamic, always flowing ceaselessly toward the ocean which is life. After Nina has left him for Dain Maroola and his wife has run away to Lakamba, Almayer burns his old house, the symbol of the only contact which he has had with reality during his years on Sambir. While the house containing Nina's dresses and Mrs. Almayer's crude treasure chest burns, Almayer, in what seems a grotesque parody of Sir Bedivere's consigning Excalibur to the Lady of the Lake, sends the key to his old house, the key to reality, "whizzing into the river" (XI, 200). He throws back at life the ugly reality which it would force upon him and moves his hammock and his blankets to the illusionary world of his decaying new house, Almayer's Folly.

Albert Guerard describes *Almayer's Folly* as a novel with no center of interest.[10] Certainly the novel does contain an almost infinitely complicated symbolic pattern, and the three patterns of imagery thus far discussed contribute to a seeming confusion of design in that their relevance to Almayer's tragedy is sometimes tangential. The fourth major pattern of imagery, however, the imagery of decay, clearly focuses on Almayer's spiritual disintegration and serves to knit up the entire complex system.

As the novel opens Almayer is standing on the verandah of "his new but already decaying house" (XI, 4), his folly, dreaming of the success of a new enterprise. When his imaginative reverie evaporates, he returns to his other decaying house:

The floor was uneven, with many withered plants and dried earth scattered about. A general air of squalid neglect pervaded the place.

---

[10]   Albert Guerard, *Conrad the Novelist* (Cambridge, Mass., 1958), p. 71.

The light breeze from the river swayed gently the tattered blinds, sending from the woods opposite a faint and sickly perfume as of decaying flowers. (XI, 16)

When Almayer entertains some Dutch colonial officers his table is laid with "ill assorted and shabby crockery . . . tin spoons . . . forks with broken prongs . . . knives with sawlike blades and broken handles" (XI, 124). The decay of Almayer's houses, the wretchedness of his standard of living, the jungle's "riot of silent destruction" (XI, 165) all reflect the decomposition of Almayer's romantic hopes and the accompanying disintegration of his spiritual being. All the imagery of decay in the novel centers in Almayer and renders his defeat almost inevitable. True, Almayer is a weak man and only in a limited sense "one of us", but his fate is so inescapable that instead of cursing his weakness we pity his helplessness.

In describing the final stage in Almayer's decline Conrad employs a grotesque imagery, the type of which has perhaps been matched in the novelistic form only by his predecessor Dickens and his successor Kafka. Before Almayer burns the old house which Lingard built for him and Mrs. Almayer, he inspects the office which it contains one final time:

He went towards the office door and with some difficulty managed to open it. He entered in a cloud of dust that rose under his feet. Books open with torn pages bestrewed the floor; other books lay about grimy and black, looking as if they had never been opened. Account books. In those books he had intended to keep day by day a record of his rising fortunes. Long time ago. A very long time. For many years there had been no record to keep on the blue and red ruled pages! In the middle of the room the big office desk, with one of its legs broken, careened over like the hull of a stranded ship; most of the drawers had fallen out, disclosing heaps of paper yellow with age and dirt. The revolving office chair stood in its place, but he found the pivot set fast when he tried to turn it. No matter. He desisted, and his eyes wandered slowly from object to object. All those things had cost a lot of money at the time. The desk, the paper, the torn books, and the broken shelves, all under a thick coat of dust. The very dust and bones of a dead and gone business. He looked at all these things, all that was left after so many years of work, of strife, of weariness, of discouragement, conquered so many times. And all for what? (XI, 199)

Almayer is a weak man, but what could he have done in the midst of the all-pervading corruption and decay which surrounded him. Had he been stronger he might have ruled his native charges as does Kurtz in "Heart of Darkness", and might have ascended to his inevitable decay rather than sinking to it with easy submission. But decay he must.

Clearly, the only salvation for Almayer would be for him to escape to the ocean as Dain and Nina do, for all the characters in the novel who remain on Sambir decay as Almayer does. Mrs. Almayer, who starts life on Sambir as a voluptuous though barbaric young Malayan, declines rapidly after Lingard takes the young Nina away and at the end of the story is a hag-like witch who watches jealously over a small pile of shiny coins. Taminah dies of grief at losing Dain Maroola. Even the old voluptuary Lakamba and his astutely deceitful prime minister Babalatchi are conquered by the impersonal forces of destruction which touch everything in Sambir. Babalatchi buys Taminah only to have her wither and die. Lakamba has increasingly more trouble with the Dutch and is forced to pay heavy fines and to curtail sharply his illegal activities. Abdulla, the Arab, who has easily overcome Almayer in the battle for native trade, suddenly realizes, as he looks at Almayer's lifeless body, that he, too, is caught up in the web of decay which stifles the small island of Sambir:

Abdulla looked down sadly at this Infidel he had fought so long and had bested so many times. Such was the reward of the Faithful! Yet in the Arab's old heart there was a feeling of regret for that thing gone out of his life. He was leaving fast behind him friendships, and enmities, successes, and disappointments – all that makes up a life; and before him was only the end. Prayer would fill up the remainder of the days allotted to the True Believer! He took in his hand the beads that hung at his waist. (XI, 208)

Almayer's Folly is a story with a definite center. The center, of course, is Almayer. In his death the various threads of imagery are connected. His death represents the triumph of the destructive powers inherent in his materialistic romanticism. It represents the triumph of the barbarity of which his wife is a symbol. It also represents the triumph of the savage jungle. Inasmuch as the imagery dealing with Almayer's materialistic vision, that dealing with woman as sorceress, and that concerned with the role of the natural world have in common the elements of decay and disintegration, and inasmuch as these elements are united in the more general imagery of decay which clearly focuses on Almayer, the novel can be demonstrated to center in him.

C. *ALMAYER'S FOLLY* AS MYTH, WITH SOME SUGGESTIONS CONCERNING THE DIGNITY OF ALMAYER'S DEATH

As Conrad subtly blended the imagery which he created in *Almayer's Folly* into a larger symbolic pattern, he likewise merged the symbols of the novel into a larger mythic pattern. Dain Maroola, as has been previously suggested, can easily be interpreted as a Malay knight-errant who carries the enchanted princess Nina off to a land where they can live happily ever after. Wiley briefly mentions the "heavy mythical and somewhat Wagnerian undertones" which are apparent in the narrative structure of *Almayer's Folly* and sees Dain Maroola as a Parsifal figure who "plays renegade rather than saviour".[11] Whether Conrad had any specific mythical knight in mind is perhaps doubtful, but it is evident that he did intend Dain Maroola to function as a chivalrous soldier figure. When he arrives in Sambir, Mrs. Almayer speaks of him as "a Son of Heaven" (XI, 51). The savage crew of his brig obey him as if he were a divinity. His dress is exceedingly handsome, and as he walks erect and indifferent he is accompanied "with a tinkle of gold ornaments" (XI, 114). In addition, he possesses the romantic love of adventure, the martial enthusiasm, and the desire for wealth and glory which are commonly associated with the knight figure.

As Wiley suggests, however, Dain Maroola might seem more of a renegade than a saviour. The quest which brings him to

---

[11] Wiley, pp. 34–35.

Sambir is by no means spiritual. He is in search of gunpowder with which his father can carry on his wars. In order to get Almayer to act as an agent in the illegal gunpowder transactions, Dain promises the Dutchman that he will furnish him with the men and the boats necessary to journey up river in quest of Lingard's buried treasure. But he never intends to keep this promise. In addition, he steals Almayer's daughter. It is easy to see, then, how Dain Maroola could be labeled a renegade.

Dain does not, however, break any of the rules of his Malay warrior code. He is loyal and generous to his followers and extremely brave in battle. And his lying to Almayer does not seem quite so deceitful in view of Dain's proud Malayan belief that the white men in the Malayan islands are there as conquerors who are bleeding the natives of their wealth. Viewed in the mythic referent of the story, his carrying Nina off is not an act of betrayal but the rescue of a maiden in distress from an ogre parent.

In Almayer's household Nina moves as if she were in an enchanted state. She sees "the days rush by into the past, without a hope, a desire, or an aim that would justify the life she had to endure in ever-growing weariness" (XI, 151). Even Almayer is "awed by the calm impassiveness of her face, by these solemn eyes looking past him on the great, still forests sleeping in majestic repose to the murmur of the broad river" (XI, 31). As Almayer's daughter Nina is exposed to the disrespect of white man and native alike. Babalatchi says Nina is "half white and has no decency" (XI, 128). A young Dutch officer who visits Almayer's household feels no shame at the lustful glances which he directs toward Nina because, as he reasons, she is "after all a half-caste girl" (XI, 126).

Dain Maroola offers Nina an escape from the sterile enchantment of her father's world, and though Nina's decision to go with Dain may represent a regression to the savage instincts of her mother, it also represents the choice of life over death. Almayer would keep Nina from Dain and prevent life from going its own way; Dain, a life force symbol, shatters the enchanted spell which the ogre Almayer has cast on his daughter. Before she leaves her father Nina says to him:

"You wanted me to dream your dreams, to see your own visions – the visions of life amongst the white faces of those who cast me out from their midst in angry contempt. But while you spoke I listened to the voice of my own self; then this man came, and all was still; there was only the murmur of his love." (XI, 179)

Concerning the Nina-Dain Maroola love affair, Thomas Moser writes:

Conrad does not tell us, however, why he felt compelled to include in his first novel the love story of Almayer's daughter, Nina, and the handsome Malay, Dain Maroola. It does not really matter; perhaps his purpose was no more mysterious than a vague feeling that since most novels he knew (particularly English ones) included a romantic love story, his should also. [12]

Conrad is perhaps guilty of telling us too much in *Almayer's Folly*, but in the case of the young lovers he does not "tell" us but makes us "see". The life-giving force of their love stands in sharp contrast to the shallow helplessness of Almayer's egoism. Perhaps their love even serves the purpose of softening Almayer's tragedy, for his disintegration might be altogether too painful were it not for the contrasting beauty of the love which Dain and Nina discover.

If the Dain-Nina love affair is interpreted in terms of the suggested mythic referent as an integral part of the narrative of Almayer's decay, a further softening of Almayer's fate presents itself. It is in fulfilling his role as the archetypal jealous father that Almayer comes to at least an imperfect self-knowledge. The actions which Almayer performs in his attempt to keep Nina from fleeing with Dain are almost comic in their impotence, but they are the first really decisive actions which he takes. When he learns that Nina intends to leave him, the spell of his destructive dream is broken. He arms himself with a revolver and pursues the lovers, intending to kill Dain. Dain, of course, easily disarms Almayer, but the quality of the gesture,

---

[12] Thomas Moser, *Joseph Conrad: Achievement and Decline* (Cambridge, Mass., 1957), pp. 51–52.

which indicates that the Dutchman has escaped at least temporarily from his egoism, remains.

Before Dain Maroola carried Nina off, Almayer was almost completely indifferent to her fate. Influenced by old Lingard, he let the young Nina be taken from him to be educated in Singapore. When she unexpectedly returned, he was so engrossed in his own plans that he asked his daughter for no explanation: "He did not care to ask" (XI, 31). He could not fathom the storm of anger and humiliation which raged in his daughter's soul, for his sight was "dimmed by self-pity, by anger, and by despair" (XI, 103). The last time Almayer speaks to Nina, however, his anger seems temporarily to transcend his egotism. He vows that he will never forgive her for leaving him. She responds:

"What is there to forgive?", asked Nina, not addressing Almayer directly, but more as if arguing with herself. "Can I not live my own life as you have lived yours? The path you would have wished me to follow has been closed to me by no fault of mine."

"You never told me", muttered Almayer.

"You never asked me", she answered, "and I thought you were like the others and did not care. I bore the memory of my humiliation alone, and why should I tell you it came to me because I am your daughter? I knew you could not avenge me."

"And yet I was thinking of that only", interrupted Almayer, "and I wanted to give you years of happiness for the short day of your suffering. I knew only of one way."

"Ah! but it was not my way!", she replied. "Could you give me happiness without life? Life!" she repeated with sudden energy that sent the word ringing over the sea." (XI, 190)

Certainly Almayer's attempted rescue of his daughter is somewhat marred by the fact that she holds a central place in his dreams of wealth and power. Yet, when he pursues Nina, his illusions have been completely shattered. He knows Dain will not help him search for Lingard's treasure. Thus, he does not pursue Nina because he sees her as a princess who will share with him a palatial mansion in Amsterdam. For the first time he realizes that she is a human being with emotions which transcend his materialistic dream. In short, Almayer finally realizes that Nina is his daughter and that losing her will make his existence even more miserable. He is disenchanted, if only for a moment.

When Nina has convinced her father that she loves Dain more than life itself, Almayer helps the couple to escape the Dutch authorities who are hoping to hang Dain for his murder of two white men. But the quality of this action is ambiguous. Almayer almost leaves the young lovers to be captured by the Dutch authorities, but at the last moment changes his mind and offers a despicably egoistic excuse:

"I cannot", he muttered to himself. After a long pause he spoke again a little lower, but in an unsteady voice, "It would be too great a disgrace. I am a white man." He broke down completely there, and went on tearfully, "I am a white man, and of good family. Very good family", he repeated, weeping bitterly. "It would be a disgrace . . . all over the island, . . . the only white man on the east coast. No, it cannot be . . . white men finding my daughter with this Malay. My daughter!" he cried aloud, with a ring of despair in his voice. . . . "You, Dain, or whatever your name may be, I shall take you and that woman to the island at the mouth of the river myself. Come with me." (XI, 184)

This is not, of course, the clear-headed act of renunciation which we expect from the typical tragic hero. It is, however, the type of act compounded of equal parts of misguided intention and muddled thinking that we have come to expect of Almayer as Conrad created him.

The classic tragic hero discovers reality and then faces it no matter what the cost. Almayer discovers reality and then shrinks further from it into the world of his Folly, where, with opium, he attempts to forget his daughter and his false hopes. At the last he does succeed:

The only white man on the east coast was dead, and his soul, delivered from the trammels of his earthly folly, stood now in the presence of Infinite Wisdom. On the upturned face there was that serene look which follows the sudden relief from anguish and pain, and it testified silently before the cloudless heaven that the man lying there under the gaze of indifferent eyes had been permitted to forget before he died. (XI, 208)

Almayer does not choose the path of courage for he is not a courageous man. Yet, in his weakness he demonstrates, at least imperfectly, some of the strength of the human spirit. He does not die because of his disappointed materialistic hopes, but because of his discovery that no man can exist without the love and compassion of another human spirit. Almayer is, then, in the strength of his imperfection, "one of us": *"Qui de nous n'a eu sa terre promise, son jour d'extase, et sa fin en exil?"* (Epigraph to *Almayer's Folly*).

D. A BRIEF INDICATION OF SOME OF THE INADEQUACIES OF *ALMAYER'S FOLLY*

Almayer's Folly, though a remarkable first novel, is, nevertheless, imperfect. The natural imagery is so overdrawn that it tends to smother plot and character development. The jungle, at times, seems to be more important and, indeed, frequently exhibits more intense emotions than do the main characters of the novel. Conrad could not, as did Hardy in *Tess of the d'Urbervilles,* make nature a highly important background and yet keep the trees and the river and the clouds from entering almost directly into the action of the narrative. The handling of much of the natural imagery in *Almayer's Folly* is certainly clumsy, and, if fallacious, truly pathetically so.

Much of the symbolism in Conrad's first novel is top heavy. Mrs. Almayer functions admirably as a symbol of the savage woman, but she seldom is probable as a flesh and blood human being. Almayer's Folly itself is an admirably conceived symbol, but Conrad, as if he were not confident of his ability to make the reader "see", must again and again "tell" him what Almayer's deserted ruin stands for. The young lovers of *Almayer's Folly,* symbol of the vital life which Almayer has forsaken, though never as ill-conceived as Moser would suggest,[13] frequently speak and act in such a stereotyped manner that they are almost ridiculous. In short, in *Almayer's Folly* Conrad reveals that he

[13] Moser, pp. 51–52.

has not yet attained either mastery of or self-confidence in the symbolic method which he conceived as such a vital part of the art of the novel. He was to have difficulty with the symbolic method again, but he demonstrated through most of his thirty years as a writer a mastery of the symbolic conception that has seldom been equalled in the novelistic form.

It took Conrad only two years to move from the partial failure of *Almayer's Folly* to the unqualified success of *The Nigger of the "Narcissus"*.

III. THE NIGGER OF THE "NARCISSUS"

"...there is both a moral and an excitement
in a faithful rendering of life."

A. CRITICAL OPINIONS AND MISCONCEPTIONS

The Nigger of the "Narcissus" contains such consummately
wrought realistic detail that the symbolic interpretation of the
narrative is often overlooked. Even some of those readers who
perceive Conrad's brilliant symbolic expression in *The Nigger*
are at times dismayed at the wealth of detail which the story
contains. Vernon Young feels that "Conrad overloaded his mun-
dane treatment of the crew"[1] and argues that the emphasis on
professional virtue almost destroys the aesthetic integrity of the
novel. Paul Wiley says that "the world of *The Nigger* is still
that of the sailing ship"[2] and that "the standard of conduct
which has formed Singleton and the rest of his generation would
come to lose meaning for a world of men of a different order".[3]

However, the argument that there is any significant fault
either in the conception or the execution of *The Nigger of the
"Narcissus"* is rather tenuous. Certainly, Conrad emphasizes the
sailors as competent workmen, for it is their devotion to duty
which enables them to master the evil Wait and his tattered
Mephistopheles, Donkin. Singleton's standard of conduct may
well come to lose meaning, but not until Marlow succumbs to
Kurtz, or MacWhirr decides that he would rather save his life
than the *"Nan-Shan"*.

---

[1] Vernon Young, "Trial by Water: Joseph Conrad's *The Nigger of
the 'Narcissus' "*, *Accent,* XII (Spring, 1952), 80.
[2] Paul Wiley, *Conrad's Measure of Man* (Madison, Wis., 1954), p. 50.
[3] Wiley, p. 49.

The world of *The Nigger* is much larger than that of the sailing ship, and would be so even if Conrad did not call the *Narcissus* "a small planet ... a fragment detached from the earth". [4] (XXIII, 29) The men of the *Narcissus* are merely rude sailors, but the problems of conduct which they encounter are the ancient, universal ones which all mankind must face. In 1916 Hugh Walpole wrote:

In *The Nigger of the "Narcissus"* the death of the negro, James Wait, immediately affects the lives of a number of very ordinary human beings whose friends and intimates we have become – but that shadow that traps the feet of the negro, that alarms the souls of Donkin, of Belfast, of Singleton, of the boy Charlie, creeps also to our sides and envelopes for us far more than that single voyage of the *Narcissus*. [5]

There is, as Walpole suggests, both a situational and a symbolic truth in the voyage of the *Narcissus*. But the symbolic elements in *The Nigger* are not, as those in *Almayer's Folly* and *An Outcast of the Islands* often are, superimposed on the narrative in an attempt to render it more universal. The symbolic elements in *The Nigger* are the cumulative effect of the narrative's realistic detail.

Before Conrad asks us to accept James Wait as a symbol of evil presumption, he skillfully creates James Wait, the malingering seaman. Wait is so well drawn on the realistic level that he could well be a private in a modern infantry company. He would receive the same distrust and the same sympathy from his fellow soldiers. He would be able to shirk his duties just as well, for the commanding officer, like Allistoun, would realize the dangers of forcing a possibly sick man to work. The nigger would receive the same curses, the same protection, the same adulation that he receives on board the *Narcissus*.

---

[4] Albert Guerard, *Conrad the Novelist* (Cambridge, Mass., 1958), p. 103, calls Conrad's references to the ship as microcosm "Victorian obviousness". Obvious as the ship-world metaphors may be, however, they are not a device employed to give a superficial universality to the plot. They are never forced, but spring quite naturally from the smaller world which Conrad has created.
[5] Hugh Walpole, *Joseph Conrad* (New York, 1916), p. 86.

The ship is in perfect order before Wait comes aboard:

The carpenter had driven in the last wedge of the mainhatch battens, and, throwing down his maul, had wiped his face with great deliberation, just on the stroke of five. The decks had been swept, the windlass oiled and made ready to heave up the anchor; the big towrope lay in long bights along one side of the main deck, with one end carried up and hung over the bows, in readiness for the tug that would come paddling and hissing noisily, hot and smoky, in the limpid, cool quietness of the early morning. (XXIII, 3–4)

Mr. Baker, the chief mate, musters the crew, and the roll call proceeds in an orderly fashion, only briefly interrupted by the appearance of the grotesque Donkin. Each man, as his name is called by Mr. Baker, steps from the darkness of the starboard side of the ship into the circle of light which Mr. Baker's lantern casts, and then again into the darkness on the port side of the ship. Only sixteen of the ship's seventeen seamen answer muster. There is one missing, but Mr. Baker cannot read the name of the missing man, for on the piece of white paper which Baker holds in his hand, where the missing man's name should appear there is only a smudge. Before the ship's company has broken formation the missing crewman appears and shouts his name:

"Wait!" cried a deep, ringing voice.
All stood still. Mr. Baker, who had turned away yawning, spun round open-mouthed. At last, furious, he blurted out: – "What's this? Who said 'Wait'? What . . ."
But he saw a tall figure standing on the rail. It came down and pushed through the crowd, marching with a heavy tread towards the light on the quarter-deck. (XXIII, 17)

When Baker asks Wait what he is doing on board the *Narcissus,* Wait simply replies: "I belong to the ship" (XXIII, 18).

There is a scrupulous attention to realistic detail in the first few pages of *The Nigger.* Conrad certainly cannot be accused of attempting some sort of symbolistic trickery in these pages. The events which he describes here are "trivial enough on the surface to have some charm for the man on the street".[6] There

---

[6] G. Jean-Aubry, ed., *Joseph Conrad, Life and Letters* (Garden City, N. Y., 1927), I, 197.

is hardly the slightest hint that these first incidents in the novel have any symbolic significance, yet when the narrative of *The Nigger* is complete, the events surrounding Wait's coming on board the *Narcissus* are seen to foreshadow the symbolic pattern of the novel. When the ship's company step from darkness into light and back into darkness, they prefigure the spiritual voyage which the *Narcissus* is to make. The *Narcissus* sails from the darkness of Bombay to the darkness of London, but it sails through a patch of light when its crew remains true to duty and overcomes the influence of Wait and his hateful emissary, Donkin. The missing crewman's name is smudged beyond recognition. Later, the smudged name is seen as a token of the perfect imperfection of James Wait. When Wait shouts his name, the crew is momentarily confused. Later they are to vacillate between the measured forms of the orders of Mr. Baker and Captain Allistoun and the chaotic influences of James Wait. James Wait "belongs" to the ship because he has been signed on by Captain Allistoun. When Wait's devilish influence is clearer, he can be seen as a symbol of that elemental, ubiquitous evil which "belongs" to any human endeavor.

B. THE SYMBOLIC AND MYTHIC REFERENTS OF *THE NIGGER*

The real and the symbolic in *The Nigger of the "Narcissus"* are one. Combining the reality of his own experience with the truth of his artistic vision, Conrad created a richly complex synthesis which reveals archetypal and mythic patterns.

1. *Allistoun as God-father figure*

Captain Allistoun is an unmistakable God-father figure. He is coeval with his ship: "He had commanded the *Narcissus* since she was built .... He, the ruler of that minute world, seldom descended from the Olympian heights of his poop. Below him – at his feet, so to speak – common mortals led their busy and insignificant lives" (XXIII, 30–31). It is significant that when the *Narcissus* turns over on her side, the crew must ascend to Allistoun's quarterdeck to escape drowning. There they gain a mysterious strength from the old captain who "seemed with his eyes to hold the ship up in a superhuman concentration of effort" (XXIII, 65). The captain's words upon leaving the ship are also highly charged with symbolism: "Don't forget to wind up the chronometers tomorrow morning" (XXIII, 165). The forces of evil represented by Wait and Donkin achieve temporary victories, but in the end they are easily overcome by the omnipotent master of this small planet.

The voyage is hardly underway before Allistoun calls Wait to his cabin and orders him to lie up. Shortly thereafter, Baker reports that Wait's presence in the forecastle is causing dissension, and Allistoun exiles the nigger from the forecastle to a cabin on deck. Jimmy's exile cheers him a bit, for now he has his own small kingdom to rule:

Knowles affirmed having heard him laugh to himself in peals one day. Others had seen him walking about on deck at night. His little place, with the door ajar on a long hook, was always full of tobacco smoke. We spoke through the crack cheerfully, sometimes abusively, as we passed by, intent on our work. He fascinated us. (XXIII, 46)

2. *Wait as Devil*

Wait is not heroic enough a figure to be "hurled headlong flaming from the etheral sky", as is Milton's Satan, nor is Wait immortal, as is the Satan of Christian mythology. Yet, the general scheme of his conflict with authority and his exile is the same as that of Christian myth. Wait is the Devil of the *Narcissus*, and his cabin is the microcosmic hell which the ship must carry with it.

Wait, like the Satan of Christian myth, is an imposing specimen:

The nigger was calm, cool, towering, superb. The men had approached and stood behind him in a body. He overtopped the tallest by half a head. He said: "I belong to the ship." He enunciated distinctly, with soft precision. The deep, rolling tones of his voice filled the deck without effort. He was naturally scornful, unaffectedly condescending, as if from his height of six foot three he had surveyed all the vastness of human folly and had made up his mind not to be too hard on it. (XXIII, 18)

In fact, Conrad's description of James Wait in Chapter One of *The Nigger* echoes Milton's description of Satan in Book One of *Paradise Lost*. Milton's Satan "above the rest/In shape and gesture proudly eminent, / Stood like a tower. His form had yet not lost / All her original brightness." There are further echoes of Milton in Conrad's description of the nigger. Milton, describing his Satan, writes:

> Darkened so, yet shone
> Above them all th' Archangel: but his face
> Deep scars of thunder had intrenched, and care
> Sat on his faded cheek, but under brows
> Of Dauntless courage, and considerate pride
> Waiting revenge. Cruel his eye, but cast
> Signs of remorse and passion, to behold
> The fellows of his crime, the followers rather
> (Far other once beheld in bliss), condemned
> For ever now to have their lot in pain –

From the face of James Wait also emanates an ugly pride:

The folly around him was confounded. He was right as ever, and as ever ready to forgive. The disdainful tones had ceased, and, breathing heavily, he stood still, surrounded by all these white men. He held his head up in the glare of the lamp – a head vigorously modelled into deep shadows and shining lights – a head powerful and misshapen with a tormented and flattened face – a face pathetic and brutal: the tragic, the mysterious, the repulsive mask of a nigger's soul. (XXIII, 18)

In spite of his magnificent physique, however, James Wait is a hollow man, and by subtle employment of images denoting insubstantiality, Conrad makes a disembodied prince of darkness out of James Wait, the St. Kitt's negro. The first time Wait's ominous cough is heard, it resounds "like two explosions in a

vault" (XXIII, 18). Shortly afterward, when several of the crew
are engaged in a noisy argument about the definition of a
gentleman, Wait, whose sleep has been disturbed, appears in the
dark doorway of the forecastle. "Wait's head protuding, became
visible, as if suspended between the two hands that grasped a
doorpost on each side of the face" (XXIII, 34). There is an
ascending intensification of the images of hollowness which
reaches its climax when Wait is rescued from his cabin during
the storm. The narrator, an unnamed member of the rescue
party, reports that when Wait was pulled through the small hole
chopped for him in the side of his cabin, "he seemed positively
to escape from our hands like a bladder full of gas. . . . He glared
with his bulging eyes, mute as a fish, and with all the stiffening
knocked out of him . . . he was only a cold black skin loosely
stuffed with soft cotton wool" (XXIII, 70, 71). He was like a
"doll that had lost half its sawdust" (XXIII, 72). These images
combine to lend to James Wait that spectral quality which he
must possess as the Devil of the *Narcissus*. When the crewmen
drag the incorporeal black mass to the poop deck, they not only
save Wait from drowning, they retrieve the evil, unearthly
hollowness which he represents.

The rescue of Wait also demonstrates the exact nature and
full power of his evil. His wickedness is not overt, and, thus, it
is all the more powerful. The officers and the crew of the
Narcissus can handle a direct attack on their solidarity relatively easily, as is evidenced by the utter defeat which Donkin
suffers each time he attempts such an attack. Wait's corrupt
influence is paradoxical in that he achieves his evil not by
directly appealing to that weakness which exists in the collective
soul of the crew, but by appealing to their noblest instincts and
perverting them.

In saving Wait, the crew evidence an instinct for solidarity.
They save their trapped shipmate even at the risk of their own
lives. But at the same time they rescue Jimmy, they retrieve an
evil which will later very nearly destroy the ship. Conrad conceived that the evil which threatens mankind's existence is seldom
of a clearcut nature. The commanding officer of the patrol ship

in "The Tale" does not fear the night, for "the night blinds you frankly". He does, however, fear the deceitful fog and mist in which it is difficult to tell whether an action shall result in good or evil.

The rescue party, after making their way across the deck to the cabin in which Jimmy is trapped, discover that in order to save Jimmy they must chop through a bulkhead which separates the carpenter's shop from the nigger's prison. The ship is on her side. All doors have become trapdoors and the bulkhead of the carpenter's shop, which has become a floor, is covered with nails:

They lay in a solid mass more inabordable than a hedgehog. We hesitated, yearning for a shovel, while Jimmy below us yelled as though he had been flayed. Groaning, we dug our fingers in, and very much hurt, shook our hands, scattering nails and drops of blood. We passed up our hats full of assorted nails to the boatswain, who, as if performing a mysterious and appeasing rite, cast them wide upon a raging sea. (XXIII, 68)

The nails, the normal function of which is to fasten things together, clearly function here as a symbol of that solidarity which must be cast overboard if Wait is to live. And the blood which is mixed with the nails as they are cast overboard is the libation which the men of the *Narcissus* must pour out before they can descend into the underworld to rescue the Devil of the *Narcissus,* James Wait. In their frantic efforts to save Wait, the men curse the Clyde shipwrights for building the bulkhead so well. Wait has caused the crew to wish to destroy the very strength of the ship which enables it to ride out the storm. The implications of this powerfully conceived scene are, of course, almost endless; but no matter how it is interpreted, it symbolizes the terrible power which Wait exercises over the crew of the *Narcissus*.

The evil of James Wait is passive. It infects the soul of the crew and initiates a process of slow decay. However, when Wait's subtle subversions are complemented by Donkin's direct ones, a sudden and complete disintegration of the ship's discipline nearly occurs. Wait, shortly before his death, threatens to come back on deck and assume his duties, but Allistoun refuses to let him do so, for the master feels humanitarian pity for Wait and also recognizes that the nigger's return represents a direct challenge to authority. Wait's emissary, Donkin, agitates for the nigger's return and succeeds in fostering a near mutiny, which reaches its peak when Donkin throws an iron belaying pin at the backs of the two mates. The mates are enraged and nearly lose control of the situation when Mr. Baker advances toward the knot of angry men. Allistoun, however, controls the situation easily. He is as remote and assured as a divinity: "He was one of those commanders who speak little, seem to hear nothing, look at no one – and know everything, hear every whisper, see every fleeting shadow of their ship's life" (XXIII, 125). The morning after the belaying pin incident, the captain musters the crew, reminds them of their duty, and in a ritual which affirms his authority, forces Donkin to replace the belaying pin in its proper place. Allistoun is the master. He is bothered no more by the active evil of Donkin than by the passive evil of Wait.

Allistoun cannot, however, protect his men from the evil influence of Wait and Donkin. The crew must overcome this evil without their captain's direct intervention. The captain, as the ruler of the small planet the *Narcissus,* can only hope that his charges will avail themselves of the crude wisdom of the patriarch Singleton and the gift of grace represented by the ship's work.

3. Work as Grace

The routine duties of the ship enable the men to conquer their weakness, to identify themselves with a value outside themselves. In the ritual of work they wring out a meaning from their sinful lives and become shareholders in their mutual joint-stock world. At every crucial point in the narrative, when the solidarity of the crew is threatened, their unconscious devotion to duty saves them.

When the ragged scarecrow Donkin comes on board, he

straightaway causes confusion in the forecastle. Donkin's crewmates pity his miserable condition and with a wave of sentiment donate their old gear to him. Donkin thanks them by threatening the man who he perceives is the most vulnerable member of the crew, the imbecilic Wamibo. But before Donkin can start a fight with Wamibo,

... many heavy blows struck with a handspike on the deck above like discharges of small cannon through the forecastle. Then the boatswain's voice rose outside the door with an authoritative note in its drawl: – "D'ye hear, below there? Lay aft! Lay aft to muster all hands! (XXIII, 14)

The forecastle of the *Narcissus* has no doubt seen many fights, and another one would not be extraordinary. However, a fight among the "people" is a breach, no matter how minor, in the orderly routine of the ship. It is significant that the fight between Donkin and Wamibo is averted by the muster call. And, it is a bit of masterful symbolism that the call comes from above, that the stimulus which dissolves the momentary chaos of the forecastle comes from outside it.

During the storm the ship turns over on her side, and the men can no longer perform the usual routines of duty. They can no longer skip up and down masts setting the sails, for the masts are in the water. It is in this difficult situation, however, that the crew exhibits its greatest devotion to duty. When the ship is on her side, she has a better chance of not turning over completely if her masts are cut. In the first moments of fright after the ship has gone over, the men yell for this to be done, but Allistoun ignores their panic:

Captain Allistoun struggled, managed to stand up with his face near the deck, upon which men swung on the ends of ropes, like nest robbers upon a cliff. One of his feet was on somebody's chest; his face was purple; his lips moved. He yelled also; he yelled, bending down: – "No! No!" Mr. Baker, one leg over the binnacle-stand, roared out: – "Did you say no? Not cut?" He shook his head madly. "No! No!" Between his legs the crawling carpenter heard, collapsed at once, and lay full length in the angle of the skylight. Voices took up the shout – "No! No!" Then all became still. They waited for the ship to turn over altogether, and shake them out into the sea; and upon the terrific noise of wind and sea not a murmur of remonstrance came from those men, who each would have given ever so many years of life to see "them damned sticks go overboard!" They all believed it their only chance; but a little hardfaced man shook his grey head and shouted "No!" (XXIII, 59)

The active ritual of work cannot restore order to the ship's crew in this situation, for they must cling to the ship to keep from sliding into the sea. In their instinctive and ready submission to the captain's decision not to cut the masts, however, they affirm, even in the chaos of the storm, their belief in the fitness of the ship's routine. It is not fear of the captain that keeps them from protesting, for in the situation in which the men of the *Narcissus* find themselves, sheer animal terror blots out any thought of charges of mutiny which may be brought against them if they disobey. They obey automatically, because in their collective soul there exists an unconscious identification, even stronger than the instinct of self-preservation, with the forces of order which the captain represents.

One man does protest – Donkin, who "knows all about his rights, but knows nothing of courage, of endurance, and of the unexpressed faith, of the unspoken loyalty that knits together a ship's company" (XXIII, 11):

Donkin, caught by one foot in a loop of some rope, hung, head down, below us, and yelled, with his face to the deck: – "Cut! Cut!" Two men lowered themselves cautiously to him; others hauled him into a safer place, held him. He shouted curses at the master, shook his fist at him with horrible blasphemies, called upon us in filthy words to "Cut! Don't mind that murdering fool! Cut, some of you!" One of his rescuers struck him a back-handed blow over the mouth; his head banged on the deck, and he became suddenly very quiet, with a white face, breathing hard, and with a few drops of blood trickling from his cut lip. (XXIII, 60)

For the second time Donkin has rebelled against the system of order which insures that the work will be done which is necessary to keep the *Narcissus* afloat. For the second time he is defeated, and his second defeat indicates more clearly than the first the exact nature of both his rebellion and the principles against which he is rebelling.[7]

The third time Donkin rebels against the order of the ship, he hurls an iron belaying pin at the officers. The ensuing confusion causes a cardinal breach in the discipline of the ship – the helmsman leaves the wheel:

...the helmsman, anxious to know what the row was about, had let go the wheel, and, bent double, ran with long, stealthy footsteps to the break of the poop. The *Narcissus,* left to herself, came up gently to the wind without any one being aware of it. She gave a slight roll, and the sleeping sails woke suddenly. (XXIII, 124)

Again it is the demands of the ship which restore order:

"Helm up!" cried the master, sharply. "Run aft, Mr. Creighton, and see what that fool there is up to." – "Flatten in the head sheets. Stand by the weather fore-braces", growled Mr. Baker. Startled men ran swiftly repeating the orders. The watch below, abandoned all at once by the watch on deck, drifted towards the forecastle in twos and threes, arguing noisily as they went – "We shall see tomorrow!" cried a loud voice, as if to cover with a menacing hint an inglorious retreat. And then only orders were heard, the falling of heavy coils of rope, the rattling of blocks. Singleton's white head flitted here and there in the night, high above the deck, like the ghost of a bird. – "Going off, sir!" shouted Mr. Creighton from aft. – "Full, again." – "All right..." – "Ease off the head sheets. That will do the braces. Coil the ropes up", grunted Mr. Baker, bustling about. (XXIII, 125)

Surely the work of the ship serves the practical purpose of keeping the men's minds occupied so that they cannot entertain mutinous thoughts, yet the work also enables the men to attain

---

[7] The device of placing a character in the same general situation several times and intensifying the importance of the character's action with each repetition of the basic frame is, of course, most noticeable in *Lord Jim.* Conrad does, however, employ this device less perfectly with Donkin in *The Nigger* and, perhaps even more artistically than in *Lord Jim,* with Marlow in "Heart of Darkness". In "Heart of Darkness" Marlow is several times placed in a situation in which he is forced to choose between order on the one hand and chaos on the other. He chooses correctly in each case, which perhaps makes the fact that he has made a decision harder to detect. However, both the difficulty and the importance of his decisions are intensified with each repetition.

a certain dignity. In the struggle to save the *Narcissus* from the storm, the crew wring out a meaning from life, and they realize this, at least imperfectly. When Donkin suggests that the entire crew sham sick, Knowles gives the naive, but effective, answer: "If we all went sick what would become of the ship?" (XXIII, 108). Knowles, with the rest of the crew, realizes that the ship is what gives his life purpose. Thomas Carlyle, some fifty years before Conrad started his literary career, expressed a philisophy regarding work that closely resembles that evinced in *The Nigger of the "Narcissus"*:

> Work is of a religious nature: – work is of a *brave* nature; which it is the aim of all religion to be. All work of man is as the swimmer's: a waste ocean threatens to devour him; if he front it not bravely, it will keep its word. By incessant wise defiance of it, lusty rebuke and buffet of it, behold how it loyally supports him, bears him as its conqueror along. "It is so", says Goethe, "with all things that man undertakes in this world." [8]

4. Singleton as Prophet

Only one seaman, old Singleton, is completely undeceived by the evil malingering of Donkin and Wait. He is "tattooed like a cannibal chief all over his powerful chest and enormous biceps ... the incarnation of barbarion wisdom serene in the blasphemous turmoil of the world" (XXIII, 6). It is not only Singleton's tattooing but his instinctive and passionate devotion to duty which recall another magnificent barbarian seaman, Melville's Queequeg. Both men are the embodiment of unconscious moral force, and both play the dual role of prophet and saviour. Queequeg foretells his own death; Singleton foretells Wait's. Queequeg fashions a coffin which saves one man;

---

[8] Thomas Carlyle, "Labour", in *Prose of the Victorian Period,* ed. William E. Buckler (Boston, 1958), p. 146. The work ethic was to be of central importance in a number of Conrad's later stories, notably *Typhoon,* "The Secret Sharer", and *The Shadow Line.* In *Lord Jim,* Jim's personal tragedy, of course, overshadows all else, but his failure to perform his duty on board the *Patna* is the basis of his guilt. It is also interesting to note the similarities between Stein's famous "to the destructive element submit" and Carlyle's remarks on work.

Singleton is the exemplar of a rigid work ethic which is instrumental in saving an entire crew.

Singleton is early identified with the forces of order. While the *Narcissus* is still at anchor before leaving Bombay, a fresh breeze comes up causing a strain on the anchor cable and necessitating an adjustment on the windlass brake. Singleton instinctively leaps to the task:

Singleton seized the high lever, and, by a violent throw forward of his body, wrung out another halfturn from the brake. He recovered himself, breathed largely, and remained for awhile glaring down at the powerful and compact engine that squatted on the deck at his feet like some quiet monster – a creature amazing and tame. "You... hold!" he growled at it masterfully, in the incult tangle of his white beard. (XXIII, 26)

The anchor which bites into the bottom of the sea keeps the ship from floating helplessly about. Singleton's intuitive wisdom, which seizes upon those very few simple ideas of loyalty, devotion, and courage, keeps the ship's crew from floating helplessly about.

Even before Singleton has discovered his own mortality, he recognizes Wait's. Shortly before the nigger is exiled from the forecastle, he becomes so abusive that he annoys Singleton:

Jimmy expressed his general disgust with men and things in words that were particularly disgusting. Singleton lifted his head. We became mute. The old man, addressing Jimmy, asked: – "Are you dying?" Thus interrogated, James Wait appeared horribly startled and confused.... "Why? Can't you see I am?" he answered shakily. Singleton lifted a piece of soaked biscuit ("his teeth" – he declared – "had no edge on them now") to his lips. – "Well, get on with your dying", he said with venerable mildness; "don't raise a blamed fuss with us over that job. We can't help you." (XXIII, 42)

Later, when Singleton is asked whether Wait will die, he straightforwardly replies: "Why, of course he will die" (XXXII, 42). The white-bearded old sailor is a prophet who disseminates the words of the master to the people and foretells his judgments. Singleton's telling Wait not to "raise a blamed fuss with us over that job" clearly prefigures Allistoun's judgment that Wait has "no grit to face what's soming to us all" (XXIII, 127).

Singleton also accurately predicts that Wait will not die until

land is sighted and that the ship will not have a fair breeze
until the nigger dies. Certainly, as Vernon Young indicates,
Singleton's last prophecy is a sort of "white magic".[9] In the
mythic frame which Conrad has constructed, however, Singleton's
divination becomes more than the mere superstitious utterance
of an old salt.

One other man in the crew, Podmore, the cook, also seems
aware of Wait's evil nature. When Wait first comes on board,
he sticks his head into the galley and shouts a greeting to the
dozing cook. The cook awakes with a start and later reports:
"The poor fellow had scared me. I thought I had seen the devil"
(XXIII, 19). But though the cook knows Wait is evil, he does
not sense the true nature of the nigger's malevolence as does
Singleton. The cook fancies himself a pious Christian, but his
sentimental evangelical Christianity is clearly ineffectual, both
in itself and when compared to the larger morality of the sailor's
craft which Singleton embodies. The chaplain in Melville's *Billy
Budd,* when faced with Billy's innocence, realizes that his
ministering has encountered a situation in which it is useless.
"With the good sense of a good heart", he insists not in his
vocation and, thus, attains a certain dignity. Podmore never
realizes that his shallow Christian ethic cannot cope with the
incarnate evil which Wait represents, and, thus, he becomes
ridiculous.

Conrad describes the cook as "a conceited saint unable to forget
his glorious reward" (XXIII, 32), and places him in situations
in which his sentimental evangelism is laughably absurd. During
the first hours of the storm, "the cook, embracing a wooden
stanchion, unconsciously repeated a prayer. In every short inter-
val of the fiendish noises around, he could be heard there,
without cap or slippers, imploring the Master of our lives not to
lead him into temptation" (XXIII, 61). The cook sees no in-
consistency in beating his son for accidentally falling in a pond
on the way to church. He reports to Mr. Baker: "I whopped
him, sir, till I couldn't lift my arm" (XXIII, 81).

The crowning absurdity, made humorous by the cook's perversion of Christian myth, is his attempt to convert Wait:

"This is no time for sleep!" exclaimed the cook, very loud. He had prayerfully divested himself of the last vestige of his humanity. He was a voice – a fleshless and sublime thing, as on that memorable night – the night when he went walking over the sea to make coffee for perishing sinners. "This is no time for sleeping", he repeated with exaltation. "*I* can't sleep."
"Don't care damn", said Wait, with factitious energy. " I can. Go an' turn in."
"Swear ... in the very jaws! ... In the very jaws! Don't you see the everlasting fire ... don't you feel it? Blind, chock-full of sin! Repent, repent! I can't bear to think of you. I hear the call to save you. Night and day. Jimmy, let me save you!" The words of entreaty and menace broke out of him in a roaring torrent. The cockroaches ran away. Jimmy perspired, wriggling stealthily under his blanket. (XXIII, 116)

James Wait is evil incarnate and cannot be saved. He is incapacitated physically and spiritually from partaking of the ritual grace of work. His evil pride is innate and cannot be purged. Wait, like Milton's Satan, is "Self-tempted, self-depraved", and, therefore, shall finally receive not pity, but justice.

As a self-conscious salesman of Christian piety, Podmore does not contribute to the solidarity which is to be the salvation of the *Narcissus*. In fulfilling his duties as ship's cook, however he is instrumental in the crew's redemption. During the storm he performs a task nearly as heroic as Singleton's thirty-hour stint at the wheel. With the ship nearly on its side, he creeps forward from the poop deck and makes a pot of hot coffee, which helps the men to endure the night. It is not his talk of unearthly joys and burning pits which the men remember. It is his fealty to the work of the ship. The narrator reports: "Later, whenever one of us was puzzled by a task and advised to relinquish it, he would express his determination to persevere and to succeed by the words: – 'As long as she swims I will cook!' " (XXIII, 84).

The cook's heroic act is overshadowed, however, by Singleton's herculean endurance during the storm. In fact, every man on board the *Narcissus,* with the obvious exception of Allistoun, is inferior to Singleton. Singleton's superiority is nowhere more apparent, of course, than in a comparison with Wait. These two men of the *Narcissus* represent antipodal attitudes toward life and death. Wait boasts of his ability to shirk duty; Singleton never mentions his ability to perform it. Wait is horrified by death; Singleton sees it as another difficult task.

When Singleton comes back to the forecastle after thirty hours at the wheel, he collapses, "crashing down, stiff and headlong like an uprooted tree" (XXIII, 97). The men give him up, but at midnight he turns out for his duty. Singleton knows he must die, but he is not frightened by this knowledge; it completes his wisdom:

Old! It seemed to him he was broken at last. And like a man bound treacherously while he sleeps, he woke up fettered by the long chain of disregarded years. He had to take up at once the burden of all his existence, and found it almost too heavy for his strength. Old! He moved his arms, shook his head, felt his limbs. Getting old ... and then? He looked upon the immortal sea with the awakened and groping perception of its heartless might; he saw it unchanged, black and flaming under the eternal scrutiny of the stars; he heard its impatient voice calling for him out of a pitiless vastness full of unrest, of turmoil, and of terror. He looked afar upon it, and he saw an immensity tormented and blind, moaning and furious, that claimed all the days of his tenacious life, and, when life was over, would claim the worn-out body of its slave. (XXIII, 99)

The burden is nearly too much, but he can shoulder it. Though when he looks at the sea he sees the terror and the pain of existence, he also imperfectly realizes that the struggle against his powerful adversary is noble because of the certainty of final defeat. In any case, he does not whine.

Wait's reaction to the certainty of death is clearly less heroic than Singleton's. When the nigger realizes his mortality he cries out in terror: "Overboard! ... I! ... My God!" (XXIII, 153). Wait, unlike Singleton, has devoted his entire life to thoughts of "his mortal self". He cannot, like Singleton, relate his existence to the work ethic of the ship or the immortal power of the sea.

Thus, he can see death only as it reflects in the mirror of his grotesque egoism. Wait fears the pain of death because his selfishness has prevented him from experiencing the preparatory pain of life.[10]

Wait, of course, does die, and his death shocks the crew:

Jimmy's death, after all, came as a tremendous surprise. We did not know till then how much faith we had put in his delusions. We had taken his chances of life so much at his own valuation that his death, like the death of an old belief, shook the foundations of our society. A common bond was gone; the strong, effective and respectable bond of a sentimental lie. (XXIII, 155)

Even after Jimmy is dead, however, his evil influence lives on. The day of his burial, the crew go about their work in a lackadaisical manner, and shortly before Wait's funeral, a fight breaks out near his lifeless body. The nigger has seized upon the collective weakness of the crew to such an extent that they nearly refuse to accept his death as the end of his monstrous falsehood. He has become to the crew a symbol of rebellion to the natural law of death. If they accept the full significance of Wait's death, they must accept the inevitability of their own, and this they are not yet ready to do.

Only when James Wait slides over the rail of the ship is his evil influence purged. Conrad effects this purgation in the burial scene by first making Wait seem to exercise an evil will even in

[10] The often shifted point of view in *The Nigger* has, of course, often been criticized. For one of the most recent indictments, see Vernon Young's "Trial by Water", *Accent,* XII (Spring, 1952), 81. Ian Watt, in his "Conrad Criticism and *The Nigger of the 'Narcissus' "*, *Nineteenth Century Fiction, XII* (March, 1958), defends the plasticity of the point of view on the grounds that reflections issuing from an individual narrator must by necessity be expressed in "an appropriate personal vernacular". This, Watt says, would have caused Conrad stylistic problems. Albert Guerard also defends Conrad. In *Conrad the Novelist* he writes: "We need only demand that the changes in point of view not violate the reader's larger sustained vision of the dramatized experience." It might also be suggested, with the contrasting reactions of Wait and Singleton to death in mind, that the changes in point of view in *The Nigger* are dictated by the aesthetic and thematic design of the novel. Singleton's reaction is presented in the third person, Wait's in the first person. The effect Conrad thus gains is obvious.

death, and then, by a subtle stroke, turning him suddenly into
a mere mortal. As Mr. Baker reads the words "to the deep",
two men lift the inboard end of the planks holding Jimmy's body:

The boatswain snatched off the Union Jack, and James Wait did not
move. – "Higher", muttered the boatswain angrily. All the heads
were raised; every man stirred uneasily, but James Wait gave no sign
of going. In death and swathed up for all eternity, he yet seemed
to cling to the ship with the grip of an undying fear. "Higher! Lift!"
whispered the boatswain fiercely. – "He won't go", stammered one of
the men, shakily, and both appeared ready to drop everything. Mr.
Baker waited, burying his face in the book, and shuffling his feet
nervously. All the men looked profoundly disturbed; from their midst
a faint humming noise spread out – growing louder ... "Jimmy!"
cried Belfast in a wailing tone, and there was a second of shuddering
dismay. "Jimmy, be a man!" he shrieked, passionately ... His fingers
touched the head of the body, and the grey package started reluctantly
to whizz off the lifted planks all at once, with the suddenness of a flash
of lightning. The crowd stepped forward like one man; a deep Ah–h–h!
came out vibrating from the broad chests. (XXIII, 159, 160)

Belfast's "be a man" in effect transforms Jimmy from a supernatural phantom of evil into a mere dead negro. When Jimmy
slides over the rail, he takes his lie with him, and the crew
members cease their murmurings against the truth by accepting
their mortality.

Before demonstrating by dying that he is a mere man, Wait
looms so large that his black skin seems to enclose all evil. At
the moment he slides from the planks, however, he changes from
an incarnation of Satan into a personification of the terror of
death. The evil he represents, though still very potent, is no
longer magnificent. Wait's illusion of immortality is seen as an
all-too-mortal artful dodge, and he himself is no longer seen
as a proud rebel, but as a sniveling malcontent. Most of the
crew of the *Narcissus*, having committed themselves to the
unwritten articles of the sailor's craft, will be able to face the
emptiness of death because their lives contain some substance.
Wait has made no such commitment, has never experienced
the adventure of life. His lie to himself and the crew is completely devoid of positive good. Wait's illusion is not of the saving

type which takes account of the "destructive element" and which permits man to perform good in the face of death, the inevitable negation of good. Thus, death terrifies him because he has lied so horribly about life.

In the powerfully conceived scene describing Wait's burial, the ubiquitous symbolism of the work ethic also functions. A fair wind comes up immediately after Wait's body is consigned to the deep, and the captain gives the order to square the yards. The men rush to the sails and the hard truth of their "completed knowledge" is immersed in the work of the ship. The postlogue to the scene is a masterful capsulization of the Wait-chaos, work-salvation themes. The boatswain confesses that the mate has dressed him down for forgetting to put a dab of grease on the planks which held Jimmy's body. As the boatswain confesses his neglect, he turns to the carpenter: "You ought to have known better, too, than to leave a nail sticking up – hey, Chips?" (XXIIII, 161). Thus, Wait's influence even at his burial is seen to be dependent upon inattention to duty. The small omissions of the boatswain and the carpenter are symbols of the delinquency of the crew which enabled Wait to attain his evil power.

C. THE CYCLIC NATURE OF THE VOYAGE OF THE *NARCISSUS*

The pilgrimage motif in *The Nigger of the "Narcissus"* is unmistakable.[11] But the pilgrimage does not end with Wait's burial. The knowledge which the crew has gained through its contact with Wait is only temporary. In mastering the savage force of the sea and the insidious evil of Donkin and Wait, the men of the *Narcissus* have stepped into a patch of light as they did at their first muster call. But when the ship docks,

[11] James E. Miller, Jr., *"The Nigger of the 'Narcissus':* a Re-examination", P. M. L. A., LXVI (December, 1951), 911–918, in one of the first symbolic readings of *The Nigger,* sees the crew's voyage as a transition "from ignorance to knowledge about life and about death". Harold E. Davis, "Symbolism in *The Nigger of the 'Narcissus'",* *Twentieth Century Literature,* II (April, 1956), 26–29, calls the pilgrimage theme "the basic pattern in the novel". Albert Guerard calls the story "a version of our dark human pilgrimage" (*Conrad the Novelist,* p. 103).

they step back into the darkness once more. Old Singleton, who performed so admirably at sea, is drunk at pay call and can "hardly find the small pile of gold in the profound darkness of the shore" (XXIII, 168). A red-faced, blowsy woman falls on young Charlie's neck. It is his mother, and he can extricate himself only by promising to give her a bob for drink out of his pay. Even Captain Allistoun is somewhat contaminated by the shore, as he sits behind a brass wire grating with a "Board of Trade bird" paying the crew off. One of the crew, in fact, has still not discovered Jimmy's lie. Belfast, the most sentimental of the crew, still confuses the evil black spectre which he helped to save during the storm with a lamb[12] (XXIII, 171).

The *Narcissus* escaped "the distant gloom of the land" (XXIII, 27) when she sailed from Bombay, but her respite is short lived. At the end of her voyage, she returns to the squalor of London, and the truth she has temporarily borne is stifled: [13]

Between high buildings the dust of all the continents soared in short flights; and a penetrating smell of perfumes and dirt, of spices and hides, of things costly and of things filthy, pervaded the space, made for it an atmosphere precious and disgusting. The *Narcissus* came gently into her berth; the shadows of soulless walls fell upon her, the dust of all the continents leaped upon her deck, and a swarm of strange men, clambering up her sides, took possession of her in the name of the sordid earth. She had ceased to live. (XXIII, 165)

[12] Belfast, recounting his part in the rescue of Wait, on several occasions says: "He went for me like a lamb." Certainly Wait is something of a scapegoat, but the sin of the crew which he carries with him to the deep is of his own creation. There is an irony here, of course, for Belfast confuses Jimmy's devilish promise of immortality through rebellion with the lamb of God's promise of eternal life to be gained through submission.

[13] Conrad has skilfully foreshadowed the return of the *Narcissus* to darkness by an extensive yet subtle employment of light and dark imagery which gives the narrative a sort of chiaroscuro effect. The quality of this imagery perfectly reveals that dynamic "incompleteness" characteristic of life which Conrad mentioned in a letter to Garnett: "As to lack of incident, well – it's life. The incomplete joy, the incomplete sorrow, the incomplete rascality or heroism – the incomplete suffering" (Aubrey, I, 197). For a complete catalogue of the more important light-dark images, see the previously cited articles by Vernon Young and Harold Davis.

James Wait has been buried. The devil has been cast into the bottomless pit and shut up for his thousand years, but he will again be "loosed a little season" to attack the weak, reckless, joyous, mad "castaways making merry in the storm ... upon an insecure ledge of a treacherous rock" (XXIII, 172).

No analysis can reveal all of the infinite implications of the masterfully wrought symbolism in *The Nigger of the "Narcissus"*, but any well-reasoned analysis reveals that in this novel Conrad attained a complete mastery of the symbolic method. The narrative contains not one violation of the facts of human experience, yet these facts have been transformed by Conrad's genius into something of larger symbolic significance – a work of art which speaks to our capacity for delight and wonder, and makes us "see".

IV. LORD JIM

"All adventure, all love, every success is resumed
in the supreme energy of an act of renunciation."

A. IMAGE AND SYMBOL IN "THE LAGOON" AND "KARAIN": PREFIGURATIONS OF *LORD JIM*

In *The Nigger of the "Narcissus"*, Conrad demonstrated the effects of evil upon a group of men. Some three years later, as if anticipating those critics who would suggest that the lack of a central consciousness in *The Nigger* detracts from its power, he finished his admirable *Lord Jim,* the story of an individual's successful fight against the "destructive element". Even while Conrad was writing the story of the *Narcissus,* he must have been contemplating a narrative which would focus on an individual hero's reaction to life's dark uncertainties. During the time *The Nigger* was in the process of composition, he wrote "The Lagoon", and shortly after he finished *The Nigger,* he started "Karain". Both of these narratives, however imperfectly, describe individual heroes in the classical tragic pattern. In each story, the hero, temporarily dominated by his own weakness, makes a wrong decision, discovers his error and, finally, faces his destiny.

Both stories contain obvious imperfections. They are rife with "second-hand Conradese" and contain an ambiguity which is, perhaps, not artful. These stories do, however, prefigure, in both their general frame and their symbolism, the second of Conrad's masterpieces, *Lord Jim*. What Conrad attempted in "The Lagoon" and "Karain" he perfected in *Lord Jim*.

Arsat, like Jim, has jumped into an "everlasting deep hole". To get to Arsat's clearing, the narrator of "The Lagoon" must pass through the jungle, a place of elemental darkness:

Here and there, near the glistening blackness of the water, a twisted root of some tall tree showed amongst the tracery of small ferns, black and dull, writhing and motionless, like an arrested snake ... Darkness oozed out from between the trees, through the tangled maze of the creepers, from behind the great fantastic and unstirring leaves; the darkness, mysterious and invincible; the darkness scented and poisonous of impenetrable forests. (VIII, 189)

The crew of the white man's boat dislike and fear Arsat, for "he who repairs to a ruined house, and dwells in it, proclaims he is not afraid to live amongst the spirits that haunt the places abandoned by mankind" (VIII, 189).

Arsat has breached tribal morality by abducting a slave woman. His crime, in a sense, resembles Jim's, for it is not a deliberate evil. It is an almost unconscious surrender to his weaker self. In yet another sense Arsat's crime may be seen to resemble Jim's, for in breaking faith with the trust his ruler has placed in him, the Malay is led to abandon his brother to certain death. In breaking faith with the morality of the seaman's craft, Jim abandons eight hundred pilgrims. In each case, the crime begins in individual passion and ends in a contravention of solidarity.

In *Lord Jim* the matured romanticism of Marlow and Stein demonstrates the shallowness of Jim's view of life. In "The Lagoon" it is Arsat's brother who is an exemplar of "how to be". When Arsat tells his brother of his love for the slave girl, his brother advises him to open his heart to the girl, and to be patient. Arsat, however, cannot wait to enjoy his beloved. His brother suffers with him and finally decides to help him carry the girl off. As they leave the village, the brother wishes to shout a parting challenge, but Arsat, blinded by his love for the girl, will not allow his brother even this small gesture. They pass from the village in cowardly silence. The brother, of course, transgresses the warrior's code both in betraying his ruler and in leaving without a challenge, but he does so not for personal reasons but in order to be true to the higher loyalty which he owes to Arsat. He broods gloomily while Arsat carries on his clandestine affair, and he aids in the abduction ably but solemnly.

He realizes that in performing one duty he is unfaithful to another. In any case, his fealty and courage offset Arsat's disloyal cowardice.

After he betrays his ruler and his brother, Arsat, with his woman, seeks a place "Where death is unknown" (VIII, 201), but like Jim he finds that by running from his fate, he only hastens to it. Death does enter his enchanted kingdom. His woman dies, and he is left with only the hollowness of his destructive illusion. As the story ends, Arsat stands "lonely in the searching sunshine" and looks "beyond the great light of a cloudless day into the darkness of a world of illusions" (VIII, 204).

Arsat's discovery of his own error and the destiny which fate has planned for him is not complete as the narrative ends. But he shall, sometime in the future, expiate. He tells the white man: "In a little while I shall see clear enough to strike – to strike. But she has died and... now... darkness" (VIII, 204). Arsat's projected return to his homeland will not, however, be a mere bloody demonstration of his bravery. Like Jim, he has demonstrated physical courage while failing morally. Arsat will undoubtedly be forced to conceive the full implications of his return as an act of duty before he can climb out of the gloomy hole into which his illusions have thrust him.[1]

---

[1] The controversy which has been carried on for some years in *The Explicator* attests to the possibly ambiguous nature of Arsat's final view into the "darkness of a world of illusions". In *The Explicator,* XIV, Item 23 (January, 1956), Thomas Gullason sees Arsat's disillusion after Diamelen's death as the first step in his purgation. In *The Explicator,* XV, Item 17 (December, 1956), Eleanor Sickels disagrees, stating that Arsat's death cannot possibly atone for the death of his brother. Robert Gleckner, in *The Explicator,* XVI, Item 33 (March, 1958), adds his voice to Gullason's arguing that Arsat does, indeed, effect a purgation. Charles McCann in *The Explicator,* XVIII, Item 3 (October, 1959), joins in on Miss Sickels' side. According to McCann, any subsequent action which Arsat takes will be meaningless since he, unlike Jim, cannot see a goal for his action. Guy Owen, *The Explicator,* XVIII, Item 47 (May, 1960), acknowledging the Gullason-Gleckner, Sickels-McCann struggle, hints that they are all mistaken and suggests that "The Lagoon" is a story of the conflict between love and duty. All five critics, it seems, pay rather too little attention to the duty ethic, those "very few simple ideas" which comprise the heart of "The Lagoon".

In "The Lagoon" Conrad succeeded in showing Arsat's nobility, but much of the natural imagery and symbolism which Conrad employed detracts from the story. One cannot quite agree with Professor Guerard that "The Lagoon" is an "incoherent performance",[2] but some of the overdrawn nature imagery and strained prose so effectively parodied by Beerbohm cannot be ignored. It is, however, a tribute to the power of Conrad's initial conception of the narrative that it succeeds in spite of its defects.

In the "Author's Note" to *Tales of Unrest,* Conrad remarked on the similarity of the motif of "The Lagoon" to that of "Karain". Both stories deal with a man's loss of moral courage and faith through a selfishly passionate love for a woman. But in "Karain" the narrative is carried beyond the point of the hero's discovery of his illusion. Arsat, whose woman is sick, asks the white man, "Have you medicine, Tuan?" (VIII, 190). In the symbolic frame of the story, Arsat is, of course, asking for some sort of charm with which he can cure his own spiritual sickness. The white man has no medicine, either for Arsat's woman or for Arsat. Karain, after betraying a friend for an even more illusory passion than that of Arsat, also asks for "medicine" from the white man. Karain receives his talisman.

Karain and his friend Matara have sworn to kill Matara's sister and the Dutchman with whom she has run off. During the many years that the two comrades search for the sister and the Dutchman, however, the woman appears to Karain in his dreams and he falls in love with her phantom. When Matara's sister and the Dutchman are finally found, Karain kills his friend rather than the woman. Thus, he, like Arsat and Jim, can never return to his homeland. To exorcise the phantom of Matara which he imagines is pursuing him, Karain employs an old man to stand behind him with a sword. When the old man dies, Karain is frantic. He pleads with his white friends: "Give me your protection – or your strength . . . A charm . . . a weapon" (VIII, 45). Out of a gilt jubilee sixpence, a bit of leather and

[2] Albert Guerard, *Conrad the Novelist* (Cambridge, Mass., 1958), p. 67.

some dark ribbon the white men make Karain a charm, "a thing like those Italian peasants wear, you know" (VIII, 50).

Professor Guerard calls the white men's giving of the hastily improvised charm to Karain a "trivial anecdote".[3] But it seems Conrad intended the charm as symbol to carry more than a trivial significance. The charm does work. Karain, almost immediately after receiving it, tells the white men that it has caused Matara's ghost to leave him forever. It is Karain's charm, his new illusion, that prevents his past from destroying him.[4] Though the white men do not believe in the illusion they have created for Karain, Conrad indicates that they, too, have their illusions. Before Karain begins his confession to the white men, his troubled stare greatly disturbs them. The narrator is reassured, however, much in the same way Karain is reassured later by the jubilee sixpence, by the steady ticking of the ship's chronometers:

The silence was profound; but it seemed full of noiseless phantoms, of things sorrowful, shadowy, and mute, in whose invisible presence the firm, pulsating beat of the two ship's chronometers ticking off steadily the seconds of Greenwich Time seemed to me a protection and a relief. (VIII, 40)

What is Greenwich Time, or any time, for that matter, except an imaginary system which the white men carry with them to give order to their lives?

When two of the white men who have heard Karain's confession meet much later in the streets of London, they see in

---

3 Guerard, p. 91.
4 Walter Wright, in discussing Karain's charm as a symbol of saving illusion, sums up Conrad's position: "The truth existed in so far as Conrad's conviction was sound – that man can live profoundly, experiencing deep sorrow and great joy, even though the structure of his world is an illusion. For Conrad an illusion expressed the genius of artistic paradox. Common sense could deny it a factual basis, that is a basis in the world of common sense. Yet it was itself the imaginative creation which gave facts meaning – in the world of the imagination. It was true or false accordingly as it was or was not consistent within itself" (Walter F. Wright, *Romance and Tragedy in Joseph Conrad*, Lincoln, Nebr., 1949, p. 27).

the confused scramble of people who rush past them, manifestations of the same dark force which haunted Karain. One
white man says: "Yes, I see it. . . . It is there; it pants, it runs, it
rolls, it is strong and alive; it would smash you if you didn't look
out" (VIII, 55). The white men must devise complicated systems
in order to "look out" for the spectres which haunt them.
Karain's propitiation, though just as effective, is much simpler.
He needs only a jubilee sixpence, a bit of leather, and some
ribbon.

Karain is, perhaps, not quite "one of us", but he does sum up
"his race, his country, the elemental force of ardent life, of
tropical nature" (VIII, 7). Conrad is here clearly looking forward to the creation of a universal hero. The mythic elements
of *Lord Jim* are also clearly prefigured in "Karain", in which
Conrad refers to his hero as an Odysseus wandering among
mankind's various illusions. The most important relationship of
"Karain" to *Lord Jim,* however, is inherent in the relationship
between Karain's talisman and Jim's sacrificial death. That is,
even if Jim's death is given the shallowest possible interpretation,
even if, as some critics vehemently insist, Jim, at the last, merely
surrenders to an illusion, that illusion can be seen as one which
makes the human spirit noble.

Jim's death, however, represents more than a mere surrender
to a saving illusion.[5] One must agree with Professor Wright
that when Jim "falls, shot through the heart, there has been
retribution; he has expiated for his human error".[6] Most Conrad
scholars do see Jim's death as an atonement, and it is a tribute
to the complexity of Conrad's art that one could proceed to
the same conclusion without referring to previous critical

---

[5] Some critics see Jim's death as rather insignificant indeed. Dorothy
Van Ghent, *The English Novel: Form and Function* (New York, 1953),
p. 244, says *Lord Jim* is a "tale that put both the law and the self to
question, and left them there". Paul Wiley, *Conrad's Measure of Man*
(Madison, Wis., 1954), p. 60, terms Jim's sacrifice "both chivalrous
and futile". Vernon Young, "Joseph Conrad: Outline for a Reconsideration", *Hudson Review,* II (Spring, 1949), 10, calls Jim's actions, even
his final one, "priggish attempts . . . to keep his head above water by
the vain consolations of gentlemanly action".
[6] Wright, p. 114.

readings of *Lord Jim*. Of all the various readings of *Lord Jim*, however, none comments in detail upon the symbolism of the novel as it relates to the nature of Jim's tragedy.

B. JIM AS MYTHIC HERO

1. *Jim as "One of us"*

Jim, himself, fulfils a symbolic function. He is "one of us", and, though he dies far from home among people who only half understand his reasons for sacrificing himself, in his death he attests to the existence of the spiritual bond which unites the community of mankind. Even were it not for Marlow's recurrent comment, "he is one of us", the reader of *Lord Jim* would identify himself with the hero of Conrad's story. Certainly Jim is more physically fearless than many of "us", and, perhaps, more introspective than most; but he possesses those mysterious blends of good and evil, strength and weakness, insight and blindness that exist, albeit in different proportions, in the noblest as well as the basest of mankind. When Marlow first sees Jim, he recognizes these blends at work in the young man. Marlow senses that there is an "infernal alloy in Jim's character – an alloy that may prove Jim to be "nothing more rare than brass" (XXI, 46). Yet, the old story teller without hesitation classifies Jim as "one of us" – one potentially able to defy human weakness and turn it into triumph:

He stood there for all the parentage of his kind, for men and women by no means clever or amusing, but whose very existence is based upon honest faith, and upon the instinct of courage. I don't mean military courage, or civil courage, or any special kind of courage. I mean just that inborn ability to look temptations straight in the face – a readiness unintellectual enough, goodness knows, but without pose – a power of resistance, don't you see, ungracious if you like, but priceless – an unthinking and blessed stiffness before the outward and inward terrors, before the might of nature, and the seductive corruption of men – backed by a faith invulnerable to the strength of facts, to the contagion of example, to the solicitation of ideas. (XXI, 43)

Through his cowardly behaviour on the *Patna,* as well as his noble behaviour in Patusan, Jim demonstrates himself to be "one of us". As Marlow says of him: "He appealed to all sides at once – to the side turned perpetually to the light of day, and to that side of us which, like the other hemisphere of the moon, exists stealthily in perpetual darkness, with only a fearful ashy light falling at times on the edge" (XXI, 93). On the *Patna* the lurking cowardice present in all mankind forces Jim to jump from the ship into the lifeboat. It is highly significant symbolically that before Jim jumps, he hears the men in the lifeboat calling to the dead third engineer. The cries of "Jump, George" communicate with that particle of cowardice present in Jim. Almost involuntarily he jumps. He is, now, literally and figuratively "in the same boat" as the despicable officers of the *Patna* Once Jim is in the boat, the captain and the chief engineer actually mistake him for George and abuse him in language which, in the dramatic situation, is highly ironic: "What kept you from jumping, you lunatic? ... What have you got to say for yourself, you fool?" (XXI, 116). Jim, like Young Goodman Brown, has been kept back a while by his Faith. Jim is a man noble, but not eminently good; and because Conrad so effectively presents the base, shrinking side of his nature, as well as the exalted, courageous side, Jim's struggle with his demon becomes a singularly dramatic experience, and Jim becomes meaningful as a symbol of universal man.

The criminal weakness which Jim demonstrates in deserting the *Patna* is, of course, magnified by his romantic failure to recognize his fault in the proper perspective. Though he is subconsciously aware of his failure, he consciously attempts to blame the other members of the crew for his "missed opportunity": "Certainly, I jumped! I told you I jumped; but I tell you they were too much for any man. It was their doing as plainly as if they had reached up with a boathook and pulled me over" (XXI, 123). Jim's shallow romantic outlook will not allow him to recognize the harsh and unpleasant truths of life.

Instead of blaming himself, he rails against the other members
of the crew and the circumstances. He flees, assuming an in-
cognito designed not "to hide a personality but a fact". By running from the truth he further identifies himself as "one of us".
In the human condition, the attainment of self knowledge is
painful. Usually before self knowledge comes a hollow self justification.

The rest of the *Patna's* officers escape from the trial. They
do not experience feelings of guilt and disgrace as Jim does.
They do not feel the need to expiate their sin. They are not
"of us". Jim, however, can be identified with the larger, sensitive
and introspective segment of mankind. As Marlow tells his rapt
audience:

He was – if you allow me to say so – very fine; very fine –and very
unfortunate. A little coarser nature would not have borne the strain;
it would have had to come to terms with itself – with a sigh, with
a grunt, or even with a guffaw; a still coarser one would have
remained invulnerably ignorant and completely uninteresting. (XXI,
177)

Before Jim establishes himself as Tuan Jim, however, his attempts to defeat a malevolent providence seem almost ludicrous.
He is forever being taken unawares, and his refusal to soil his
ideal standard of conduct by an acknowledgement of his all-too-
human weakness does, indeed, seem priggish. In fact, it almost
seems as if Conrad created Jim as a heroic archetype for ironic
purposes alone. Certain of Marlow's comments to Jim during the
confession scene are extremely sarcastic, and Jim's actions in the
first half of the novel seem more characteristic of the helpless
hero of modern realism than the flawed protagonist of classical
tragedy. However, Marlow insists on Jim's nobility and repeatedly
says that "our" fate is tied up in Jim's. And it attests to Conrad's
complete mastery of his material that he can make the heroic
overtones which he creates serve a double purpose. Jim's nobility
is, if not diminished, certainly qualified by his failure to measure
up to the absolute standards of conduct of the mythic hero.
Yet his stature is increased in that he comes closer to these
standards than do a host of minor characters that appear in
Lord Jim.

2. *Structural relationship of minor characters*

All these minor characters fail in some way which parallels and mitigates Jim's failure. Though few of these individuals directly affect Jim's life, each of them provides a symbolic insight into the exact nature of Jim's failure and the psychological characteristics which caused it. They are, as it were, metaphors by which Conrad expresses complex and subtle ideas regarding his hero, ideas that could perhaps be only imperfectly expressed otherwise.

Jim's romanticism makes him, at times, seem rather absurd. Marlow is sometimes so exasperated by it that he nearly wishes to throttle Jim. Conrad, however, mitigates the absurdity of this most striking aspect of Jim's character by presenting several realists and, in so doing, stressing the limits of the realistic view.

The captain of the *Patna,* one of the most grotesque and despicable characters that Conrad created in any of his stories, represents the utter debasement to which the realist may sink. He apparently has no pride whatsoever in the seaman's craft. Working on ships in the Eastern seas is the best means he can think of to permit him to lounge safely through existence. In "Typhoon", Captain MacWhirr indicates that he considers the Chinese coolies in the hold of the *Nan-Shan* as cargo rather than passengers; yet MacWhirr's callow attitude is somehow not self-damning, as is the fat German's "look at dese cattle" (XXI, 15) when he views the eight hundred Moslem pilgrims on board the *Patna.* His remark sums up his incompetence as both a sailor and a human being. When the *Patna* seems on the verge of sinking, the skipper is, however, a leader of sorts – he leads the panic of the miserable crew. He is a realist who views the sailor's law that the captain must go down with his ship as a useless and dangerous bit of nonsense.

At the trial, the skipper appears in a dirty green and orange sleeping suit, straw slippers, and a cast-off pith hat two sizes too small for him. Marlow carefully explains that a man the size of the captain of the *Patna* would find it utterly impossible to borrow any suitable clothing. But though the captain is dressed as he is by necessity, his clothing destroys any vestige of dignity which he might have retained. The awning-striped sleeping suit not only turns him into a fat clown, it stands as a symbol of the laziness and sloth which render this New South Wales German, this ridiculous realist, totally incapable of attaining even a particle of human nobility. Better Jim's shallow romanticism than the absurdly criminal realism of the skipper.

Chester and Robinson, representatives of a somewhat higher type of realism than that which the *Patna*'s master represents, hover like vultures over Jim. They hope to use the dishonored Jim as a foreman in their guano shipping enterprise. Chester is an outcast and has, apparently, during his checkered career, broken faith with the community of mankind; but his coarsely realistic nature has allowed him to come to terms with his disgrace. He tells Marlow: "You must see things exactly as they are – if you don't, you may as well give in at once. You will never do anything in this world. Look at me. I made it a practice never to take anything to heart" (XXI, 162). Robinson, former opium smuggler and seal hunter turned cannibal, is also a realist. After being shipwrecked and forced to dine off his companions, Robinson is apparently able to turn a deaf ear to the horrid stories about him which circulate after his rescue. Such cool realism suits Chester very well; "That's the man for me", he says, "He didn't allow any fuss that was made on shore to upset him; he just shut his lips tight, and let people screech. It was bad enough to have lost his ship, and all he was worth besides, without paying attention to the hard names they called him" (XXI, 163). Marlow, however, sees the realism of Chester and Robinson for the dishonesty that it is. Jim may turn out to be no rarer than brass, but Marlow, with the reader, is beginning to sense the fineness of Jim by seeing what he is not.

The highest form of the unimaginative, realistic view of life is, perhaps, represented by the *Patna*'s two native helmsmen. Not having received any order from the frightened captain to abandon their post, they remained at their job until the *Patna* was taken in tow by the French ship. When questioned at the trial as to what he thought about after the *Patna* hit the derelict, one lascar reports he "thought nothing" (XXI, 98). He and his

companion thus represent a state of mind completely opposite
to that of Jim, who is tricked into jumping by his forestalling
imagination. Conrad has demonstrated, however, with the lascar
seamen, that there can be no courage without the fear which is
generated by the imagination.

Even the French Lieutenant who functions as "the mouthpiece
of abstract wisdom" (XXI, 147) possesses a hint of dross realism
which makes him, even in his heroism, seem, somehow, a less
impressive character than Jim in his failure. The French
Lieutenant, however, nearly approaches that stern romantic
standard of conduct which Jim has envisioned for himself. He
has known fear: "One is always afraid. One may talk, but . . .
the fear, the fear – look you – it is always there" (XXI, 146).
He submits to the "destructive element" in that he is familiar
with the universal condition of mankind: "Man is born a coward
(*L'homme est né poltron*). It is a difficulty – *parbleu:* it would
be too easy otherwise" (XXI, 147). But in immersing himself
in the "destructive element", the French Lieutenant can call upon
natural abilities, can disengage himself from his imagination as
Jim never could: "But habit – habit – necessity – do you see? –
the eye of others – *voilà*. One puts up with it. And then the
example of others who are no better than yourself, and yet make
good countenance" (XXI 147). And, it is significant that the
French Lieutenant did not perform his heroic thirty-hour stint
aboard the crippled *Patna* totally unaided. He was never completely isolated from the traditions of the sailor's craft as was
Jim. Though the Lieutenant is alone on board the *Patna,* the
hawser which connects the towed ship to his own is a sort of
umbilical cord, attaching the Frenchman to abstract notions of
honor and courage.

Marlow expresses both the instinctive abilities of the French
Lieutenant and the limitation of his intelligence and conception
of honor. Marlow sees the Frenchman as a sort of priest-like
figure who years before abnegated the more troublesome elements of his imagination so that each new challenge could be
responded to almost automatically:[7] "He ought to have had a

[7] Robert Haugh calls the French Lieutenant a "natural athlete, morally

threadbare black 'soutane' buttoned smoothly up to his ample
chin, instead of a frock-coat with shoulder-straps and brass buttons" (XXI, 139). The French Lieutenant's conception of honor
is not so elevated as Jim's. In his conversation with Marlow this
stolid man of duty hints that his courage has, at one time,
failed him:

"It's evident – *parbleu!*" he continued; "for, make up your mind as
much as you like, even a simple headache or a fit of indigestion *(un
dérangement d'estomac)* is enough to ... Take me, for instance – I
have made my proofs. *Eh bien!* I, who am speaking to you, once ..."
(XXI, 147)

But he has not run from his imperfection:

"One may get on knowing very well that one's courage does not come
of itself *(ne vient pas tout seul)*. There's nothing much in that to get
upset about. One truth the more ought not to make life impossible ..."
But the honour – the honour, monsieur!... "The honour... that is
real – that is! And what life may be worth when"... he got on his
feet with a ponderous impetuosity, as a startled ox might scramble
up from the grass... "when the honour is gone – *ah ça! par exemple*
– I can offer no opinion. I can offer no opinion – because – monsieur
– I know nothing of it." (XXI, 148)

There is ever so little coarseness in the Frenchman's conception
of honor, and by the ox metaphor Marlow expresses this. Surely,
Jim, like the French Lieutenant, will have to live with "one truth
the more"; he will be forced to recognize and come to terms
with "the destructive element". But he will do so in a slightly
different manner than the Frenchman – by integrating the circumstances into his dream and, thus, making his dream larger
rather than qualifying it. The Frenchman seems, after all,
to be only "one of those steady and reliable men" (XXI, 143)
who possess an acute sense of honor. When, at the end of their
conversation, Marlow asks the Lieutenant to qualify the sense
of honor he has recently defined, the grizzled sailor answers:

---

speaking" (*Joseph Conrad: Discovery in Design,* Norman, Okla., 1957,
p. 69). Such a label is useful but must be qualified by taking notice of
the fact that the Frenchman, who is no stranger to fear, has had to
come to terms with his imagination.

"This monsieur is too fine for me – much above me – I don't think about it" (XXI, 149).

In Big Brierly, one of the assessors at the trial, Conrad presents a perspective from which the very special type of romanticism which Jim represents may be judged. He is self-conscious like Jim: "He had one of the best commands going in the Eastern trade – and, what's more, he thought a lot of what he had . . . . He was acutely aware of his merits and his rewards" (XXI, 57). He does not, however, possess the fortitude to face up to Jim's trial. He attempts to induce Marlow to help him bribe Jim to run away. Marlow, of course, refuses, perceiving that there is a kind of courage in Jim's facing it out. Shortly after the trial Brierly commits suicide.

Brierly's studied boredom during the trial betrays his inner tensions. He is not, as he would wish to indicate, indifferent to Jim's case. Marlow reports: "He was probably holding silent inquiry into his own case. The verdict must have been of unmitigated guilt, and he took the secret of the evidence with him in that leap into the sea"[8] (XXI, 58). By committing suicide, Brierly "cleared out" as Jim refused to do. While Jim was in the lifeboat with the officers of the *Patna,* he also contemplated suicide, but the knowledge that the captain and the scurvy second engineer would like to see him jump again gives him the impetus to hang on. He refuses Brierly's easy way.

The circumstance surrounding Brierly's jump and those surrounding that of Jim also seemingly mitigate Jim's dishonor. Brierly religiously attends to the ship's duties before his leap. He carefully sets the log and makes certain that the mate knows

[8] Both E. K. Brown, "James and Conrad", *Yale Review,* XXXV (Winter, 1946), 271, and Frederick Karl, *A Reader's Guide to Joseph Conrad* (New York, 1960), p. 124, see Brierly's suicide as motivated by the fear that he may sometime commit a cowardly act like Jim's. But one must agree with Walter Wright, *Romance and Tragedy in Joseph Conrad* (Lincoln, Nebr., 1949), p. 211, that such explanations seem "unpsychological and untenable". The powerful effect of Brierly's suicide is in part traceable to the very vagueness which surrounds its cause. Brierly is, after all, only important as his situation relates to Jim. If Conrad had given the exact cause of Brierly's death, Brierly would, perhaps, have loomed too large for a minor character.

the exact course to steer. He has his dog locked up in the chart room; he puts four iron belaying pins in his pocket to weight him down; he hangs his gold watch on the rail and leaps. Certainly, Brierly deserves a sort of backhanded praise for attending to his duties so carefully before he runs out on them for all time, but it is perhaps not Brierly's devotion to duty which Conrad wishes to express here. The point he is trying to make is that Brierly's leap is coolly premeditated, while Jim's is not. Were he to return to report on his jump, Brierly could not say, as Jim does, "I had jumped, it seems". The captain of the crack White Star liner is not "taken unawares". He "clears out" knowing the full implication of his dereliction. Thus, though he is a romantic like Jim and, therefore, by definition, self-conscious, his romanticism is the self-worshipping kind that Jim's never is. Jim, even at his most self-centered moments, is thinking more of an ideal standard of conduct than of himself.

The chief engineer is the most pathetic minor character which Conrad creates by way of comment on Jim. His physical appearance, like Jim's, is noble. His lean bronzed head and white moustaches make him resemble the famous knight of La Mancha, and Marlow is tricked into thinking that he can learn from this lean ghost "some profound and redeeming cause, some merciful explanation, some convincing shadow of an excuse (XXI, 50). But the chief engineer cannot lay the ghost of doubt for Marlow. When Marlow questions him about the *Patna* affair, the engineer, in guarded tones, tells him that the crew was forced to abandon the *Patna* because she was full of reptiles:

"Millions of pink toads.... The ship was full of them, you know, and we had to clear out on the strict 'Q.T.' ", he whispered with the extreme rapidity. "All pink. All pink – as big as mastiffs, with an eye on the top of the head and claws all round their ugly mouths." (XXI, 52–53)

The original Don Quijote's delirium was initiated by reading too many books of romance. Conrad's Don Quijote is not so noble, not funny at all, and gets his illusions from a bottle.

The chief engineer's pink toads represent Jim's illusion gone mad. Surely, Jim is not so utterly self-deceived as the engineer, but there are some interesting parallels between Jim's situation on the *Patna* and the alcoholic vision which the chief engineer describes to Marlow. While relating his version of the *Patna* story to Marlow, the chief engineer imagines that the floor of the hospital is also populated with pink toads. Marlow, to calm him, tells him that the toads are asleep, but the chief engineer's imagination rises to the occasion:

"Bash in the head of the first that stirs. There's too many of them, and, she won't swim more than ten minutes." He panted again. "Hurry up", he yelled suddenly, and went on in a steady scream: "They are all awake – millions of them. They are trampling on me! Wait! Oh, wait: I'll smash them in heaps like flies. Wait for me! Help! H-e-elp!" (XXI, 54)

When Marlow has heard Jim's story he comments: "His confounded imagination had evoked for him all the horrors of panic, the trampling rush, the pitiful screams, boats swamped – all the appalling incidents of a disaster at sea he had ever heard of" (XXI, 88). Jim's pilgrims, like the engineer's toads, are asleep. When one awakes and asks Jim for water, Jim bashes him on the head:

"As calmly as I could I ordered him to let go. He was stopping me, time was pressing, other men began to stir; I wanted time – time to cut the boats adrift. He got hold of my hand now, and I felt that he would begin to shout. It flashed upon me that it was enough to start a panic, and I hauled off with my free arm and slung the lamp in his face. The glass jingled, the light went out, but the blow made him let go, and I ran off – I wanted to get at the boats." (XXI, 90)

As the resident surgeon at the hospital tells Marlow about the chief engineer, "there's some sort of method in his raving" (XXI, 54).

Brierly, Robinson, the French Lieutenant, the chief engineer, none can exorcise Marlow's doubt. He must look to Jim, and it is through Marlow's reaction to him that Conrad reveals yet another facet of Jim's complex character. Marlow, however, is not a mere observer. It is through his consciousness that the facts of Jim's case are filtered.[9] And, Marlow's interest in Jim is not simple curiosity. He hopes to discover something about himself by inquiring into Jim's life. Marlow could be no more firmly bound to Jim if Jim were his son.

In the journey which Jim makes from coward to lord, Marlow functions as his Mentor. He not only is a spiritual participant in Jim's trials, he gives him practical aid. On two occasions he literally keeps him from starving. At first, however, Marlow evidences a vindictive motive for attending Jim's trial: "I tell you I wanted to see him squirm for the honour of the craft" (XXI, 46). But when Marlow listens to Jim's story, he perceives that it is more than a simple case of dereliction of duty. He identifies himself with Jim and realizes that he, too, given a certain set of circumstances in which he was unable to forget himself, might have jumped. It is Marlow's belief "that each of us has a guardian angel" and "a familiar devil as well" (XXI, 34). The devil that haunts Jim is his shallow idealism; the guardian who helps him is Marlow. After writing for Jim a letter of introduction to Denver, Marlow says: "It was borne upon me suddenly and with unaccountable force that should I

[9]   William York Tindall, "Apology for Marlow", in *From Jane Austen to Joseph Conrad* (Minneapolis, 1959), pp. 274–285, defends well against F. R. Leavis's attack on Marlow as a disciple of cheap glamor, and demonstrates that Conrad's inclusion of Marlow in "Heart of Darkness" and *Lord Jim* helps to indicate the thematic intention of the stories. It might also be noted that, though Conrad does, perhaps, misuse the recording consciousness of Marlow in *Chance*, in "Heart of Darkness" and *Lord Jim*, Marlow's being in the proper place to learn all the facts is not at all strained. In *Lord Jim* Marlow's occasional verbosity and his inconclusive profundities concerning "how to be" are perfectly consistent with the situation and character which Conrad has created. Marlow is, after all, telling a story and groping for its meaning. The strained nature of some of his generalities about life is obviously designed by him in order to keep his auditors interested. Also, as Conrad tells us in the "Author's Note", "we may presume that there must have been refreshments on that night, a glass of mineral water of some sort, to help the narrator on" (XXI, vii). As for the "inconclusive" nature of Marlow's experience, he is by nature a cautious man and, Conrad hints, is sure that his audience would neither accept nor comprehend a "conclusive" experience.

let him slip away into darkness I would never forgive myself"
(XXI, 180).

Marlow may be verbose, but he is not stupid. He senses a
quality in Jim which is perhaps strong enough to enable him
to defy his fate. Marlow has seen many men fail to realize their
dreams. He has seen them rot in a sea of alcohol; he has seen
them break down on the upswing of a promising career; he has
seen them compromise their dreams and turn them into destructive weapons. As Jim detects, Marlow himself has had his dream
and has not achieved it. For Jim's sake, for the sake of the
dream, and for the sake of all the men who have ever dreamed
or ever will, Marlow wants Jim to succeed.[10] And, Marlow's
failure to commit himself positively as to the quality of Jim's
final action seems to be prompted more by a cautious realization
of unhoped-for success than by honest doubt.[11]

By introducing several analagous father-son relationships into
the narrative of *Lord Jim*, Conrad not only emphasizes the importance of the Marlow-Jim relationship, he universalizes Jim
as a messianic son figure. When Jim, on the strength of Marlow's
recommendation, finds work with Denver, the old man treats
him as his son. In fact, all Jim's employers during his period of
flight take a paternal interest in him. Marlow has been a father-

---

[10]   The Jamesian dialogue which occurs when Jim thanks Marlow for
the letter of recommendation to Denver indicates that Marlow's
romanticism is of much the same type as Jim's:
"Well. Thanks – once more. You've been – er – uncommonly –
really there's no word to ... Uncommonly! I don't know why, I am
sure. I am afraid I don't feel as grateful as I would if the whole thing
hadn't been so brutally sprung on me. Because at bottom ... you,
yourself ..." He stuttered.
"Possibly", I struck in. (XXI, 180)
[11]   Gerald Levin, "The Scepticism of Marlow", *Twentieth Century
Literature*, III (January, 1958), 183, says Marlow is a disillusioned
idealist, one "who never ceases to regard all solutions as means of
escaping from reality, of pursuing an impossible dream rather than as
means to dignifying the human struggle for moral identity". But
Conrad and that part of him which is Marlow do recognize a
dignity even in a hopeless struggle. Bob Stanton cannot hope to save
the stupid woman from the deck of his sinking ship, but his try makes
him noble. Singleton cannot beat his old adversary, the sea, but his
struggle lends him dignity.

instructor to a whole generation of ship's officers. Even the patriarchal Stein has, in his time, been treated as a son by old McNeil, and Stein passes on to Jim a part of the old Scotsman's legacy.

To the ordered ideas of conscience and duty inherent in the Marlow-Jim, Stein-Jim relationships, Jim's natural father, the good parson who "fancies" his son, adds a naive but chaotic note. Employing the dislocated time scheme of the novel for the best dramatic and thematic advantage, Conrad has Marlow discover, in the effects of the dead Jim, a letter from the parson. Marlow reports:

> I've looked in at a sentence here and there.... The old chap goes on equably trusting Providence and the established order of the universe, but alive to its small dangers and its small mercies.... Virtue is one all over the world, and there is only one faith, one conceivable conduct of life, one manner of dying. He hopes his "dear James" will never forget that "who once gives way to temptation, in the very instant hazards his total depravity and everlasting ruin. Therefore resolve fixedly never, through any possible motives, to do anything which you believe to be wrong." (XXI, 341–342)

Certainly virtue is the same all over the world, but the parson has only an abstract and imperfect conception of this reality. It requires a genius as great as Conrad's to parody a shallow understanding of universal notions of virtue and at the same time to indicate their serious value. When the parson tells his son never to do anything wrong, he obviously cannot imagine the complexity of the problem with which Jim is faced; yet, the very irritating naiveté of the old man's advice images, by contrast the enormity of Jim's task. It is significant that the letter from Jim's father reached Jim a few days before the *Patna* affair, and Marlow can find no later letter. Apparently the parson abandoned his son to his disgrace.

Besides functioning along with Marlow as a spiritual father to Jim, Stein fulfils an oracular function. Marlow, exasperated in his efforts to give Jim practical aid, decides to "consult" Stein, "an eminently suitable person to receive my confidences about Jim's difficulties as well as my own" (XXI, 203):

Late in the evening I entered his study, after traversing an imposing but empty dining-room very dimly lit. The house was silent. I was preceded by an elderly grim Javanese servant in a sort of livery of white jacket and yellow sarong, who, after throwing the door open, exclaimed low, "O master!" and stepping aside, vanished in a mysterious way as though he had been a ghost only momentarily embodied for that particular service. Stein turned round with the chair, and in the same movement his spectacles seemed to get pushed up on his forehead. He welcomed me in his quiet and humorous voice. Only one corner of the vast room, the corner in which stood his writing-desk, was strongly lighted by a shaded reading-lamp, and the rest of the spacious apartment melted into shapeless gloom like a cavern. (XXI, 204)

The imagery here unmistakably equates Stein's house with the oracle's cavern.

Stein does not disappoint Marlow's desire to hear a pronouncement on Jim's case, but Stein's words are enigmatic: "No! I tell you! The way is to the destructive element submit yourself, and with the exertions of your hands and feet in the water make the deep, deep sea keep you up"[12] (XXI, 214). Stein does, of course, give a practical illustration of his philosophy's meaning when he tells Marlow how he captured the prize butterfly in his collection. Stein recalls this episode as a story about catching butterflies. The unpleasant facts of the case, the seven men who were trying to kill him, are subdued so that he can pursue the important thing, the butterfly, the dream. But the "destructive element" is a necessity. Had it not been for the thugs' delaying him, he might never have captured the butterfly.

In Stein's insect collection is seen another clue as to the meaning of "how to be". Stein speaks most of his butterflies, but his collection also contains beetles. In fact, when Marlow enters

---

[12] Albert Guerard, *Conrad the Novelist*, pp. 162–166, attempting an unorthodox reading of Stein's famous ordination, sees the dream equated with the destructive element. This reading, of course, makes the metaphor illogical. Attempting to justify his rather doubtful reading of the passage, Professor Guerard writes: "There are several possibilities here, including one seldom considered in discussions of famous passages: that Conrad produced without much effort a logically imperfect multiple metaphor, liked the sound of it, and let matters go at that."

Stein's work room, he sees written in gold letters on one of the wooden tablets which hang in the room the word "Coleoptera". The ugly "Coleoptera", the beetles, are ranged alongside the beautiful "Lepidoptera", the butterflies. Stein's collection is, of course, a symbolic comment on Jim's shallow romanticism. Had Jim on Patusan recognized Cornelius's ugliness – "His slow laborious walk resembled the creeping of a repulsive beetle, the legs alone moving with horrid industry, while the body glided evenly" (XXI, 285) – Dain Waris would not have been killed. But, paradoxically, if the native prince had lived, Jim would not have had his last glorious opportunity.

There is yet another complex symbolic element to be seen in Stein's insect collection. The butterfly, in Christian iconology, is a symbol of Christ's resurrection, and the three stages of the butterfly's life cycle – the caterpillar, the chrysalis, and the butterfly – traditionally represent life, death and resurrection. Jim's life as messianic hero corresponds to this pattern. He fails on board the *Patna*, he is buried on Patusan, and he gains immortality by his last unselfish act. Significantly enough, the last word of the novel is "butterflies".

Frederick Karl believes "Stein's sufficiency is such that he overshadows Jim, and rather than supplying merely a comment on him, he engulfs and swallows up the young man in a way like that of the experienced professional in his relations with the green apprentice".[13] But for all his preternatural qualities, Stein is, after all, mortal. He asks Marlow, "And do you know how many opportunities I let escape; how many dreams I had lost that had come in my way?" (XXI, 217). And, as the witches' prophecies are meaningful after the fact of Macbeth's actions and do not cause his actions, the full significance of Stein's "to the destructive element submit" is not revealed by his life but by Jim's sacrificial death on Patusan. Stein's counsel does not, at first, seem even to Marlow to possess the shining brilliance of absolute truth. It is "crepuscular" (XXI 215).

[13] Karl, *A Reader's Guide to Joseph Conrad*, p. 127.

3. *Jim's Patusan experiences interpreted with reference to the mythic hero's period of trial and descent into the underworld*

Stein and Marlow decide "something practical" must be done for Jim. They, in fact, decide to "bury him in some sort" (XXI, 219). Thus begins Jim's mythic journey into the underworld, the bottomless pit which is Patusan. It is when Jim is on Patusan that the "burial" imagery which Conrad has so subtly injected at significant points in the narrative reaches its climax. Running from Tunku Allang's men, Jim attempts to jump across the river. He falls short, barely reaching the other bank: "He reached and grabbed desperately with his hands and only succeeded in gathering a horrible cold shiny heap of slime against his breast — up to his very chin. It seemed to him he was burying himself alive" (XXI, 254). Earlier, Brierly has said of Jim: "Well, then, let him creep twenty feet underground and stay there!" (XXI, 66). Marlow, commenting on the easy way which Chester's scheme offers to Jim echoes the imagery of Brierly's speech: "I wished heartily that the only course left open for me were to pay for his funeral. Even the law had done with him. To bury him would have been such an easy kindness!" (XXI 174). And, when Jim ran from Denver's kindness, he remarked: "This thing must be buried" (XXI, 191).

Patusan is, indeed, a "yawning grave" (XXI, 221). The river which runs through Jim's small kingdom rolls "silent and black as the Styx" (XXI 312). Coming out of the jungle after a visit to Jim, Marlow feels as if he has again returned to the land of the living. The Patusan jungle in *Lord Jim* represents the same dark evil as the Sambir jungle in *Almayer's Folly*. An examination of one of the better passages of natural description in *Lord Jim* serves at the same time to illustrate the underworld quality of the Patusan jungle and the progress which Conrad made in handling natural imagery from *Almayer's Folly* to *Lord Jim*:

For a moment it looked as though the smooth disc, falling from its place in the sky upon the earth, had rolled to the bottom of that precipice: its ascending movement was like a leisurely rebound; it disengaged itself from the tangle of twigs; the bare contorted limb of some tree, growing on the slope, made a black crack right across its face. It threw its level rays afar as if from a cavern, and in this mournful eclipse-like light the stumps of felled trees uprose very dark, the heavy shadows fell at my feet on all sides, my own moving shadow, and across my path the shadow of the solitary grave perpetually garlanded with flowers. In the darkened moonlight the interlaced blossoms took on shapes foreign to one's memory and colours indefinable to the eye, as though they had been special flowers gathered by no man, grown not in this world, and destined for the use of the dead alone. Their powerful scent hung in the warm air, making it thick and heavy like the fumes of incense. The lumps of white coral shone round the dark mound like a chaplet of bleached skulls, and everything around was so quiet that when I stood still all sound and all movement in the world seemed to come to an end ((XXI, 322)

The archetypal hero's descent into the underworld is traditionally a probationary period during which he undergoes various ordeals and gains the knowledge which will enable him to fulfil his destiny. After his arrival in Patusan, Jim's first task is to escape almost certain death at the hands of Tunku Allang. His next feat is to lead a raiding party against the outlaw Sherif Ali's stockade. This latter accomplishment makes him a living legend to the natives of Patusan. He is credited with supernatural powers and wins the title "Lord Jim". The mythic hero, because of his martial achievements, is granted the power to make laws. Jim, as an archetypal hero, settles everything from divorce cases to matters of commerce.

The temptation of sexual pleasure, or, at least, love of woman which will keep the hero from fulfilling his destiny, is also common in the archetypal pattern. The hero, Odysseus with Calypso, Aeneus with Dido, succumbs for a time, but is finally reminded of his destiny by the gods and forsakes the woman. Such is the case with Jim and his Jewel. The words of Dido, "Not unacquainted with distress, I have learned to succor the unfortunate" could well be uttered by Jewel. She has seen her mother die, abused by the evilly weak Cornelius, and is herself doomed to a life in the lightless depths of Patusan.

No matter how sincere Jim's love for Jewel is, she does symbolize the weak, feminine facet of his nature. When Jewel

questions Marlow as to whether Jim will ever return to his own
people, Marlow replies: "You've got his heart in your hand", a
certain echo of the pronouncement of Arsat's brother, "There
is half a man in you now – the other half is in that woman"
(VIII, 198). Jewel's love nearly keeps Jim from his destiny.
When she weaves garlands of flowers about the posts which mark
the grave of her mother, she is symbolically decorating the larger
grave, Patusan, so that Jim will continue to be imprisoned by
its promise of love, wealth, and power.[14] Jewel senses that Jim's
fate will take him from her, so she loves him jealously. She
knows, however, the call, the thing invisible which he can neither
see nor hear, will come: "They always leave us" (XXI, 309).

In myth, when it seems the hero shall live his life out in peace,
wealth, and pleasure, the gods send a messenger to remind him
of his high destiny. So it is with Jim. Brown, "running his appointed course.... a blind accomplice of the Dark Powers",
comes to Patusan and indirectly forces Jim to fulfil his fate.
Brown represents the extremest perversion of Jim's romantic outlook. Like Jim, he blames the world instead of himself for his
failure, but unlike Jim, he does not run – he strikes out in mad,
destructive anger. Both Brown's despicable life and his title are
a cruel parody of Jim. Brown has robbed and slaughtered his

---

[14] Thomas Moser, *Joseph Conrad: Achievement and Decline* (Cambridge, Mass., 1957), pp. 85–86, interprets this symbolism as further evidence of Conrad's misogyny – Jewel will destroy Jim. Jewel seems, however, more of an impediment than an active destructive force. What Conrad says of women in general in *Lord Jim* indicates he does not hate them
but is fascinated, as all men must be, by their strange other-worldness:
"Our common fate fastens upon the women with a peculiar cruelty.
It does not punish like a master, but inflicts lingering torment, as if
to gratify a secret, unappeasable spite. One would think that, appointed
to rule on earth, it seeks to revenge itself upon the beings that come
nearest to rising above the trammels of earthly caution; for it is only
women who manage to put at times into their love an element
just palpable enough to give one a fright – an extra-terrestrial touch.
I ask myself with wonder – how the world can look to them – whether
it has the shape and substance *we* know, the air *we* breathe! Sometimes
I fancy it must be a region of unreasonable sublimities seething with the
excitement of their adventurous souls, lighted by the glory of all possible
risks and renunciations" (XXI, 277). One suspects that those who accuse
Conrad of misogyny do not understand the masculine point of view.

fellow man and called himself Gentleman Brown. Jim has masochistically punished himself, and others have called him Lord Jim.

The scene in which Brown insinuates a common bond between himself and Jim is, perhaps, the most perfect of its type ever written. Not only does Conrad reveal Brown's cruel cleverness and Jim's hypersensitive self-consciousness, he repeats a number of the significant motifs of the story. "Let us agree", says Brown, "we are both dead men . . . . I am starving for next to no offence. But I am not a coward. Don't you be one . . . . This is as good a jumping off place for me as any other . . . . There are my men in the same boat – and by God, I am not the sort to jump out of trouble and leave then in the d–d lurch . . . . I was afraid once in my life" (XXI 381-382-383). Jim failed the first time because he would not recognize his common bond with the loathsome crew of the *Patna*. He fails the second time because he cannot recognize that Brown and he are at heart totally different.

Brown goes free to kill Dain Waris. Jim makes his atonement with the preternatural father figure, Doramin, and for a brief instant the darkness of Patusan has beheld light. Jim has rid himself of his hollow romanticism, but has not forsaken his dream. His triumph is complete because he does not blame the circumstances but integrates them into his dream, enlarging the dream beyond the self, transforming it into an ideal which will serve all mankind. Stein's ring, Jim's talisman, rolls in the dust at his feet before Doramin kills him. Jim no longer needs the old German's charm, for he has forged an ideal mightier even than Stein's.

The obscure truth involved in Jim's fate is, indeed, momentous enough to affect mankind's conception of itself. Jim's fate is hard, "and yet is not mankind itself, pushing on its blind way, driven by a dream of its greatness and its power upon the dark paths of excessive cruelty and of excessive devotion? And what is the pursuit of truth, after all?" (XXI, 349–350).

V. "HEART OF DARKNESS"

" To be hopeful ... it is not necessary to think that the world is good".

A. PREFIGURATION OF THE SYMBOLISM OF "HEART OF DARKNESS" IN "AN OUTPOST OF PROGRESS"

In the "Author's Note" to *Tales of Unrest,* Conrad referred to "An Outpost of Progress" as "the lightest part of the loot carried off from Central Africa". Earlier, in a letter to Garnett, he admitted that he felt the opening pages of this story to be inferior:

You are right in your criticism of *Outpost.* The construction is bad. It is bad because it was a matter of conscious decision, and I have no discrimination – in the artistic sense. Things get themselves written – and you like them.... But when *I* want to write – when *I* do consciously try to write or try to construct, then my ignorance has full play and ... is disclosed to the scandalized gaze of my literary father... I always told you I was a kind of inspired humbug.... Let me assure you that your remarks were a complete disclosure to me... It's very evident that the first 3 pages kill all the interest. And I wrote them of set purpose!! I thought I was achieving artistic simplicity!!!! ... Am I totally lost? Or do the last few pages save the thing from being utterly contemptible? You seem to think so – if I read your most kind and friendly letter aright.[1]

"An Outpost of Progress" is clearly not the work of an "inspired humbug". In fact, as a satiric treatment of the process of spiritual decay, it is almost unexcelled. In addition, it is particularly important in terms of the totality of Conrad, in that a

[1] *Letters from Joseph Conrad: 1895–1924,* ed. Edward Garnett (Indianapolis, 1928), pp. 66–67.

great many of the symbolic elements of this story definitely prefigure the masterful "Heart of Darkness".

Carlier, Kayerts, and their negro assistant, Henry Price, comprise the staff of a remote trading station. The white men, cut off from the "high organization of civilized crowds" (VIII, 89), slowly succumb to the hostile jungle, and, as they weaken, Price becomes stronger. The jungle so debilitates the moral fiber of these incompetent colonials that they neglect to perform the normal housekeeping tasks of the station. Buildings go unrepaired; the food supply runs out; very little ivory is collected. Kayerts and Carlier, who wish desperately to return to civilization, ignore the jungle and the simple demands of their position and immerse themselves in the torn novels which the former station manager has left behind. Richelieu, d'Artagnan, Hawk's Eye, and Father Goriot become more real to them than Henry Price and the negro laborers of the station. When Price sells the black workers into slavery in exchange for ivory, his white masters are at first shocked, but in time they are converted to that savage and expedient realism which Conrad so hated. They reason that the workers are, after all, irretrievably gone, and it would be foolish not to salvage the ivory from the unfortunate situation. Kurtz, too, must have at one point in his spiritual decline made just such an expedient decision. As Carlier says: "It's deplorable, but, the men being Company's men, the ivory is Company's ivory. We must look after it" (VIII, 106). When the white men decide to accept the ivory, Price shrewdly senses that he has become the master.

Kayerts and Carlier finally quarrel violently over their hoarded sugar supply, a symbol of the last vestige of order these two incompetents are able to maintain. Carlier chases Kayerts around the verandah of their decaying house, collides with him during this mad chase, and in a moment of extreme fright shoots him. Henry Price, called Makola by the natives, is present to make the crime easier:

After meditating for a while, Makola said softly, pointing at the dead man who lay there with his right eye blown out —

"He died of fever." Kayerts looked at him with a stony stare.
"Yes", repeated Makola thoughtfully, stepping over the corpse, "I
think he died of fever. Bury him to-morrow." (VIII, 114)

Kayerts has so completely lost touch with the ordered forms of
society that he somehow fancies his inadvertent murder of Carlier is a manifestation of his superiority. Like Kurtz, he imagines
himself as a sort of God:

His old thoughts, convictions, likes and dislikes, things he respected
and things he abhorred, appeared in their true light at last! Appeared
contemptible and childish, false and ridiculous. He revelled in his
new wisdom while he sat by the man he had killed. He argued with
himself about all things under heaven with that kind of wrong-headed
lucidity which may be observed in some lunatics. Incidentally he
reflected that the fellow dead there had been a noxious beast anyway;
that men died every day in thousands; perhaps in hundreds of
thousands – who could tell? – and that in the number, that one death
could not possibly make any difference; couldn't have any importance,
at least to a thinking creature. He, Kayerts, was a thinking creature.
He had been all his life, till that moment, a believer in a lot of
nonsense like the rest of mankind – who are fools; but now he thought!
He knew! He was at peace; he was familiar with the highest wisdom!
(VIII, 114–115)

When the relief steamer for which Kayerts and Carlier have
been waiting arrives, Kayerts's evil illusion dissolves. He cannot
face a return to civilization and the ensuing judgment of his
actions, so he hangs himself on an arm of the cross which marks
the former manager's grave. Only Henry Price is left to greet
the Managing Director of the Great Civilising Company.

In "An Outpost of Progress", though Conrad succeeds in
demonstrating the disintegrative horror of weak men isolated
from the surface routine of organized society, the decay of Carlier and Kayerts lacks the overwhelming impact of that of Kurtz.
That is, neither of these flabby individuals is "one of us". In
fact, they must seem almost as insignificant to the reader as
they do to the Managing Director, who says:

"Look at those two imbeciles. They must be mad at home to send
me such specimens. I told those fellows to plant a garden, build
new storehouses and fences, and construct a landing-stage. I bet
nothing will be done! They won't know how to begin. I always

thought the station on this river useless, and they just fit the station!"
(VIII, 88).

Henry Price is clearly meant to be a symbol of the disintegrative
powers of the jungle. When Conrad first introduces him, he
describes him as a half-savage man who worships evil spirits,
who placates his god by "a promise of more white men to play
with, by and by" (VIII, 87). There is, however, no motive for
Price's selling the black workers into slavery. If he were as
powerfully identified with the decivilizing forces of savage man
and hostile nature as is Kurtz's preternatural black consort in
"Heart of Darkness", he would need no motive. Price, however,
never assumes the symbolic role necessary to render his actions
completely valid.

Conrad surrounds Kayerts and Carlier with some powerfully
conceived images of decay. Their rooms are littered with torn
clothes, dirty and uncared-for equipment, "all the things dirty,
and all the things broken, that accumulate mysteriously round
untidy men" (VIII, 87). Grass begins to sprout in the courtyard
of their small clearing; they are ill from time to time; and
because they have not planted a garden as they were instructed
to do, they actually face the prospect of running out of food.
The contest of Kayerts and Carlier with the decivilizing forces
inherent in themselves and in the jungle is, however, altogether
too unequal. Their efforts are too feeble to bear any tragic
significance and, thus, the most significant effect of "An Outpost
of Progress" is ironical. When the Managing Director steps off
the steamboat and finds Kayerts dead, the scene does not inspire
pity and fear, but devilish laughter:

He had found one of them! And even he, the man of varied and
startling experience, was somewhat discomposed by the manner of
this finding. He stood and fumbled in his pockets (for a knife) while
he faced Kayerts, who was hanging by a leather strap from the cross.
He had evidently climbed the grave, which was high and narrow,
and after tying the end of the strap to the arm, had swung himself
off. His toes were only a couple of inches above the ground; his
arms hung stiffly down; he seemed to be standing rigidly at attention,
but with one purple cheek playfully posed on the shoulder. And,

irreverently, he was putting out a swollen tongue at his Managing
Director. (VIII, 117)

The ending of "An Outpost of Progress" is, somehow, "altogether
too dark". The Managing Director's cynical ideas concerning
the weakness of human nature have been given substance by the
failure of Kayerts and Carlier, and the savagery of the jungle
seems more powerful than the very few simple ideas which
contribute to the solidarity of mankind.

Frederick Karl's statement that "the manner and the meaning
of the story are never more than its physical equipment"[2] is
perhaps too harsh. The story is a remarkable study of the process
of spiritual disintegration. It is plainly evident, however, that
certain of the symbolic elements which Conrad conceived in "An
Outpost of Progress" function imperfectly and do not possess
the power of similar elements present in "Heart of Darkness".
The descriptions of the jungle in "An Outpost of Progress" seem
expository, rather than lyric: "Strechting away in all directions, surrounding the insignificant cleared spot of the trading post, immense forests, hiding fateful complications of fantastic life, lay
in the eloquent silence of mute greatness" (VIII, 94). Carlier,
like Kurtz, at first believes that the forces of imperialist commerce will bring civilization to the dark continent. Among the
things that the former station manager has left, Carlier discovers
an old newspaper which includes an article entitled "Our Colonial Expansion". He reads it and begins to fancy himself a
noble emissary of light:

Carlier said one evening, waving his hand about, "In a hundred years,
there will be perhaps a town here. Quays, and warehouses, and
barracks, and – and – billiard-rooms. Civilisation, my boy, and
virtue – and all. And then, chaps will read that two good fellows,
Kayerts and Carlier, were the first civilised men to live in this very
spot!" (VIII, 95)

Later, when Carlier shoots a hippopotamus for food, he fails to
secure it and it floats downstream providing a feast for the
natives. For the negroes "it was the occasion for a national holi-

---

[2] Frederick Karl, *A Reader's Guide to Joseph Conrad* (New York,
1960), p. 118.

day, but Carlier had a fit of rage over it, and talked about the necessity of *exterminating all the niggers* [italics mine] before the country could be made habitable" (VIII, 108). Clearly, Carlier's second-hand notions about his white man's burden and his subsequent ranting against the natives carry neither the symbolic nor the dramatic force of Kurtz's pamphlet for the International Society for the Suppression of Savage Customs, with its brutally simple postscript, "Exterminate all the Brutes".

There are many more elements common to both "An Outpost of Progress" and "Heart of Darkness". Ivory plays an important role in the corruption of Kayerts and Carlier as well as that of Kurtz. The negro laborers assigned to the outpost of progress resemble the cannibals who form the crew of Marlow's battered steamer, in that they have no conception of the period of time for which they have been contracted or the wages they are to be paid. The fog which settles on the river when Marlow is very near Kurtz's station is prefigured by the fog which wreathes Kayert's landing when the relief steamer arrives. Kayerts' cry of "Help ... My God!" (VIII, 115) as he views the body of Carlier is a less effectual form of Kurtz's "The horror". But though there are these resemblances in certain matters of detail between "An Outpost of Progress" and "Heart of Darkness", there is not in the former story either the wealth of imagery and symbolism or the brilliant dramatic strokes which render the latter one of the finest symbolic studies of the depths of the human mind and heart in all literature. "An Outpost of Progress" reads almost as if it were an outline for "Heart of Darkness" – an outline lacking the powerfully conceived symbols which were so characteristic of Conrad's greatest efforts.

Dr. Johnson, when asked what poetry was, replied that he could more easily tell what it was not. Conrad, though he was obviously not as dissatisfied with "An Outpost of Progress" as his letter to Garnett would indicate,[3] must have felt that the

---

[3] Gordan reports that Conrad allowed "An Outpost" to be printed in the *Grand Magazine* with an accompanying article "My Best Story and Why I Think So" (*Joseph Conrad: The Making of a Novelist*, Cambridge, Mass., 1940, p. 244).

story did not satisfy his own conception of what should be made of the experiences which he carried off from Central Africa, for some two years after he finished this story he wrote "Heart of Darkness". "Heart of Darkness" is, like "An Outpost of Progress", the story of man pitted against the savage jungle, but the struggle of Marlow and Kurtz is of greater significance simply because they are more capable men than Carlier and Kayerts. And there is in "Heart of Darkness" a mythic framework which lends the story's brilliantly evoked images and symbols an almost epic significance. Finally, though "Hearth of Darkness" is not in any sense an optimistic story, there is an affirmation of those very few simple ideas which give a significance to human existence. It was clearly within Conrad's power as a creative artist to write a story possessing an even more ironic tone and an even more grotesquely horrid comment on human incompetence than "An Outpost of Progress". It is significant, however, that in his second artistic expression of his African experiences, while certainly not ignoring "the horror", he chose to demonstrate something of the resiliency of the human spirit.

In his February 8, 1899 letter to Cunninghame Graham, Conrad implied that the full implications of the complex "Heart of Darkness" might well escape even the trained and perceptive eye. [4] Certain criticisms of the story lend substance to Conrad's apprehensions. Muriel Bradbook sees the Marlow of "Heart of Darkness" as a device employed by Conrad to transcend a genuine creative incapacity:

Marlow's function is to comment. Although a complete character and not a puppet, he shares Conrad's fundamental outlook, and so can speak for him. Comment is necessary since Conrad could not draw a character from the inside; he could not dramatise another man's mind – as for example Browning dramatises all the characters of *The Ring and the Book,* Henry James the characters of *The Awkward Age,* or E. M. Forster some of the characters of *A Passage to India.* [5]

Leonard Dean, though recognizing that Conrad was searching

[4] G. Jean-Aubry, ed., *Joseph Conrad: Life and Letters* (Garden City, N. Y. 1927), I, 268.
[5] M. C. Bradbrook, *Joseph Conrad: Poland's English Genius* (Cambridge, 1942), p. 21.

for "a new affirmative myth" in this story, also criticizes the role played by Marlow: "It is Marlow rather than Kurtz who returns to affirm his faith in The Intended. This is unsatisfactory because Marlow has only observed Kurtz's horror".[6] Neither of these criticisms recognizes that "Heart of Darkness" is Marlow's story as well as Kurtz's. Kurtz is, of course, the tragic hero of "Heart of Darkness", but the action of the story is not essentially motivated by him, but by Marlow's insatiable curiosity about the human heart and his irrevocable commitment to the business of living. The situation is, in fact, somewhat akin to that in *Othello,* in which the tragic hero and the protagonist are not the same.

Recent criticisms of "Heart of Darkness" recognize that the symbolism of the story is that of the underworld, and that Marlow, far from being a mere commentator, functions as a sort of mythic hero. Lillian Feder indicates some interesting parallels between Marlow's voyage up the Congo and Aeneus's descent into the underworld;[7] and Robert Evans likens Conrad's underworld to Dante's.[8] But though both of these perceptive studies offer a new perspective on the imagery and symbolism of the narrative, they do not relate these elements to Marlow's all-important "lie". It can be demonstrated, however, that Marlow's "lie" to Kurtz's Intended unites the complicated symbolic and thematic patterns of "Heart of Darkness".

B. INTERPRETATION OF THE THREE SYSTEMS OF IMAGERY IN "HEART OF DARKNESS"

Conrad's method in "Heart of Darkness", as in all his best work, is exceedingly complex. In fact, he sustains three distinct patterns of imagery in this tale, first emphasizing one, then another,

---

[6] Leonard F. Dean, "Tragic Pattern in Conrad's 'Heart of Darkness' ", *College English,* VI (November, 1944), 104.

[7] Lillian Feder, "Marlow's Descent into Hell", *Nineteenth Century Fiction,* IX (March, 1955), 280–292.

[8] Robert O. Evans, "Conrad's Underworld", *Modern Fiction Studies,* II (May, 1956), 56–62.

and finally uniting all three in the brilliantly conceived final scene. In the section of the narrative which begins with Marlow's accepting the job as captain of the "twopenny steamer" and ends with his starting to repair the sunken wreck of the ship, the imagery and symbolism center on the black futility which Marlow feels in his own soul, and on his initiation into a knowledge of the horrible smallness of mankind. In the section of the story which starts with Marlow's repairing the steamer and continues through the death of his helmsman, the dominant imagery focuses on work as a saving grace. When Marlow meets Kurtz, the emphasis is again shifted. At this point Marlow becomes a sort of mythic hero whose task is to discover a beneficent talisman which will aid all mankind. These systems of imagery are by no means mutually exclusive. Images of darkness occur in all three sections. Even as Marlow concentrates on his work as ship's captain in section two, it is evident he is already engaged in a sort of mythic quest. In section three the symbolism emphasizes Marlow's discovery and his return with the restorative boon, yet work imagery is an ever-present undertone.

1. *Images reflecting Marlow's despair*

In "Heart of Darkness" Conrad continued the use of character as metaphor which he so brilliantly conceived in *The Nigger of the "Narcissus"* and *Lord Jim*. As Marlow pursues his quest for Kurtz, he encounters various individuals who offer him and the reader a perspective on both the darkness of man's heart and the nobility of his spirit. After accepting a job as steamboat captain for a Belgian Congo trading company, Marlow takes a physical examination from the company's doctor. The doctor has a morbid interest in the fate of those who go to the Congo, and he asks to measure the dimensions of Marlow's head. The doctor "has a little theory" (XVI, 58) which he hopes to prove by his crude measuring of the cranial displacement of those going out to spread light in the Congo. "It would be interesting for

science", says the doctor, "to watch the mental changes of individuals, on the spot" (XVI, 58). The doctor does not realize,
as Marlow later does, that the mutations in the individuals who
front the elemental forces of the Congo are not physical, but
spiritual. The doctor speaks of the advantages his country will
reap "from the possession of such a magnificent independency"
(XVI, 58) as the Congo. He is the first and one of the wickedest
of those whom Marlow meets who completely miscomprehend
the relationship of man to himself as it is demonstrated in the
Congo, and when Marlow leaves his examining room he is almost totally disillusioned as to the possible value of the Congo trip.

   The doctor thinks that the disease which the white man in
the Congo must avoid is one which can be measured by the
instruments of science. Marlow's aunt, who has been helpful
in getting him the job, is equally deceived, though not in quite
the same manner as the doctor. She has been taken in by the
humbug of the civilizing duties of the imperialist: "She talked
about 'weaning those ignorant millions from their horrid ways',
till upon my word, she made me quite uncomfortable" (XVI,
59). Marlow abruptly suggests to her that the trading company
is run for profit, but she is quite undismayed: "You forget, dear
Charlie, that the labourer is worthy of his hire" (XVI, 59).
Marlow's aunt is, of course, a representative of the naive Victorian faith that civilization inevitably follows commerce, and
her remarks to him, coupled with his anxiety about not being
able to find a suitable position, make his mood even more somber.
Marlow's conversation with his aunt is also significant in that
it bears at least a surface resemblance to the interview which
he has with Kurtz's Intended. The Intended, too, has some rather
naive notions about the Congo, and the reader can see how far
Marlow has come in the completion of his knowledge by observing that, because of what he has learned from Kurtz's
tragedy, he does not attempt to shatter the young woman's
illusions as he does those of his aunt.

   The people whom Marlow meets on the other side of the
Portal of Darkness, though they know the Congo firsthand,
understand as little about it as the company doctor and Marlow's

aunt. Shortly after Marlow has come out of the unearthly grove of death, he meets an elegantly dressed accountant whose appearance is in striking contrast to the black disorder and decay which is everywhere present at this station of progress: "I saw a high starched collar, white cuffs, a light alpaca jacket, snowy trousers, a clean necktie, and varnished boots. No hat. Hair parted, brushed, oiled, under a greenlined parasol held in a big white hand. He was amazing, and had a penholder behind his ear" (XVI, 67). Marlow at first fancies that this man, the company's chief accountant, has performed some sort of a miracle in maintaining himself and his books in apple-pie order in the midst of the great demoralization of the land: "He had kept up his appearance. That's backbone" (XVI, 68). But Marlow is quick to see that clothes do not make the man. When a dying agent is moved into his office, the accountant complains: "The groans of this sick person distract my attention. And without that it is extremely difficult to guard against clerical errors in this climate" (XVI, 69). As he looks at the dying man, who is being ignored by the accountant bent over his books making correct entries only fifty feet from the grove of death, Marlow sees that the bookkeeper has, in fact, sold his soul to the flabby devil in exchange for starched shirts and pressed trousers.

Later, when Marlow immerses himself in the duties of his craft to stave off the flabby devil, it almost seems as if he is following the example of the accountant. There is, however, a quite obvious difference between the reaction of the accountant and the reaction of Marlow to the suffering of a fellow human being. When the native helmsman is killed, we see that Marlow's almost fanatical devotion to his duties as ship's captain has not destroyed his compassion: "The intimate profundity of that look he gave me when he received his hurt remains to this day in my memory – like a kind of distant kinship affirmed in a supreme moment" (XVI, 119). The accountant, like the company doctor and Marlow's aunt, functions as a symbolic touchstone enabling the reader to judge the full significance of Marlow's actions.

After leaving the first station, Marlow, with a white com-

panion and sixty native carriers, travels two hundred miles up
the river to the Central Station. This trip represents a further
ingress into the heart of darkness, and with each step, Marlow's
mood becomes blacker. The country between the two stations
has been completely deserted by natives, who have fled the white
man's law. All is chaos; even the natural growth and geography
of this two hundred mile stretch lack uniformity. Long grass
gives way to burnt grass, burnt grass to impenetrable thickets;
there are stony hills ablaze with heat, and chilly ravines. The
only semblance of order which Marlow encounters on this journey
is a drunk and disheveled white man who has a vague notion
that he is responsible for the upkeep of the road and who
discharges his responsibility by wandering up and down the road
shooting negroes. The other white man becomes ill; some of
the negro bearers run off, and Marlow's mood of black despair
becomes ever deeper: "I remembered the old doctor – 'It would
be interesting for science to watch the mental changes of individuals on the spot'. I felt that I was becoming scientifically
interesting" (XVI, 72).

The Central Station is not an oasis at which the weary
traveler can refresh himself either physically or spiritually. It is
bordered on three sides by scrub forest and on the other by
smelly mud. It is inhabited by a group of listless pilgrims who,
instead of contesting the elemental evils about them, spend all
their time plotting hollow schemes which will enable them to
return to Europe rich men. Marlow, who is certainly not
altogether contemptuous of the desire for wealth, sees, however,
that there is something horribly evil about the attitude of these
men:

The only real feeling was a desire to get appointed to a trading-post
where ivory was to be had, so that they could earn percentages. They
intrigued and slandered and hated each other only on that account,
– but as to effectually lifting a little finger – Oh, no. By heavens!
there is something after all in the world allowing one man to steal
a horse while another must not look at a halter. Steal a horse straight
out. Very well. He has done it. Perhaps he can ride. But there is a
way of looking at a halter that would provoke the most charitable
of saints into a kick. (XVI, 78)

The station manager is the worst of the lot:

> He had no genius for organizing, for initiative, or for order even. That was evident in such things as the deplorable state of the station. He had no learning, and no intelligence. His position had come to him – why? Perhaps because he was never ill... He had served three terms of three years out there... Because triumphant health in the general rout of constitutions is a kind of power in itself. (XVI, 73–74)

The station manager, in a highly symbolic phrase, has said: "Men who come out here should have no entrails" (XVI, 74). But Marlow senses that a man's "entrails" are the only thing which will prevent him from giving in to the flabby devil. The manager has succumbed, for though his health will allow him by default to rise in the colonial service, he has, like the accountant of the first station, lost all vestiges of humanity. His health keeps him going, and while the Central Station rots around him, he exercises a tyranny over its inhabitants, both white and black, which is limited only because he has no imagination. The station manager, like Kurtz, would take a high seat among the devils of the land if he were not congenitally incapable of doing so.

Before the Central Station, Marlow was already a scientifically interesting case. Like Melville's Ishmael, Marlow had gone to sea with "drizzly November" in his soul. His attempts to secure a position on an ocean-going vessel had been unsuccessful, and to get a job, any job, he had had to humble himself and ask the help of the women in his family. Marlow's reasons for accepting the position in the Congo were, then, a compound of his childhood ambition to visit the Congo and his desire to escape the futile task of attempting to get a job on a sea-going ship.[9] Attempting

---

[9] Ian Watt, in "Conrad Criticism and *The Nigger of the 'Narcissus'* ", *Nineteenth Century Fiction*, XII (March, 1958), 257–283, argues that Conrad should be allowed his Greek chorus in the form of Marlow as Percy Lubbock had not yet codified James' masterful handling of point of view. Conrad, however, does not seem to require this type of defence. If Marlow, in "Heart of Darkness", generalizes a great deal concerning his experience, this is because it is, after all, his story, and he is desperately searching for some sort of a meaning in it. Marvin

to recreate for his listeners the somberness of his mood at the
time he undertook his Congo voyage, Marlow clusters together
a great many images of blackness. His predecessor was killed in
an argument over two black hens. Brussels is described as a
tomb. At the trading company's office he meets the two preternatural women knitting black wool, and they seem to him to
be guarding the door of Darkness.

When Marlow reaches the coast of Africa he sees not only
blackness, but futility. A French warship is shelling the unin-
habited coastal bush; the captain of Marlow's ship, a Swede,
tells of another Swede engaged in the noble colonizing effort
who recently committed suicide. Marlow asks: "Why, in God's
name?" The captain shrugs: "Who knows? The sun too much
for him, or the country perhaps" (XVI, 63). There seems to
Marlow to be no reason behind anything he sees at this early
stage in his journey. All is futility and decay:

I came upon a boiler wallowing in the grass, then found a path
leading up the hill. It turned aside for the boulders, and also for
an undersized railway-truck lying there on its back with its wheels in
the air. One was off. The thing looked as dead as the carcass of
some animal. I came upon more pieces of decaying machinery, a
stack of rusty rails. To the left a clump of trees made a shady spot,
where dark things seemed to stir feebly. I blinked, the path was steep.
A horn tooted to the right, and I saw the black people run. A heavy
and dull detonation shook the ground, a puff of smoke came out of
the cliff, and that was all, No change appeared on the face of the
rock. They were building a railway. The cliff was not in the way
or anything; but this objectless blasting was all the work going on.
(XVI, 63–64)

During the exploratory walk which he takes at the first station,
Marlow discovers further evidences of the addle-headed folly of
the colonial powers:

I avoided a vast artificial hole somebody had been digging on the
slope, the purpose of which I found it impossible to divine. It wasn't

Mudrick's heavy-handed criticism of Marlow's "inconceivables", "im-
penetrables", "smiles of indefinable meaning", and "unspeakable rites"
either ignores or grossly misinterprets Marlow's role in "Heart of
Darkness" ("The Originality of Conrad", *The Hudson Review*, XI,
Winter, 1958–1959, 551).

a quarry or a sandpit, anyhow. It was just a hole.... Then I nearly
fell into a very narrow ravine, almost no more than a scar in the
hillside. I discovered that a lot of imported drainage-pipes for the
settlement had been tumbled in there. There wasn't one that was
not broken. It was a wanton smash-up. (XVI, 65–66)

After his dark experiences in the grove of death and his meeting
with the weak, greedy pilgrims, Marlow nearly loses his faith
in the redeeming idea at the back of the colonial operation.
The horror of his experiences has driven him ever deeper into
his own consciousness, and he nearly falls into that everlasting
deep hole in which even honor, courage, and honest devotion
to duty seem hollow. Kurtz strikes out in blind, revengeful egoism
because he can discern no system of order in the elemental
jungle, the passive stupidity of its black inhabitants, or the
disguised avarice of the colonial enterprise. In the face of this
enormous stupidity, why should an intelligent man not make his
own laws?

2. Work imagery

Through work Marlow is saved from the spiritual disintegration
to which unrestrained egoism leads. The job of repairing the
battered steamer permits him "to come out a bit", to immerse
the morbidity of his self-consciousness in some fixed value outside himself:[10]

[10] The following letter from Conrad to Mme. Poradowska offers ample
evidence that Conrad did, indeed, feel that man could find in work
the measure of his worth: "One becomes useful only on realizing the
utter insignificance of the individual in the scheme of the universe.
When one well understands that in oneself one is nothing and that a
man is worth neither more nor less than the work he accomplishes with
honesty of purpose and means, and within the strict limits of his duty
towards society, only then is one the master of his conscience, with the
right to call himself a man. Otherwise, were he more attractive than
Prince Charming, richer than Midas, wiser than Doctor Faust himself,
the two-legged featherless creature is only a despicable thing sunk in
the mud of all the passions" (John A. Gee and Paul J. Sturm, ed., *Letters
of Joseph Conrad to Marguerite Poradowska,* New Haven, Conn., 1940,
pp. 45–46).

No, I don't like work. I had rather laze about and think of all the fine things that can be done. I don't like work – no man does – but I like what is in the work, – the chance to find yourself. Your own reality – for yourself, not for others – what no other man can ever know. They can only see the mere show, and never can tell what it really means. (XVI, 85) [11]

Certainly Marlow's work is more than a device to retain his sanity. This is clearly seen when his devotion to duty is compared with that of the chief accountant at the first station. The accountant substitutes starched shirts and faultlessly kept account books for being human. His work makes him stop asking questions, makes him stop searching for a meaning in the absurd jumble of noble ideas, white men, jungle, disease, black men, and death. Marlow's work, however, offers him a secure position from which he can continue his quest for the redeeming idea, the small grain of truth which he is sure exists even in the depths of the Congo. His work is not a retreat but an opening out.

At the Central Station Marlow sees the degeneration of men who have no object in life except the accumulation of wealth, but now that he has firmly anchored himself in his work, they do not cause him to despair so much. He can observe that their lack of any unselfish objective, not the illogic of the universe, accounts for their inhumanity. The station's brick-maker symbolizes the plight of all the pilgrims. He is apparently not an altogether unpromising young man, but deprived af any possibility of fulfilling his job of making bricks, he turns into a spy

---

[11]   Conrad undoubtedly was familiar with Carlyle's essay on "Labour". Carlyle writes: "Consider how, even in the meanest sorts of Labour, the whole soul of a man is composed into a kind of real harmony, the instant he sets himself to work! Doubt, Desire, Sorrow, Remorse, Indignation, Despair itself, all these like helldogs lie beleaguering the soul of the poor dayworker, as of every man: but he bends himself with free valour against his task, and all these are stilled, all these shrink murmuring far off into their caves. The man is now a man. The blessed glow of Labour in him, is it not as purifying fire, wherein all poison is burnt up, and of sour smoke itself there is made bright blessed flame!" From *Prose of the Victorian Period,* ed., William E. Buckler (Boston, 1958), p. 144.

for the station manager. Marlow describes him as a papier-maché Mephistopheles and comments ironically on his moral weakness:

The business intrusted to this fellow was the making of bricks – so I had been informed; but there wasn't a fragment of a brick anywhere in the station, and he had been there more than a year – waiting. It seems he could not make bricks without something, I don't know what – straw maybe. Anyways, it could not be found there, and as it was not likely to be sent from Europe, it did not appear clear to me what he was waiting for. An act of special creation perhaps. (XVI, 77)

The brickmaker needs straw, and Marlow needs rivets. He has sufficient plates to cover the holes in the side of the ancient steamer, but he has no rivets, and the station manager is not particularly disposed to get him any. Rivets become an obsession with Marlow. He dreams of the wealth of rivets at the first station:

You kicked a loose rivet at every second step in that station yard on the hillside. Rivets had rolled into the grove of death. You could fill your pockets with rivets for the trouble of stooping down – and there wasn't one rivet to be found where it was wanted. (XVI, 83)

In his conversation with the brick-maker, who apparently has some influence with the station manager, Marlow demands rivets. When he and the boiler-maker with whom he has been working are confident that they shall, indeed, have some rivets, they dance a grotesque jig on the deck of the steamer. Rivets have clearly become to Marlow a symbol of the redeeming ideas of civilization, the ideas of humanity and solidarity which enable man to constrain hostile nature: "What I wanted was a certain quantity of rivets – and rivets were what really Mr. Kurtz wanted, if he had only known it" (XVI, 84). It is also significant that in order to obtain rivets for his ship, Marlow goes "near enough to a lie" (XVI, 82). When the brick-maker overestimates the importance of Marlow's connections in Europe, Marlow does not correct him. The brick-maker apparently reports that this influential man wants rivets desperately, and the station manager has them sent. Marlow's first "lie", then, enables him, if the

symbolic significance of the rivets is accepted, to gain access to
the strength which he must have to front the elemental evil
which would turn him into a scheming animal. His second "lie"
is of much the same nature.

Slowly, Marlow, though never ignoring the ever-present danger
which the jungle represents, begins to see order where before he
could see only chaos. There is a certain fitness in the boiler-
maker's tying up his waist-length beard in a serviette to keep
it clean as he crawls in the mud underneath the ship repairing
her. He immerses himself in the destructive element. the river's
primeval ooze, but by the force of his imagination he keeps a
part of himself clean.

When Marlow gets the ship underway, he travels further yet
into the heart of darkness. During this part of his voyage, the
exercise of his craft becomes even more important to the maintenance of his spiritual sanity, for now he realizes that he possesses a heritage in common with the savages whom he sees on
the river banks:

It was unearthly, and the men were – No, they were not inhuman.
Well, you know, that was the worst of it – this suspicion of their
not being inhuman. It would come slowly to one. They howled and
leaped and spun, and made horrid faces; but what thrilled you was
just the thought of their humanity – like yours – the thought of your
remote kinship with the wild and passionate uproar. Ugly. Yes, it
was ugly enough; but if you were man enough you would admit to
yourself that there was in you just the faintest trace of a response
to the terrible frankness of that noise, a dim suspicion of there being
a meaning in it which you – you so remote from the night of first
ages – could comprehend. (XVI, 96)

Yet, since he is protected from the primeval ugliness by the ritual
of his work, he can begin to discern the truth for which he is
searching:

What was there after all? Joy, fear, sorrow, devotion, valour, rage
– who can tell? – but truth – truth stripped of its cloak of time....
You wonder I didn't go ashore for a howl and a dance? Well, no – I
didn't. Fine sentiments, you say? Fine sentiments, be hanged! I had
no time. I had to mess about with white-lead and strips of woollen
blanket helping to put bandages on those leaky steam-pipes – I tell
you. I had to watch the steering, and circumvent those snags, and get

the tin-pot along by hook or by crook. There was a surface-truth enough in these things to save a wiser man. (XVI, 96–97)

In his fireman and his cannibal crew, Marlow reads the story of mankind's faltering and painful journey out of the dark jungle. The fireman tends the boiler with assiduous care because he believes that if he lets the water fall below a certain mark on the gauge, the spirit inside the boiler will become angry and devour him. He does not understand his work, but he is useful to the ship, and the knowledge of the ship's operation which he possesses is "improving knowledge" (XVI, 97).

It is an indication of how far Marlow has pierced into the heart of darkness that his not being eaten by a fellow human being is to him a hopeful sign. It is also a tribute to Conrad's ability to present the primary, unadorned realities of existence that, in describing the cannibal's restraint, he gives an infinitely more meaningful perspective on the solidarity of mankind than can volumes of preaching about the brotherhood of man. The cannibals have no inherited experience to teach them a code of behaviour. They do not understand the contract under which they are bound, and their pay – three pieces of brass wire a month – is useless to them. They are hungry, but yet they perform their duties and apparently never think of dining on Marlow and the pilgrims. Marlow jokes that he, if he were a cannibal, would not eat the pilgrims either – they are unwholesome in any sense of the word – but he is mystified by the cannibals' restraint:

Restraint! What possible restraint? Was it superstition, disgust, patience, fear – or some kind of primitive honour? No fear can stand up to hunger, no patience can wear it out, disgust simply does not exist where hunger is; and as to superstition, beliefs, and what you may call principles, they are less than chaff in a breeze. (XVI, 105)

Marlow sees that the nobility of the human spirit is in fact a greater mystery than the nameless brute thing waiting in the jungle:

But there was the fact facing me – the fact dazzling, to be seen, like the foam on the depths of the sea, like a ripple on an unfathomable enigma, a mystery greater – when I thought of it – than the curious, inexplicable note of desperate grief in this savage clamour that had swept by us on the river-bank, behind the blind whiteness of the fog. (XVI, 105)

He is beginning to fit the facts of his experience into some meaningful pattern, and Conrad skilfully guides the reader along the path of Marlow's ever-more-hopeful quest.

One of the most effective symbols in this, the second section of "Heart of Darkness", is the tattered book, *An Inquiry into Some Points of Seamanship*. Marlow, when he discovers this volume in the deserted hut of the Russian harlequin, can be said to be almost cheerful:

Not a very enthralling book; but at the first glance you could see there a singleness of intention, an honest concern for the right way of going to work, which made these humble pages, thought out so many years ago, luminous with another than a professional light. The simple old sailor, with his talk of chains and purchases, made me forget the jungle and the pilgrims in a delicious sensation of having come upon something unmistakably real. (XVI, 99)

He has in his hands at last a tangible manifestation of the honor which he has been able to salvage from the chaos of Africa.

Marlow's devotion to his work is a code which enables him to find value in life. In fact, some twenty years before Hemingway began to write, Conrad had conceived in the Marlow of "Heart of Darkness" the "code hero". Cayetano, Harry Wilson, the "non-messy" people in *The Sun Also Rises,* and old Santiago are direct descendants of Marlow. Perhaps their code is a bit narrower, and perhaps it allows them to come out of themselves a bit less, yet Hemingway's characters who are true to the code must, like Marlow, "breathe dead hippo and not be contaminated". In fact, it would not at all violate the character of Harry Wilson for him to offer exactly the aforementioned advice to Francis Macomber.

3. *Marlow as mythic hero*

Conrad blends the first and second parts of the story together by bringing the work imagery to the fore just at the moment when Marlow seems to have lost all faith in making his mind triumph over the futility which he observes around him. The second section of the story flows perfectly into the third section, in which the emphasis is on Marlow as mythic hero, in the scene in which Marlow's helmsman is killed. Here Marlow's work ethic enables him to come even further out of himself. He acknowledges his personal tie to his helmsman, and, in a blood ritual, purges himself of the heritage of guilt which his predecessor Fresleven has left him. Lillian Feder, in tracing the parallels between Marlow's descent into the underworld and that of Aeneas, likens Marlow's helmsman to Aeneas's, Palinurus, and certainly there is ample evidence that these two helmsmen fulfil generally the same function in their respective stories.[12] However, when Miss Feder says that "both die 'insontes'" (guiltless), and loyal to their leaders, she seemingly overlooks an important difference between Palinurus and Marlow's helmsman. Palinurus slips and falls accidentally into the sea, but is so intent on his job of steering that he holds to the tiller even as he falls and carries it with him. Marlow's helmsman leaves the tiller and throws open the shutter of the deck house to fire a rifle at the natives on the bank. He does not die guiltless; he has failed in his duty. Like the helmsman of the "Narcissus" who left his post during the near mutiny, Marlow's helmsman has been overcome by the evil, insidious powers which abhor solidarity. The helmsman's death, which comes as a direct result of his leaving the wheel, is Conrad's symbolic comment on the wages of dereliction of duty. Kurtz has also, in a sense, left the tiller.

The death of the helmsman fulfils additional important symbolic functions. As has been previously noted, when the native falls dead at Marlow's feet, Marlow realizes that his work has enabled him to understand and sympathize with a fellow human being. The helmsman is by no means proficient at his job, but

[12] The Sibyl tells Aeneas:

> "make
> Sacrifice of black sheep: only when you are thus
> Purified, shall you see the Stygian groves and the regions
> Not visible to the living."

Marlow's helmsman seems to be his master's "black sheep".

Marlow perceives that there is something mystic and profoundly human about this native's imperfect attempts to steer the ship when it would be more reasonable for him to be ashore howling and dancing. Marlow is a nineteenth-century Englishman, and Conrad never allows him to express views inconsistent with the "idea at the back" of Victorian colonial policy. The Negroes of the Congo have been represented to Marlow by his society as an inferior species of human being; thus, he feels almost defensive as he expresses his sympathy for one:

> I missed my late helmsman awfully, – I missed him even while his body was still lying in the pilot-house. Perhaps you will think it passing strange this regret for a savage who was no more account than a grain of sand in a black Sahara. Well, don't you see, he had done something, he had steered; for months I had him at my back – a help – an instrument. It was a kind of partnership. He steered for me – I had to look after him, I worried about his deficiencies, and thus a subtle bond had been created, of which I only became aware when it was suddenly broken. (XVI, 119)

The solidarity of mankind, Marlow realizes, does not rest on the irrelevancies of skin color. The sympathy which Marlow gains for his helmsman through the ritual of work has enabled him to identify with the soul of black Africa as Kurtz, with all the eloquence of his seventeen page pamphlet, never could.

The death of the helmsman also amounts to a symbolic blood purge. When the helmsman falls dead, his blood drenches Marlow's shoes. Marlow is more than naturally anxious to get out of his shoes. In fact, his actions are frantic. Instead of waiting until danger is past, taking the shoes off, washing the blood out of them, and setting them in a corner to dry, Marlow entrusts the wheel to an unreliable pilgrim, sits down on the deck, madly pulls his bloody shoes from his feet and throws them into the river. Certainly his actions indicate how far toward irrationality the powers of darkness have driven him, and when the early reference to Fresleven is recalled, Marlow's throwing his shoes into the river assumes a highly symbolic meaning. Marlow has mentioned his search for Fresleven's remains, saying that nobody troubled much about the body of the dead man "till I got out

and stepped into his shoes" (XVI, 54). Marlow is, indeed, in
Fresleven's shoes until the helmsman dies. Up to this point in
the narrative Marlow, too, could die for something as ridiculous
as two black hens – a handful of rivets, or a piece of brass wire,
perhaps. The helmsman's death, however, enables Marlow to
symbolically cast off Fresleven's shoes. He is no longer merely
Fresleven's replacement, but a new sort of adventurer who will
progress even further into the heart of darkness.

At this point in the narrative, Conrad shifts the imagery to a
mythic referent. Marlow is transformed from the captain of a
river steamer into a hero who has as his mission the simultaneous
discovery of his own destiny and a beneficent talisman which
will work for the good of all mankind. Keeping his ship on
course is no longer his primary task. He is to wrestle with the
soul of Kurtz and effect a return from the nether world with no
powers to invoke save his own inborn courage. Though it is now
certain that Marlow will not succumb to the powers of darkness
over a thing as small as two black hens, his return from Kurtz's
hellish world is by no means assured. Marlow has already heard
the report that Kurtz once traveled almost three hundred miles
down river before deciding to go back, and the significance of
Kurtz's return, though at first understood by neither the reader
nor Marlow, becomes increasingly apparent as Marlow continues
his voyage upriver. Kurtz, in fact, did not change his mind, but
was recalled by the dark powers whose intimate he had become.
As the Sibyl warns Aeneas:

> The descent to Avernus is easy
> The gate of Pluto stands open night and day
> But to retrace one's steps and return to the upper air
> That is the toil, that the difficulty.

The mythic theme of Marlow's journey is ever present in "Heart
of Darkness", but in the first two sections it plays a subordinate
role. In the first section of the narrative he sees the two knitters
of black wool as preternatural creatures guarding the portal of
darkness, but there are not yet sufficient symbolic referents to
render these two women full significance as mythic figures.
When, in the second section of the story, Marlow speaks of

Kurtz as an "enchanted princess", the mythic framework has been more firmly established, but is, nevertheless, subordinate to the symbolism of work as a saving grace. In the third section, however, the symbolic elements emphasized earlier are submerged in the myth of the hero's discovery of the saving talisman in the nether world, and his carrying it back to the upper world.

As Marlow travels up the Congo on the last stage of his journey, the jungle steps "leisurely across the water to bar the way for our return" (XVI, 95). He has learned to look on the jungle as on a treacherous human being and has mastered it, at least temporarily, by never turning his back on it. It is clear, however, that Marlow will need to discover a more powerful stabilizing force than the ritual of work to return from the depths to which he has descended. Marlow, when he brings Kurtz on board, is "numbered with the dead" (XVI, 147) by the greedily complacent pilgrims, and he accepts this "unforeseen partnership" which has been forced on him. He, too, feels that he is a lonely spirit wandering in the land of the dead, and he knows that he must learn the secret of the heart of darkness before he can return.

The ingress into the heart of darkness has been slow, and Conrad does not jostle the deliberately unhastened sequence of action in this last stage of Marlow's journey. Before Marlow meets Kurtz, he meets the youthful Russian harlequin, one of the most enigmatic characters in "Heart of Darkness". At first Marlow almost laughs at the young adventurer: "His aspect reminded me of something funny I had seen somewhere" (XVI, 122). Marlow finally decides that the strange fellow reminds him of a harlequin:

His clothes had been made of some stuff that was brown all over, with bright patches, blue, red, and yellow, – patches on the back, patches on elbows, on knees; coloured binding around his jacket, scarlet edging at the bottom of his trousers; and the sunshine made him look extremely gay and wonderfully neat withal, because you could see how beautifully all this patching had been done. (XVI, 122)

But this harlequin is not funny, for he is completely under the mad influence of Kurtz. He has given Kurtz his small hoard of

ivory and has nursed him through two illnesses. In return, Kurtz
has lectured him on love, justice, honor, and courage and has
threatened to kill him. Kurtz is destroyed by his egoism; the
Russian is nearly destroyed by a supreme lack of self-
consciousness. Marlow says:

> If the absolutely pure, uncalculating, unpractical spirit of adventure
> had ever ruled a human being, it ruled this be-patched youth. I
> almost envied him the possession of this modest and clear flame.
> It seemed to have consumed all thought of self so completely, that
> even while he was talking to you, you forgot that it was he – the
> man before your eyes – who had gone through these things. I did
> not envy him his devotion to Kurtz, though. He had not meditated
> over it. It came to him, and he accepted it with a sort of eager fatalism.
> I must say that to me it appeared about the most dangerous thing
> in every way he had come upon so far. (XVI, 126–127)

The crazy quilt pattern of the harlequin's clothing seems symbolic of his moral and intellectual being. He has had experiences
in the jungle which should have exploded his juvenile notions,
but, unlike Marlow, he has been unable to assimilate these experiences. His ideas are as colorful as his clothing, but, like his
clothing, they are an absurd and ineffectual superficiality with
which he hopes to disguise his nakedness.

As the receptacle of Kurtz's noble ideas, the harlequin symbolically illustrates their impractical sentimental bases, but he also
functions as a sort of guide to aid Marlow in his heroic quest.
It is the Russian who has left the strange message for Marlow:
"Hurry up. Approach cautiously" (XVI, 98). And it is the Russian who confirms Marlow's suspicions about Kurtz's devilish
practices, advises him about the influence of the savage woman,
and tells him of the dangers of approaching the "pitiful Jupiter".[13]

The harlequin is, however, a desperately lonely human being,
and Marlow, who has sympathized with the oppressed negroes in
the grove of death, the cannibal crew of his steamer, and his
incompetent helmsman, likewise sympathizes with this addled
young man. In fact, it seems Marlow wishes to bring the young
Russian, as well as Kurtz, out of the Congo. Towson's *An In-*

[13] In the Russian's warning there is a definite echo of Agamemnon's
advice to Odysseus.

quiry into Some Points of Seamanship, which has come to possess
such symbolic importance to Marlow, is the young man's property, and Marlow restores it to him. Perhaps this book on navigation will help the Russian to find his way out of the heart
of darkness. It is also significant that Marlow, who has stepped
into Fresleven's shoes, and has thrown a new but bloodstained
pair of his own overboard, gives the harlequin a pair of his old
shoes. It is, of course, a mythic tradition that an article of clothing retains the spiritual and physical attributes of its original
owner. Perhaps, then, when the young man steps into Marlow's
shoes he will be able to negotiate the painful ascent to the world
of light even as Marlow does. In any case, Marlow's restoring
of the Russian's book and his gift of a pair of old shoes echo
the magical and magnanimous deeds of the mythic hero.

The jungle is ever present, ever ready to spring on the unwary;
but Marlow, by this time, regards it almost affectionately, as one
would an old enemy. He is ready for a severer test. He is ready
to meet Kurtz himself. Conrad, of course, has to handle this
meeting with consummate artistry to keep it from turning into
a horrible anti-climax, for though the narrative of Marlow's
journey is nearly over, we have still not seen Kurtz. A lesser
artist than Conrad would, no doubt, at this point include some
detailed accounts of the "unspeakable rites" and cruel atrocities
in which Kurtz has indulged.[14] Conrad, however, delineates
Kurtz's character with a few direct strokes. Kurtz comes out of
the jungle borne on a litter like a king. He is long and lean,
belying his name: "Kurtz – Kurtz – that means short in German,
don't it? Well, the name was as true as everything else in his
life – and death. He looked at least seven feet long"[15] (XVI,

---

[14]   Conrad, in giving Garnett an oral account of what he intended to
write in "Heart of Darkness", included a scene in which Kurtz, attended
by an old Negress, lay ill in a native hut (Gordan, p. 267). This scene,
of course, does not appear in "Heart of Darkness", for it would
obviously have made Kurtz less effective as both a symbolic and a
tragic character.

[15]   The manuscript of "Heart of Darkness" indicates that Conrad had
originally intended to use the name Klein for his hero, after the
Georges-Antoine Klein whom he met on his Congo voyage. In the

134). How better to indicate a man is not what he is supposed to be and how better to indicate that his failure is not a result of his conscious will than to note that his name is not fitting. Kurtz has with him a small arsenal – "two shot guns, a heavy rifle, and a light revolver carbine" (XVI, 134), absurd when the only enemy from whom he needs protection is himself.

Kurtz is, indeed, a "hollow man". Marlow, when he carries him out of the forest, reports that "he was not much heavier than a child" (XVI, 145). Kurtz is also hollow in that his "gorgeous eloquence" is wholly ethereal. Ill as he is when he is brought on board the steamer, he has not lost the ability to expound his noble ideas:

Kurtz discoursed. A voice! a voice! It rang deep to the very last. It survived his strength to hide in the magnificent folds of eloquence the barren darkness of his heart. Oh, he struggled! he struggled! The wastes of his weary brain were haunted by shadowy images now – images of wealth and fame revolving obsequiously round his unextinguishable gift of noble and lofty expression. My intended, my station, my career, my ideas – these were the subjects for the occasional utterances of elevated sentiments. (XVI, 147)

But these words are meaningless. In fact, the only words which he utters to Marlow which possess truth enough to mitigate his emptiness are his last: "The horror! The horror!" (XVI, 149).

Kurtz has allowed himself to be regarded as a God. "He has kicked himself loose of the earth" (XVI, 144), reports Mar- low. He has murdered and robbed; he has crawled through the grass like a snake in order to reach those who would worship him. His last words, however, at least partially expiate.[16] They

---

manuscript, he has several times crossed out "Monsieur Klein" and substituted "Mr. Kurtz" (Gordon, p. 37). It seems obvious that Conrad wished to retain the symbolic significance of the German "Klein" and was influenced in his happy choice of "Kurtz" by the "Kayerts" of "An Outpost of Progress".

[16] Robert Haugh, in *Joseph Conrad: Discovery in Design* (Norman, Okla., 1957), p. 40, interprets "The horror" as the talisman which Marlow has descended to discover. Lillian Feder, "Marlow's Descent into Hell", *Nineteenth Century Fiction,* interprets "The horror" in much the same way: "Kurtz's last cry, 'the horror', does not indicate that he has had a last minute conversion." Robert Evans, in "Conrad's Under-

represent for both Marlow and Kurtz a "supreme moment of complete knowledge ... an affirmation, a moral victory paid for by innumerable defeats, by abominable terrors, by abominable satisfactions" (XVI, 151). Marlow discovers that the human spirit is stronger than the powers of darkness, and this is the ultimate boon which he must carry to the upper world.

Joseph Campbell, in *The Hero with a Thousand Faces*, describes the problem of the returning hero:

> How teach again, however, what has been taught correctly and incorrectly learned a thousand thousand times, throughout the millenniums of mankind's prudent folly? That is the hero's ultimate difficult task. How render back into light-world language the speech-defying pronouncements of the dark? ... The first problem of the returning hero is to accept as real, after an experience of the soul-satisfying vision of fulfilment, the passing joys and sorrows, banalities and noisy obscenities of life. Why re-enter such a world? Why attempt to make plausible, or even interesting, to men and women consumed with passion, the experience of transcendental bliss.[17]

Conrad's description of the psychological state of his returning hero, Marlow, closely parallels that of the traditional mythic hero which Campbell describes:

> I found myself back in the sepulchral city resenting the sight of people hurrying through the streets to filch a little money from each other, to devour their infamous cookery, to gulp their unwholesome beer, to dream their insignificant and silly dreams. They trespassed upon my thoughts. They were intruders whose knowledge of life was to me an irritating pretence, because I felt so sure they could not possibly know the things I knew. Their bearing, which was simply the bearing of commonplace individuals going about their business in the assurance of perfect safety, was offensive to me like the outrageous flauntings of folly in the face of a danger it is unable to comprehend. I had no particular desire to enlighten them, but I had some difficulty in restraining myself from laughing in their faces, so full of stupid importance. (XVI, 152)

---

world", *Modern Fiction Studies*, says: " 'The horror' may not only refer back to his Satanic service but may also look ahead to an ever-lasting horror." All three of these interpretations seemingly slight Marlow's explicit statements, which indicate that Kurtz's last words represent a moral victory.

[17] Joseph Campbell, *The Hero with a Thousand Faces* (New York, 1956), p. 218.

Marlow's experience with Kurtz is not accurately one of "transcendental bliss", but though he has learned about the darkness of the human heart, he has also learned about the resiliency of the human spirit, and it is his duty, though he is at first reluctant to acknowledge it, to translate his vision of truth into a form which will "redound to the renewing of the community, the nation, the planet". [18] He "lies" to Kurtz's Intended. [19]

When Marlow recounts his experiences at the Central Station, he says:

You know I hate, detest, and can't bear a lie, not because I am straighter than the rest of us, but simply because it appalls me. There

[18] Campbell, p. 193.
[19] There is also substantial disagreement concerning Marlow's interview with the Intended. Marvin Mudrick, in "The Originality of Conrad", *The Hudson Review,* calls the lie "sentimental" and the final scene "cheaply ironic doubletalk". Thomas Moser, *Joseph Conrad: Achievement and Decline* (Cambridge, Mass., 1957), p. 79, writes: "Marlow has come there hoping to surrender to her the memory of Kurtz. She instead maneuvers him into telling her a lie: that Kurtz's last words were, not "The horror", but her name .... Marlow's lie certainly weakens the scene; he has made truth seem too important throughout the novel to persuade the reader now to accept falsehood as salvation." Lillian Feder, in "Marlow's Descent into Hell", *Nineteenth Century Fiction,* says Marlow experiences "a kind of spiritual death in the sacrifice of lying for Kurtz". Robert Evans, "Conrad's Underworld", *Modern Fiction Studies,* says Marlow's action is "selfless though intrinsically sinful". The evidence of the text would indicate, however, that Marlow's lie is not sinful, sentimental or weak. Walter Wright says: "The scene in which Marlow conceals from the girl the nature of Kurtz's death is really a study of the nature of truth. If he had told the girl the simple facts, he would have acknowledged that the pilgrims in their cynicism had the truth, that goodness and faith were the unrealities. Marlow appreciates this temptation, and we are hardly to suppose that sentimental weakness made him resist it. He does not preach to us about the wisdom he has achieved; the fact is, he deprecates it, and now he says merely that to tell her would be 'too dark altogether'. He is still perplexed as to the ethics of his deception and wishes that fate had permitted him to remain a simple reporter of incidents instead of making him struggle in the realm of human values. Yet in leaving in juxtaposition the fiancée's ideal, a matter within her own heart, and the fact of Kurtz's death, Marlow succeeds in putting before us in his inconclusive way the two extremes that can exist within the human mind, and we realize that not one, but both of these are reality" (Walter Wright, *Romance and Tragedy in Joseph Conrad,* Lincoln, Nebr., 1949, p. 159).

is a taint of death, a flavour of mortality in lies – which is exactly
what I hate and detest in the world – what I want to forget. It
makes me miserable and sick, like biting something rotten would do.
(XVI, 82)

If, however, the nature of the truth which Marlow has learned
in Africa is carefully examined, and if Marlow is viewed as a
sort of mythic hero who has returned from the nether world
with a restorative boon, his words to Kurtz's Intended do not
constitute a lie, in the normal sense of the word.

At the Central Station Marlow sees Kurtz's painting of
"justice":

I noticed a small sketch in oils, on a panel, representing a woman,
draped and blindfolded, carrying a lighted torch. The background
was sombre – almost black. The movement of the woman was stately,
and the effect of the torch-light on the face was sinister. (XVI, 79)

When Marlow stands before the door of Kurtz's Intended, he
remembers one of the dying man's remarks: "I want no more
than justice". One cannot tell whether Marlow is cynical or
pensive as he repeats: "He wanted no more than justice – no
more than justice" (XVI, 156), but after his interview with
the Intended, it is obvious that Marlow, at the last, perceives
that Kurtz, in fact all mankind, wants not justice, but love.
Justice, especially Kurtz's stark, sentimental type of justice, as
symbolized in his painting, has a sinister countenance; it is not
only dark, but terribly destructive.

When Kurtz's Intended says: "Don't you understand I loved
him – I loved him – I loved him" (XVI, 161), she in truth has
little conception of the love which transcends sexuality – the
solidarity which gives meaning to the universe. However, Marlow instantaneously perceives, when he hears the Intended speak
of her love, that only in affirming the deeper meaning of Kurtz's
expiating words "the horror" can he soothe his own troubled
imagination, keep back the dark wilderness, and make the human
adventure meaningful: "Hadn't he said he wanted only justice?
But I couldn't. I could not tell her. It would have been too dark
– too dark altogether" (XVI, 162). If Marlow tells the "truth",

his Congo experiences and Kurtz's life will be completely without value.

As Kurtz's savage consort symbolizes the soul of the jungle, the Intended, with her "great and saving illusion" (XVI, 159) shining in the darkness, symbolizes the soul of civilization. The soul of the latter is, of course, not without its darkness also. As Marlow sits in the drawing room waiting for the Intended, the imagery is dominantly dark, but there are significant patches of light and whiteness:

> The dusk was falling. I had to wait in a lofty drawing-room with three long windows from floor to ceiling that were like three luminous and bedraped columns. The bent gilt legs and backs of the furniture shone in indistinct curves. The tall marble fireplace had a cold and monumental whiteness. A grand piano stood massively in a corner; with dark gleams on the flat surfaces like a sombre and polished sarcophagus. (XVI, 156)

When Marlow meets the Intended, he has a vision of her and Kurtz united in the same being, and when she says: "I have survived" (XVI, 157) though "The horror" still echoes in Marlow's ears, he perceives that a part of Kurtz, the noblest part, the part he "Intended" has in fact survived the powers of darkness. It would be deceitful of Marlow to kill this surviving nobility.

"And this also has been one of the dark places of the earth" (XVI, 48), says Marlow before he begins the narrative of his Congo voyage. London, the city to which Marlow refers, is, however, no longer as devoid of light as the African jungle, for it has had light brought back to it by men like Charlie Marlow. A long and unbroken line of heroic adventurers have gazed into the pit and perceived this light where there seemed to be none. The illumination these knight-errants have brought back with them is imperfect and fleeting, in fact may be enfolded in a lie:

> Yes; but it is like a running glaze on a plain, like a flash of lightning in the clouds. We live in the flicker – may it last as long as the old earth keeps rolling! (XVI 49)

VI. THE SHADOW LINE STORIES

"... it is a question whether it is not a more subtle and
more human triumph to be the sport of the waves and
yet survive, achieving your end."

A. IMAGERY OF THE "GLAD ANIMAL MOVEMENTS"
OF "YOUTH"

Wordsworth, in his "Lines Written a Few Miles Above Tintern
Abbey", describes the maturation of his soul. The "glad animal
movements" of his childhood blend into the restless, uncertain
mood of his youth, and finally he arrives at spiritual maturity
– a state in which he possesses a mature conception of human
tragedy and can accept "the still sad music of humanity" as
inevitable and not altogether meaningless. In four of his stories
of initiation, Conrad also deals with the different stages in the
progress to spiritual maturity. Though as an older man Marlow
contemplates the wondrous nature of his experiences on board
the *Judea,* the young hero of "Youth" is like the young
Wordsworth described in the "Tintern Abbey" poem – a healthy
young animal with "no need of remoter charm,/ By thought
supplied, nor any interest / Unborrowed from the eye". And in
the young Marlow is seen the same type of animal fear which
overcame the young Wordsworth as he sensed the dark powers
inherent in nature. The two heroes of "Typhoon", Jukes and
Captain MacWhirr, traverse the second stage of spiritual development; they look at the fierce, seemingly malicious violence of
nature but stop short of realizing the deepest significance of
their trial. In "The Secret Sharer", Conrad brings his young
captain across the final threshold. The narrator-hero of this tale
has listened to the harsh, grating noise of the Universe and has
understood it as a part of his destiny, though he could perhaps

only imperfectly articulate this understanding. In any case, the story ends before he can speculate on his hard-won self-knowledge and relate it to the external world. As such, the young captain's experience remains highly individual. Of course, the knowledge which the narrator-hero of *The Shadow Line* attains is also primarily concerned with self recognition, yet his discovery is of a more universal nature. As Carl Benson says: "Whereas the captain of 'The Secret Sharer' has ended 'striking out for a new destiny', the captain of *The Shadow Line* has reached the destination of the common human lot".[1] In each of these four stories, Conrad dealt with the general theme of initiation, and with each treatment of this theme, brought his hero to a successively higher stage of spiritual development.

Both Wordsworth's poem and Conrad's four-story unit are intellectual reveries with wide metaphysical implications, though the focus in these descriptions of the metamorphosis from child to man is not primarily philosophical. These two artists are essentially concerned with narrating the distinct joy and the distinct pain of the three stages of spiritual awakening. They are engaged in a quest for the truth of human experience which goes too deep for logical explanation, and their methods, a subtle combination of lyricism and symbolism, are indeed similar.

In his discussion of "Youth", Walter Wright points out that Conrad might have proceeded to tell about the glamor of youth by using "a few stock phrases and incidents that would in their very generality bring up associations in any reader's mind with incidents in his own 'youth' ". This sort of confused and indistinct evocation of emotion, Professor Wright is quick to add, is not, however, Conrad's purpose in "Youth", for in this tale Conrad is concerned with isolating and intensifying the youthful experience of wonder.[2] In effecting this isolation of emotion and its consequent intensity, Conrad again employs the symbolic method which is a hallmark of his art.

[1] Carl Benson, "Conrad's Two Stories of Initiation", *P.M.L.A.*, LXIX (March, 1954), 45–56.
[2] Walter Wright, *Romance and Tragedy in Joseph Conrad* (Lincoln, Neb., 1949), pp. 9–12.

One must agree with Douglas Hewitt that in "Youth", "the glamour and the enthusiasm are so powerfully conveyed because they have the beauty of threatened things".[3] Images of light and darkness are juxtaposed in such a manner that the dark seems of value only as a contrast, and the magic quality of the light permeates all. Old Captain Beard, the archetype of the aged neophyte, appears alongside Marlow, the uninitiated youth, and Conrad so skillfully manages the point of view that old Beard's disappointment over losing his first command is completely eclipsed by the ecstatic rapture which is Marlow's when he takes charge of his first command, a small life boat. Disaster looms everywhere, but in Marlow's mind there exists only a boundless enthusiasm. Finally the reader is nearly prompted to ask: "What, then, is the reality – Marlow's romanticism or the blackness which he cannot see?" Both, of course, are reality, and in his masterful juxtaposition of these two extremes, Conrad creates a truth which communicates to the reader something almost more powerful than a first-hand experiencing of the earliest stage of spiritual development.

The *Judea,* the ship which carries Marlow on his first voyage as second mate, is, like the *Narcissus,* a small planet detached from the earth, and she is symbolic of the two extremes which exist in the world: "She was all rust, dust, grime – soot aloft, dirt on deck" (XVI, 5). Yet, there is an element of the sublime in her hackneyed motto, "Do or Die", and this early image of decay juxtaposed with naive, yet strangely wonderful romanticism, powerfully foreshadows the nature of the enchanting experience which Conrad is to describe in the story.

Marlow does not ignore "the destructive element" which is omnipresent in what he himself calls a symbolic voyage, nor does he mutate the actuality of his experience and attempt to cast a false rosy glow over it. He does, however, report the slow inevitable decay of the *Judea* in such a manner that it partakes of the romance of adventure which dwells in his youthful spirit. Before the *Judea* has picked up her cargo of coal, she

[3] Douglas Hewitt, *Conrad: A Reassessment* (Cambridge, 1952), p. 27.

runs into a storm and the sand ballast which she is carrying shifts dangerously. The crew descends into the hold, and by shovelling the ballast, attempts to right the listing ship. The ship's hold is like an infernal region: "gloomy like a cavern, the tallow dips stuck and flickering on the beams" (XVI, 6). The men, engaged in "that gravedigger's work" (XVI, 6) cannot keep their feet and are tossed helplessly about. But Conrad, through Marlow, reports the men's difficulties as a sort of adventure. The men do not fall down cursing at their barked knuckles and their almost hopeless task; they fall down "with a great flourish of shovels" (XVI, 6). The captain's wife is "an old woman, with a face all wrinkled and ruddy like a winter apple" (XVI, 7), but Marlow is quick to notice she has the figure of a young girl. When the *Judea* is caught in an Atlantic gale, the wind nearly tears her to pieces. Marlow is well aware of the danger, but to him there is an enchanted quality even in the merciless storm: "The long-boat changed, as if by magic, into matchwood where she stood in her gripes" (XVI, 11). The ship takes on so much water that the pumps must be manned around the clock. It is, Marlow reports, "as though we had been dead and gone to a hell for sailors" (XVI, 12), yet he exults in the experience:

And there was somewhere in me the thought: By Jove! this is the deuce of an adventure – something you read about; and it is my first voyage as second mate – and I am only twenty – and here I am lasting it out as well as any of these men, and keeping my chaps up to the mark. I was pleased. I would not have given up the experience for worlds. I had moments of exultation. Whenever the old dismantled craft pitched heavily with her counter high in the air, she seemed to me to throw up, like an appeal, like a defiance, like a cry to the clouds without mercy, the words written on her stern: "*Judea,* London. Do or Die." (XVI, 12)

When the coal dust in the hold of the ship explodes, Marlow is thrown into the after hatch atop the flaming cargo. Even this nearly fatal experience Marlow relates with a certain animal gusto:

I seemed somehow to be in the air. I heard all round me like a pent-up breath released – as if a thousand giants simultaneously had said Phoo! – and felt a dull concussion which made my ribs ache suddenly No doubt about it – I was in the air, and my body was describing a short parabola. But short as it was, I had the time to think several thoughts in, as far as I can remember, the following order: "This can't be the carpenter – What is it? – Some accident – Submarine volcano? – Coals, gas! – By Jove! we are being blown up – Everybody's dead – I am falling into the afterhatch – I see fire in it." (XVI, 22–23)

The image of the battered Marlow climbing out of the hold is an unforgettable symbol of the blind self-confidence of youth. When old Mahon sees Marlow scramble back on deck he is amazed and horrified. Marlow, whose ecstatic strength has never left him, is, in turn, amazed at Mahon's wide-eyed stare: "I did not know that I had no hair, no eyebrows, no eyelashes, that my young moustache was burnt off, that my face was black, one cheek laid open, my nose cut, and my chin bleeding" (XVI, 23).

In spite of the romantic hopes of her young second mate, the *Judea* is doomed. The burning coal slowly consumes her, and Marlow thinks: "Now, this is something like. This is great. I wonder what will happen" (XVI, 26). The ship burns, and as she burns the flame of Marlow's youth is united with the flame of the destructive element, and the image which Conrad draws at this point evokes pure and unrestrained the emotion of youth too subtle for the intellect to comprehend:

Oh, the glamour of youth! Oh, the fire of it, more dazzling than the flames of the burning ship, throwing a magic light on the wide earth, leaping audaciously to the sky, presently to be quenched by time, more cruel, more pitiless, more bitter than the sea – and like the flames of the burning ship surrounded by an impenetrable night. (XVI, 30)

F. R. Leavis decries Marlow's "cheap insistence upon the glamour" in "Youth",[4] but to accept Leavis's view of Marlow is to ignore the symbolic presence of Captain Beard. The old captain's age and disappointment counterpoint Marlow's youth and enthusiasm, and his tempered, unglamorous optimism offers

4   F. R. Leavis, *The Great Tradition* (New York, 1948), p. 190.

a touchstone from which the reader can better see the young second mate's ardor as an honest welling up of the magic energy of youth. That is to say, if Beard were not present in the narrative, the reader might well accuse Conrad of creating the glamor of youth merely by neglecting to show the other side of the coin – age and failure. The *Judea* is the old captain's first command, and he undertakes to bring her from London to Bankok with something of the enthusiasm with which young Marlow undertakes his first really responsible position. Beard, however, has lost most of that youthful enthusiasm which makes the ill-fated voyage an adventure for Marlow. The last time we see the captain, he is a weary old man tricked by fate out of his first command and probably doomed never to have another: "He sat, a broken figure in the stern, wet with dew, his hands clasped in his lap... 'I had a terrible time of it', he murmured" (XVI, 38). The captain is a victim of those incomprehensible quirks of fate which keep an inherently good and capable man like himself from succeeding, a victim of all those blindly cruel forces with which Marlow is as yet unacquainted.

As Marlow cannot fully comprehend the horrible possibilities inherent in the *Judea*'s plight, so he fails to understand why Captain Beard has not had a command before he was sixty. Beard is certainly not incompetent, for he handles the ship and her crew well in difficult circumstances. The perfect love of the work has not escaped him. He is, however, somewhat of a doleful latter-day Parson Adams in that fate inevitably perverts his good intentions. When the *Judea* has taken on her load of coal, the captain the same evening takes her from her dockside berth out to the dock-gates, hoping to get an early start the next morning. He does not, however, save any time, for in the dark his ship is rammed by a steam-collier, and is delayed three weeks for repairs. Before the collier collides with his ship, the captain hears Marlow's warning cry and runs to save Mrs. Beard. "Just imagine", says Marlow "that old fellow saving heroically in his arms that old woman – the woman of his life" (XVI, 9). The captain scoops his wife up in his arms, runs across the deck, down a ladder and deposits her in the ship's boat. His action, however, is doomed to be pathetic rather than heroic. The painter holding the boat to the ship comes loose. The captain and his wife are adrift in the harbor for more than an hour, and the captain is not with his ship while she is in trouble – a serious breach of the ship officer's code. Marlow does not sense the tragic turmoil of his captain's soul, not because he does not care for the old man, but because he is caught up in the magic of being alive. Because we have the potentially tragic nature of Captain Beard's existence juxtaposed with Marlow's romantic spirit of adventure, we are better able to discern the exact quality of the emotion which grips the young second mate and are able to see that the power of the emotion which Conrad evokes in "Youth" is as much attributable to the nature of the men and events which the young Marlow fails to fully under-stand as to the glamor on which the old Marlow, who is recalling his youth, insists.

The fire which smolders in the hold of the *Judea* is also highly symbolic. It cannot be quenched; it is "the destructive element", a symbol of the evil which accompanies any human endeavor. At one point in the voyage, the crew attempts to dig down through the smouldering coal to uncover the fire. Mahon, the first who descends, is overcome by the coal gas. The man who goes to bring him out also faints. When these two are rescued, Marlow leaps down on the pile of coal "to show how easily it could be done" (XVI, 21). But the magic which he carries in his heart is ineffectual against carbon monoxide – he too faints. This incident, however, does not destroy his confidence, for he still feels he can outlast the fire in the *Judea*'s hold and that he is stronger than any other man aboard the ship. He follows his dream, and even when the *Judea* sinks, with "Do or Die" burned off her hull by the fire, Marlow is undaunted. The sinking of the old bark is an opportunity for further adven-ture. He is now the master of his own small boat.

Marlow's spirit of adventure is, of course, not the same as Stein's. He cannot consciously immerse himself in the destructive element for he cannot as yet fully recognize it. Yet the splendor of youthful vision will guide him until he is ready to take the second step in his spiritual growth. It is significant in this respect that when Marlow and his lifeboat crew pull into the Eastern port, Marlow can see the red light set out by the caretaker at the end of the jetty. When he attempts to arrange passage for the castaway crew of the *Judea* on the *Celestial,* an English ship which steams into the Javanese harbor shortly after his boat and that of his captain have arrived, the *Celestial*'s captain mistakes the young mate's boat for a native shore boat and curses him violently. When he recognizes Marlow as a fellow English sailor he apologizes and begins abusing the caretaker for not setting out the red guiding light:

"The light is out, and I nearly ran foul of the end of this damned jetty. This is third time he plays me this trick. Now, I ask you, can anybody stand this kind of thing? It's enough to drive a man out of his mind. I'll report him.... I'll get the Assistant Resident to give him the sack, by....! See – there's no light. It's out, isn't it? I take you to witness the light's out. There should be a light, you know. A red light on the –"
"There was a light", I said, mildly.
"But it's out, man! What's the use of talking like this? You can see for yourself it's out – don't you? If you had to take a valuable steamer along this Godforsaken coast you would want a light, too." (XVI, 40)

The *Celestial*'s captain, who obviously has lost most of his enthusiasm for the sea and the "romantic East", cannot see the light. Marlow, who savors the romance of every moment of his existence, can.

Several times while he is narrating his *Judea* voyage, Marlow pauses for an instant and says, "Pass the bottle". Marlow's requests for the bottle never allow the reader to forget that "Youth" is "emotion recollected in tranquillity". There was a truth and intensity to the original experience, and the older Marlow, looking back on his *Judea* voyage, can recapture the joy of his youth. At sea the crew of the *Narcissus* wring out a meaning from their sinful lives, and even though, when the ship returns to the London docks, the crew is contaminated by the filth of the city, the purity of their experience in bringing the ship through the storm can be neither defiled nor destroyed. The elder Marlow has seen the evil of the world, has seen a stealthy Nemesis unmercifully track men down, but the youthful sensations of his first voyage as second mate can never be lost, even though he knows that the sea and old age are the eventual victors. Youth may be only "a flick of sunshine upon a strange shore", but through the paradox which is art, Conrad demonstrates that once this momentary light is perceived clearly, it is inextinguishable.

B. "TYPHOON"

The beginnings of the second stage of spiritual development, that middleground between the enchantment of youth and the tempered optimism of maturity, Conrad describes in "Typhoon". There are, of course, certain close resemblances between the character and the action of "Youth" and that of "Typhoon".

1. *The symbolic significance of the characters and actions of Jukes and MacWhirr as they face the storm*

MacWhirr offsets Jukes, his young, sometimes irresponsible mate, as the aged Captain Beard contrasts with the youthful Marlow. The captain and first mate of the *Nan-Shan* face a disaster at sea just as do Captain Beard and Marlow. But while "Youth" is essentially lyric, "Typhoon" contains a drama which is almost epic. MacWhirr and Jukes are not much changed at the end of their voyage, but they have had a somewhat more difficult struggle with elemental nature than Captain Beard and Marlow. The *Nan-Shan*, in fact, sights, "the coast of the Great Beyond, whence no ship ever returns to give up her crew to the dust of the earth" (XX, 91), and her physical appearance at the end of the voyage seems to indicate that she has by some special dispensation been allowed to return from the nether world: "She was encrusted and gray with salt to the trucks of her masts and to the top of her funnel; as though (as some facetious seaman said) 'the crowd on board had fished her out somewhere from the bottom of the sea and brought her in here for salvage' " (XX, 91).

Marlow never doubts that the *Judea* will reach Bankok; when she sinks and he assumes command of a tiny life-boat, it never occurs to him that he and his crew may be lost at sea before he reaches the romantic East. There is not so much of this blind self-confidence in either MacWhirr or Jukes. Both, like Marlow, immerse themselves in the moment, seldom looking either to the past or the future, but they do, albeit infrequently, doubt that the universe is a wonderful adventurous place, as young Marlow never could. Jukes rails against his captain and the blind force of the sea. MacWhirr only once indicates that he doubts the ship will pull through the storm. His "I wouldn't like to lose her" (XX, 90), of course sums up his matter-of-fact type of courage, but it also indicates that he has, at least momentarily, lost faith in the order of the universe and in the doctrine that it is foolish to run about over the sea dodging dirty weather. Both Jukes and MacWhirr look for a brief moment into the chaos of the universe. Both wonder whether their struggles are completely without meaning. They cannot completely immerse themselves with Marlow's enthusiasm in the adventure which the storm represents, nor can their spirits truly comprehend the seemingly unimaginative standards of conduct which enable them to conquer the storm. That is, though the actions of Jukes and MacWhirr are embodiments of the third and highest stage of spiritual development in which the destructive element is recognized and made a part of the dream, their lack of imagination will not permit them to understand this. Singleton, "the incarnation of barbarian wisdom serene in the blasphemous turmoil of the world", never understands that he is an exemplification of the art which is the seaman's craft, just as MacWhirr does not see that his faith that one cannot avoid facing "the dirty weather knocking about the world" (XX, 34) contains a profoundly imaginative thesis. He cannot imagine the fury of a typhoon, but he can, somehow, understand that by running from fate one only hastens to it. Conrad says of MacWhirr:

It was, in truth, as impossible for him to take a flight of fancy as it would be for a watchmaker to put together a chronometer with nothing except a two-pound hammer and a whip-saw in the way of tools. Yet the uninteresting lives of men so entirely given to the actuality of the bare existence have their mysterious side. (XX, 4)

Captain MacWhirr the man is sometimes ridiculous, but Captain MacWhirr the ship's officer is a symbol of the understanding of both good and evil which allows man to achieve a spiritual triumph over the dark powers symbolized by the typhoon. Even the seemingly absurd remarks which MacWhirr makes in his conversations with Jukes possess a subtle truth, though the captain does not understand this truth any better than Jukes. When the owners of the *Nan-Shan* transfer her from the British flag to the Siamese, Jukes is indignant. The first morning the new flag flies over the stern of the ship, Jukes says: "Queer flag for a man to sail under, sir" (XX, 10). Captain MacWhirr looks in his International Signal Code Book and finds that the flag is quite all right:

No. I looked up the book. Length twice the breadth and the elephant exactly in the middle. I thought the people ashore would know how to make the local flag. Stands to reason. You were wrong, Jukes.... All you have to do is to take care they don't hoist the elephant upside-down before they get quite used to it. (XX, 10–11)

Shortly before the typhoon strikes, a high swell hits the ship. "I wonder where that beastly swell comes from", says Jukes. "Northeast", MacWhirr answers (XX, 22). When Jukes complains that the sultry air makes him feel as if he had his head wrapped up in a blanket MacWhirr refuses to accept the metaphor:

"D'ye mean to say, Mr. Jukes, you ever had your head tied up in a blanket? What was that for?... Some of you fellows do go on!... I wish you wouldn't talk so wild.... And what's a blanket got to do with it – or the weather either.... And what's the good of your talking like this?" (XX, 25)

These scenes are among the most humorous that Conrad ever wrote, and, of course, indicate that he is more of a writing virtuoso than those who label his point of view as monotonously somber and pessimistic would care to admit. But these encounters between Jukes and MacWhirr are not merely humorous. They are intensely ironical, for they possess an underlying reality which runs counter to their humorous surface. There is, in fact, nothing wrong with the Siamese flag, and a change in flag does not lessen the responsibilities or decrease the capabilities of the *Nan-Shan*'s officers. The swell indeed comes from the Northeast, and it ill-behooves a sailor to think too much beyond this literal fact when his ship is in danger. Cursing the heavy air runs counter to Mac-Whirr's ideas of the "fittness of things", for though he does not quite understand it, the captain senses that Jukes's complaining is an evidence of the young man's inability to fathom the full demands of his position as a ship's officer.

MacWhirr doubts himself and his unimaginative ethic only once – when he enters his disordered cabin while the *Nan-Shan* is in the eye of the typhoon. Jukes is constantly given to moods of self-doubt, and, as such, is a much better symbol of the second, restless stage of spiritual development. Though the storm represents somewhat of an adventure to Jukes, it profoundly weakens his faith in himself, and before the storm is over he wants " to be dismissed from the face of that odious trouble intruding on the great need of the ship" (XX, 72). Unlike young Marlow, he does not desire the responsibility of command, for he is well enough acquainted with the fury of the sea and his own short-comings to realize that there is more dangerous work than romance to the captain's job. On the other hand, his spirit cannot comprehend the saving truth inherent in MacWhirr's stolid contest with the typhoon. After the *Nan-Shan* has safely docked at Fu-Chau, Jukes writes a letter to a friend in which he says he thinks MacWhirr "got out of it very well for such a stupid man" (XX, 102). MacWhirr's example has not caused Jukes to see the typhoon as a necessary element in an epic struggle which proves the strength of the human spirit.

But whether Jukes realizes it or not, during the worst moments of the storm he desperately clings to the truth which MacWhirr represents. A moment before the typhoon hits the *Nan-Shan* she seems almost to have descended into hell:

> A faint burst of lightning quivered all round, as if flashed into a cavern – into a black and secret chamber of the sea, with a floor of foaming crests. It unveiled for a sinister, fluttering moment a ragged mass of clouds hanging low, the lurch of the long outlines of the ship, the black figures of men caught on the bridge, heads forward, as if petrified in the act of butting. The darkness palpitated down upon all this. (XX, 40)

When the full fury of the storm strikes, the men lose touch with one another. Jukes is tossed about the bridge and half-drowned, and as he claws for a grip to keep himself from being washed overboard, he finds MacWhirr:

> As soon as he commenced his wretched struggles he discovered that he had become somehow mixed up with a face, an oilskin coat, somebody's boots. He clawed ferociously all these things in turn, lost them, found them again, lost them once more, and finally was himself caught in the firm clasp of a pair of stout arms. He returned the embrace closely round a thick solid body. He had found his captain. (XX, 42)

Jukes cries out in his great need to communicate with something the storm cannot destroy:

> He started shouting aimlessly to the man he could feel near him in that fiendish blackness. "Is it you, sir? Is it you, sir?" till his temples seemed ready to burst. And he heard in answer a voice, as if crying far away, as if screaming to him fretfully from a very great distance, the one word "Yes!" (XX, 42)

As soon as Jukes hears the reassuring voice of his captain over the turmoil of the wind, a huge sea sweeps over the bridge and baptizes him.

To reinforce the symbolism of the first embrace, Conrad brings MacWhirr and Jukes together again when the next monstrous sea sweeps the deck of the *Nan-Shan*. Jukes believes the ship is done for: "Nothing could be prevented now, and nothing could be remedied. The men on board did not count, and the ship could

not last. This weather was too impossible" (XX, 45). Again
Jukes's courage is renewed in an embrace with the captain:

Jukes felt an arm thrown heavily over his shoulders; and to the
overture he responded with great intelligence by catching hold of
his captain round the waist. They stood clasped thus in the blind
night, bracing each other against the wind, cheek to cheek and lip
to ear, in the manner of two hulks lashed stem to stern together.
(XX, 45–46)

Again MacWhirr speaks to Jukes, and the captain's voice is as
reassuring as that of a supernatural being, "bearing that strange
effect of quietness like the serene glow of a halo" (XX, 46).
Jukes even dares hope the *Nan-Shan* will not go down, and
he shouts, not to Captain MacWhirr the man, but to MacWhirr
the incarnation of supernatural wisdom, "Will she live through
this?" He hears MacWhirr's affirmative answer, "the frail and
resisting voice in his ear, the dwarf sound, unconquered in the
giant tumult" (XX, 49). The symbolic nature of MacWhirr's
embrace is further emphasized when the captain takes his hand
from Jukes's shoulder. At that moment Jukes becomes dangerously
self-conscious, his mind becoming "concentrated upon himself in
an aimless, idle way" (XX, 48).

The typhoon, the lyric description of which is perhaps ex-
celled in English literature only by the storm description in *The
Nigger of the "Narcissus"*, becomes a symbol of that universal
power which Conrad felt was omnipresent attempting to shatter
the solidarity of mankind:

This is the disintegrating power of a great wind: it isolates one from
one's kind. An earthquake, a landslip, an avalanche, overtake a man
incidentally, as it were – without passion. A furious gale attacks him
like a personal enemy, tries to grasp his limbs, fastens upon his mind,
seeks to rout his very spirit out of him. (XX, 40)

The storm drives a wedge of wind and sea between Jukes and
MacWhirr, but, paradoxically, it is only during the typhoon that
these two men can communicate effectively. Before the storm
they cannot even discuss matters of such relative unimportance
as the Siamese flag, an ocean swell, or the sultry air without
arriving at a ludicrous misunderstanding. During the storm they

speak of matters of life and death and understand one another perfectly.

MacWhirr, like Allistoun of the *Narcissus,* seems to hold his ship up by sheer spiritual effort, and, like Allistoun, he seems to be an almost supernatural figure in the midst of the storm. Only his voice pierces the shrieking wind and raging seas, and when he sends Jukes to the hold to stop the Chinese coolies from fighting, he assumes something of the stature of a divine father commissioning his son with the errand of restoring order to the lower world. In one sense, of course, MacWhirr's concern for the Chinese is ridiculous. If the ship sinks no one will know about the disorder below decks, and if she survives, surely the typhoon is a sufficient excuse for ignoring the Chinese. But for MacWhirr to let them continue fighting would be for him to "ignore the dirty weather knocking about the world". Mac Whirr's sending Jukes to the hold possesses, like all of the captain's actions, a subtler truth than is at first evident in the dramatic situation. When MacWhirr's symbolic role is understood, however, this truth seems very clear – the destructive element, though it can be ignored by MacWhirr, the unimaginative man, cannot be ignored by MacWhirr in his symbolic role as ship's captain.

The between-decks area into which Jukes descends represents the mythic nether world. It is " a place deep as a well, black as Tophet" (XX, 70), and the boatswain refers to it as a "regular little hell' (XX, 62). Though the engine room through which Jukes must travel to get to the Chinamen's compartment is a well-ordered place, and though the chief engineer is carrying on his part of the struggle as heroically as MacWhirr, there is an eerie, otherworldly quality about the furnaces and the great iron walls of the engine-room:

Painted white, they rose high into the dusk of the skylight, sloping like a roof; and the whole lofty space resembled the interior of a monument, divided by floors of iron grating, with lights flickering at different levels, and a mass of gloom lingering in the middle, within the columnar stir of machinery under the motionless swelling of the cylinders. A loud and wild resonance, made up of all the noises of the hurricane, dwelt in the still warmth of the air. There was in it the smell of hot metal, of oil, and slight mist of steam. (XX, 68)

The Chinamen look like those inhabitants of Hades who have died in battle and carry their wounds even in death:

Here and there a coolie would fall on his knees as if begging for mercy; several whom the excess of fear made unruly, were hit with hard fists between the eyes, and cowered; while those who were hurt submitted to rough handling, blinking rapidly without a plaint. Faces streamed with blood; there were raw places on the shaven heads, scratches, bruises, torn wounds, gashes. The broken porcelain out of the chests was mostly responsible for the latter. Here and there a Chinaman, wild-eyed, with his tail unplaited, nursed a bleeding sole. (XX, 78)

When Jukes returns to the deck, the *Nan-Shan* has taken on the aspect of a ghost-ship:

He saw faint outlines. They recalled not the familiar aspect of the *Nan-Shan,* but something remembered – an old dismantled steamer he had seen years ago rotting on a mudbank. She recalled that wreck. (XX, 81)

Clearly, Jukes's experience resembles that of Jim on Patusan and that of Marlow in the Congo, for he, too, discovers a meaning, though he quickly loses sight of it, in his trial in the darkness. When he comes back to the bridge and reports his success, MacWhirr does not praise him, but gives him a lecture about the dangers of facing trouble half way. The captain's chiding, however, strangely inspires Jukes. The captain's voice "spoke much louder than Jukes had ever heard it before":

For some reason Jukes experienced an access of confidence, a sensation that came from outside like a warm breath, and made him feel equal to every demand. The distant muttering of the darkness stole into his ears. He noted it unmoved, out of that sudden belief in himself, as a man safe in a shirt of mail would watch a point. (XX, 89)

2. *Ironic symbol at the conclusion of "Typhoon"*

The officers of the *Nan-Shan,* like the crew of the *Narcissus,* leave behind their special powers and mystic discoveries about the nature of life when they return again to the land. There are no images of the filth and corruption of the land in "Typhoon" to compare with those at the conclusion of *The Nigger of the "Narcissus"*. There are, however, the letters of MacWhirr, Jukes, and Solomon Rout to indicate that once the voyage is over these men fall back into their old habits of mind.

MacWhirr's letter to his wife does not indicate that he has understood the significance of his experience in the typhoon or that he will ever understand the power of the tradition which he paradoxically embodies. His letter indicates that he is still the same man whom Conrad described at the beginning of the story, "the past being to his mind done with, and the future not there yet" (XX, 9). He will, perhaps, again have uncomfortable periods, such as the few moments he spent in his cabin at the height of the typhoon, in which the tragic profundity of life will press him for recognition, but these moments will be fleeting and possibly never again occur. And, underlining the irony of MacWhirr's not understanding his experiences is Mrs. MacWhirr's complete lack of interest in the laconic message which she receives from her husband. MacWhirr's steward becomes so absorbed in reading the captain's letter while it is in the process of composition that he is several times nearly caught in the act, but Mrs. MacWhirr, as she reads the letter, stifles a yawn. She does not even give the letter sufficient attention to note that on the overleaf MacWhirr has written that at one time he doubted if the ship could best the storm. When neighbors question Mrs. MacWhirr about her husband, she replies: "Of course, it's very sad to have him away, but it's such a comfort to know he keeps so well . . . . The climate there agrees with him (XX, 95).

Solomon Rout perhaps understands the typhoon a bit better than either Jukes or MacWhirr. His awareness of his narrow escape from death, however, though it makes him wish he could spend more time with his wife, awakens in him no sense of the magnificence of the struggle which he has just undergone. To create the ironical tone here, Conrad chooses Solomon's mother. The younger Mrs. Rout reads of Solomon's desire to spend more time with her, but reports to her mother-in-law only that Solomon is well. The elder Mrs. Rout replies: "He always was a strong healthy boy" (XX, 97).

Jukes's letter is to a young fellow officer in the merchant marine. He reports MacWhirr's actions in a bantering tone, and there is also an uncommonly frequent reference to the first person, considering that Jukes's role in bringing the *Nan-Shan* through the storm was quite inconsequential compared with MacWhirr's. The closing sentence of Jukes's letter, also the last sentence in the book, indicates that Jukes, too, though he may now be expected to discharge his obligations to the seaman's craft in much the same fashion as MacWhirr, has no sense of the significance of these traditions as they relate to the human soul: "I think he got out of it very well for such a stupid man" (XX, 102).

In "Typhoon", Conrad has demonstrated the purifying power of the destructive element, but he has also shown that some people may immerse themselves in this element, and in fact overcome it, with no sense of the significance of their struggle. They are those people who catch Stein's butterfly without being able to mount it, behold it, and enjoy its full beauty.

C. "THE SECRET SHARER"

In "The Secret Sharer", one of the most complex tales which Conrad wrote, the hero makes the destructive element a part of his dream, and at the same time realizes a perfect understanding of the paradoxical nature of the evil which he has faced. In contrast with MacWhirr and Jukes, the young captain of this story breaks the code of his craft, but in so doing he finally realizes that the breach was necessary in order for him to become the master of his destiny.

1. *The "double" imagery of "The Secret Sharer"*

The symbolic nature of the young captain's "secret sharer" is obvious – so obvious, in fact, that one critic says: "The constant parallel descriptions of the two men, the use of doubles, doubling,

second self, secret self, other self, and so on, are tedious".[5] The
very emphasis which Conrad places upon the doubling process
in this story, however, is an integral part of his aesthetic design,
and to overlook his subtle employment of the seemingly monot-
onous rhythm of doubles is to miss much of his art. The Young
narrator several times straightforwardly refers to his lack of self-
confidence, but a more subtle indication of his unsureness than
his self-doubting comments is his readiness to "see double".
Before Leggatt climbs on board the ship, the narrator-captain has
demonstrated a fondness for pairing things off. With the ship
anchored at the mouth of the Meinam river the captain looks
at the shore, and it is significant that he describes what he sees
on his right, and then, as if for balance, immediately describes
the landscape on his left hand. He associates the deserted aspect
of the sea with that of the land, and compares the ruinous decay
of the shore to the purity of the sea. The small islets of the sea he
balances with two small clumps of trees, one on each side of
the mouth of the river. He sees himself and his ship as doubles,
and when he describes the mastheads of the *Sephora*, the
reader does not need to be told that the captain sees her as a
double of his own ship. The opening pages of the story, containing the aforementioned imagery, serve two purposes. They
establish the story's rhythm of "doubles", and they subtly suggest
that the narrator has an uncomprehended horror of solitude.
That is, having little self-confidence, he unconsciously feels the
need of an alter ego to accompany him as he meets his test as
ship's captain. He does not wish to be alone, and he cannot bear
to see natural objects as solitary. One clump of trees must be
paired with another clump of trees, one ship with another. Even
the momentousness of Leggatt's arrival cannot shock the narrator
out of his desire to see the world as symmetrical. Midway
through the story, the captain, going up on deck after leaving
his secret self in his cabin, notices "two bunches of bananas hung
from the beam symmetrically, one on each side of the rudder
casing" (XIX, 104).

[5] Frederick Karl, *A Reader's Guide to Joseph Conrad* (New York, 1960), p. 231.

The captain-narrator is like the Marlow of "Youth" in that he looks forward to his first voyage as a master-mariner with a sense of adventure, yet he is notably more self-conscious than Marlow in that he fears that he will prove incapable of the task. When Leggatt scrambles up out of the water, the neophyte captain uses him as an excuse to avoid making the step from aware youthfulness to mature responsibility. He sees Leggatt as his double, even though "he was not a bit like me, really" (XIX, 105). At one point during the voyage, the steward enters the captain's cabin to hang up a wet jacket. The captain watches him helplessly, with no chance to warn Leggatt. When the steward emerges from the cabin, showing no sign that he has discovered Leggatt, the captain is sure that his alter ego has left the ship: "Saved, I thought. But no! Lost! Gone! He was gone!" (XIX, 129). If Leggatt is gone, the captain, of course, will no longer have to live with the constant fear that his fugitive self will be discovered. But in another sense the captain is lost, in that if Leggatt has left, he will have to devote his full attention to the demands of the ship and he is terribly uncertain that he can handle her. Before the narrator understands his relationship to Leggatt he whispers orders to his mates, shouts through his closed cabin door for the ship to be gotten underway, and finds it "most trying to be on deck" (XIX, 123) at all. Ostensibly he is worried that Leggatt will be discovered, but secretly he is afraid of the ship. Only when Leggatt's leaving becomes inevitable can the captain see that he has used his secret sharer as an excuse for not accepting his responsibilities:

I felt suddenly ashamed of myself. I may say truly that I understood – and my hesitation in letting that man swim away from my ship's side had been a mere sham sentiment, a sort of cowardice. (XIX, 132)

When he achieves this stage of self-knowledge, the young captain is ready to pass the shadow line.

Leggatt is, of course, an incarnation of the fearful lack of self-possession which the young captain must identify in himself before he can sail his ship with confidence. To say, however, that the narrator need only sympathize with Leggatt's situation and see his own weaknesses in the fugitive from the *Sephora* is to oversimplify Conrad's conception of the symbolic relationship between these two men. While the narrator insists that Leggatt is his "double", "his secret self", "his hidden self", the character of the secret sharer, as it penetrates through the haze of the young captain's self-deception, appears to be quite different from that of his protector.

Leggatt has, after all, killed a man, and his explanation of the act bears a close resemblance to the artful dodges of Gentleman Brown, and to those of Lord Jim before he has made his self-discovery. Leggatt blames not himself, but the situation – the storm, the rebellious sailor, the *Sephora*'s incompetent captain. He could, with Jim, say: "I ask you, has any man ever been so sorely tried?" The *Sephora*'s mate also has a terror of explaining to a jury the murder which he has committed, and in this fear there is an unmistakable echo of Gentleman Brown's unnatural fright at the prospect of being imprisoned:

"You don't suppose I am afraid of what can be done to me? Prison or gallows or whatever they may please. But you don't see me coming back to explain such things to an old fellow in a wig and twelve respectable tradesmen, do you? What can they know whether I am guilty or not – or of *what* I am guilty, either? That's my affair." (XIX, 131–132)

A fact concerning the murder on the *Sephora* which both the self-doubting narrator and the somewhat egoistic Leggatt ignore makes it difficult to argue for the necessity of the rebellious seaman's being killed. That is, Leggatt strangled the disobedient man after the sail which saved the ship had already been set. Thus, Leggatt's murdering the seaman is not clearly established as a necessary consequent of saving the ship.

Leggatt, as his protector recognizes, is not a "homocidal ruffian", but the image of him clutching the insubordinate sailor's neck as a heavy sea washes over the deck of the *Sephora* hints that he was temporarily mad:

"They say that for over ten minutes hardly anything was to be seen of the ship – just the three masts and a bit of the forecastle head and of the poop all awash driving along in a smother of foam. It was a miracle that they found us, jammed together behind the forebits. It's clear that I meant business, because I was holding him by the throat still when they picked us up. He was black in the face." (XIX, 102)

In addition, Leggatt seems a bit too ready to refer to his desire to escape as bearing fatal consequences for those who would attempt to stop him. He says: "I did not mean to get into a confounded scrimmage. Somebody else might have gotten killed – for I would not have broken out only to get chucked back" (XIX, 107); and: "Do you see me being hauled back, stark naked, off one of those little islands by the scruff of the neck and fighting like a wild beast? Somebody would have got killed for certain" (XIX, 109). Leggatt, like Jim, runs from his disgrace while it is his guilt alone that matters. He, in fact, is almost proud that he has killed the rebel: "That's all right. I was ready enough to go off wandering on the face of the earth – and that was price enough to pay for an Abel of that sort" (XIX, 107).

Leggatt is, of course, not a villain like Brown. He shows too much concern for his protector to be likened to that evil vagabond. His moral equity is, however, at best ambiguous, but the very ambiguity contributes to his effectiveness as a symbolic character. That is, if Leggatt's actions on board the *Sephora* were completely unjustified, the narrator-captain would be too much an accomplice of evil in helping him. On the other hand, if Leggatt were completely without guilt, the young captain would not be justified in purging himself, however unconsciously, of his secret sharer.

Purge himself of Leggatt the narrator must, or he shall end his days at sea a timid incompetent like Captain Archbold of the *Sephora*. One of the functions of Gentleman Brown in *Lord Jim* is to demonstrate what Jim might become were he not to assume responsibility for his own actions. Captain Archbold fulfils an analogous role in "The Secret Sharer" in that he is a symbol of the man who has not crossed the shadow line, who has not recognized his weakness and purged it. The young captain's description of Archbold leaves little doubt as to the old man's indecisive nature:

The skipper of the *Sephora* had a thin red whisker all round his face, and the sort of complexion that goes with hair of that color; also the particular, rather smeary shade of blue in the eyes. He was not exactly a showy figure; his shoulders were high, his stature but middling – one leg slightly more bandy than the other. He shook hands, looking vaguely round. A spiritless tenacity was his main characteristic, I judged. I behaved with a politeness which seemed to disconcert him. Perhaps he was shy. He mumbled to me as if he were ashamed of what he was saying; gave his name (it was something like Archbold, but at this distance of years I hardly am sure), his ship's name, and a few other particulars of that sort, in the manner of a criminal making a reluctant and doleful confession. He had had terrible weather on the passage out – terrible – terrible – wife aboard, too. (XIX, 115)

As Kurtz's name belied his physical appearance, Archbold is an ironic name for this whimpering creature to bear. Archbold mentions his wife again during his conversation with the narrator, as if her presence on the *Sephora* should make Leggatt's crime more horrible. In describing his own actions during the storm, Archbold lends credence to Leggatt's story that his captain "started raving like the rest of them" (XIX, 103) when the *Sephora*'s plight seemed hopeless. Archbold says: "I hardly dared give the order. It seemed impossible that we could touch anything without losing it, and then our last hope would have been gone" (XIX, 118).

2. The symbolic relationship between the young captain, Leggatt, and Archbold

Captain Archbold is a weak man. He took Leggatt on as first mate because he did not have the courage to argue that he instead of the owners should pick the crew of the *Sephora*. Before he leaves the narrator's ship, Archbold decides to take the easy way of rescinding his responsibility for Leggatt. Rather than acknowledge that he has allowed his mate to escape, he decides to report him as a suicide. As we have no reason to disbelieve Leggatt's report that Archbold did not give the order to set the sail which saved the ship, but stood on the quarter-deck blank-eyed and whimpering while Leggatt performed this vital task, so we have no reason to disbelieve Leggatt's report that Archbold is, in fact, only nominally master of the *Sephora:*

He was afraid of the men, and also of that old second mate of his who had been sailing with him for years – a grey-headed old humbug; and his steward, too, had been with him for devil knows how long – seventeen years or more – a dogmatic sort of loafer who hated me like poison, just because I was the chief mate. No chief mate ever made more than one voyage in the *Sephora,* you know. Those two old chaps ran the ship. Devil only knows what the skipper wasn't afraid of (all his nerve went to pieces altogether in that hellish spell of bad weather we had) – of what the law would do to him – of his wife, perhaps. Oh, yes, She's on board. (XIX, 107)

The narrator of "The Secret Sharer" realizes that his ship must not have two captains. Archbold, a representation of what the young captain may become if he does not complete the paradoxical action of both accepting responsibility for Leggatt and purging himself of his influence, has struggled along for seventeen years with a ship that has three, perhaps four, commanders.

The narrator-captain feels he and his ship are united twice during the narrative, first during the opening frame, and again when Leggatt strikes out for the dark mass of Koh-Ring. Before Leggatt comes on board, the captain, albeit in a dreamy, immature way, refers to himself and his ship collectively:

In this breathless pause at the threshold of a long passage we seemed to be measuring our fitness for a long and arduous enterprise, the appointed task of both our existences to be carried out, far from all human eyes, with only sky and sea for spectators and for judges. (XIX, 92)

Once Leggatt is on board, however, the captain, who was only unconsciously apprehensive before, is now split between loyalty to his ship and loyalty to his secret sharer:

There are to a seaman certain words, gestures, that should in given conditions come as naturally, as instinctively as the winking of a menaced eye. A certain order should spring on to his lips without thinking; a certain sign should get itself made, so to speak, without reflection. But all unconscious alertness had abandoned me. I had to make an effort of will to recall myself back (from the cabin) to the conditions of the moment. I felt that I was appearing an irresolute commander to those people who were watching me more or less critically. (XIX, 126)

The captain's unconscious, which must with his conscious mind be focused on the demands of the ship for him to be her master in a real sense, is occupied with Leggatt. Only when the captain can recognize Leggatt as a separate human being, only when his protection of Leggatt becomes sympathy for a fellow human being rather than a disguised self-indulgence can he re-establish the rapport with his command which he anticipated before actually assuming duties as captain.

In helping Leggatt to escape, the captain establishes a solidarity with weak, yet strangely courageous mankind, and discovers, once this solidarity is established, that it is the element necessary for the self-confidence without which one cannot undertake a job so demanding as that of ship's captain. To illustrate the nature of his young captain's discovery, Conrad creates a closing frame which contains an abundance of well-drawn symbols and symbolic action.

3. Image and symbol in the closing frame

In the opening pages of the story, the narrator exults in the tranquility of the sea as compared to the turmoil of the land:

I rejoiced in the great security of the sea as compared with the unrest of the land, in my choice of that untempted life presenting no disquieting problems, invested with an elementary moral beauty by the absolute straightforwardness of its appeal and by the singleness of its purpose. (XIX, 96)

To help Leggatt to escape, however, the young captain must take himself and his ship dangerously close to the treacherous shore:

At noon I gave no orders for a change of course, and the mate's

whiskers became much concerned and seemed to be offering themselves unduly to my notice. At last I said:

"I am going to stand right in. Quite in – as far as I can take her."

The stare of extreme surprise imparted an air of ferocity also to
his eyes, and he looked truly terrific for a moment.

"We're not doing well in the middle of the gulf", I continued,
casually. "I am going to look for the land breezes tonight."

"Bless my soul! Do you mean, sir, in the dark amongst the lot of
all them islands and reefs and shoals?"

"Well – if there are any regular land breezes at all on this coast
one must get close inshore to find them, mustn't one?" (XIX, 133–134)

Nearly every word in this dialogue bears a symbolic importance.
The captain realizes he is "not doing well in the middle of the
gulf". He must commit himself wholeheartedly to his command,
must search among "all them islands and reefs and shoals" for
the saving knowledge which paradoxically comes from a recognition of evil. The narrator himself unconsciously recognizes that
his dream, full command of his ship, can only be realized by his
approaching the gates of Hell. A hush falls on the ship as she
approaches the dark shore of Koh-Ring looming out of the
water: "She might have been a bark of the dead floating in
slowly under the very gate of Erebus" (XIX, 140). Yet the
ship must go nearer the shore: "I had shut my eyes – because
the ship must go closer. She must" (XIX, 139).

When the ship is so close to Koh-Ring that it seems she
cannot be saved, the second mate explodes: "She will never get
out. You have done it, sir. I knew it'd end in something like
this. She will never weather, and you are too close now to stay.
She'll drift ashore before she's round. O my God!" (XIX, 140–
141). In a variation on Leggatt's choking of the seaman on board
the *Sephora*, the young captain clutches the arm of his insolent
and frightened mate:

I caught his arm as he was raising it to batter his poor devoted head,
and shook violently.

"She's ashore already," he wailed, trying to tear himself away.

"Is she? ... Keep good full there!"

"Good full, sir", cried the helmsman in a frightened, thin, childlike
voice.

I hadn't let go the mate's arm and went on shaking it. "Ready about, do you hear? You go forward" – shake – "and stop there" – shake – "and hold your noise" – shake – "and see these head sheets properly overhauled" – shake, shake – shake.

And all the time I dared not look toward the land lest my heart should fail me. I released my grip at last and he ran forward as if fleeing for dear life. (XIX, 141)

The narrator has been pushed as far as Leggatt was, and though his response is the same in kind, it is notably different in degree. He is clearly a different man from Leggatt, clearly not the kind of man to lose his self possession entirely in a crisis.

The incidents surrounding the cap which the narrator-captain gives to Leggatt perhaps constitute the most important symbolism in these last few pages of the story. When the captain, in a burst of sentiment, attempts to put his cap on his secret sharer's head, the latter, not sure of his protector's intention, shies away. Leggatt's action is quite plausible in a realistic sense, and it demonstrates that he and the captain are not, in fact, "doubles". They do not think each other's thoughts. Leggatt apparently accepts the hat and puts it on his head before he climbs into the water to make good his escape. But the captain's hat is not meant for Leggatt's head. It falls off as he swims away, and the captain uses it as a mark in swinging his ship away from the shore. The cap, then, is a masterfully drawn symbol of the paradoxical nature of the captain's relationship to Leggatt. Had the cap fit, had it not fallen off Leggatt's head, had the captain and Leggatt indeed been doubles, the ship would have torn her bottom out on the rocks of Koh-Ring. However, had the captain not given his cap to Leggatt, had he not sympathized with this fugitive, he would not have brought his ship through the dangerous reefs off Koh-Ring and would never have mastered her.

At the last, the captain in "The Secret Sharer" fits the destructive element into the pattern of his dream. Conrad has brought him near to insanity, but has permitted him to recognize the paradoxical nature of evil and to pass the shadow-line which separates youth from maturity. He has permitted him to relate himself to humanity and to his craft.

D. THE SHADOW LINE

Though "The Secret Sharer" is, perhaps, a more complicated statement of the experience of the passing from youth to maturity in that it is richer in symbolism than *The Shadow Line,* the latter story seems to present this experience in more universal terms. "The Secret Sharer" ends at the moment of discovery, with the young captain "striking out for a new destiny", whereas in *The Shadow Line,* the narrator returns to the land to evaluate the significance of what he has learned from his first command. And, the canvas of *The Shadow Line* seems a bit larger in that its characters bear a more obvious archetypal significance than those in "The Secret Sharer".

Conrad would almost seem to have written the opening paragraphs of *The Shadow Line* as an epilogue to "Youth":

Only the young have such moments. I don't mean the very young. No. The very young have, properly speaking, no moments. It is the privilege of early youth to live in advance of its days in all the beautiful continuity of hope which knows no pauses and no introspection.

One closes behind one the little gate of mere boyishness *—* and enters an enchanted garden. Its very shades glow with promise. Every turn of the path has its seduction. And it isn't because it is an undiscovered country. One knows well enough that all mankind had streamed that way. It is the charm of universal experience from which one expects an uncommon or personal sensation — a bit of one's own.

One goes on recognizing the landmarks of the predecessors, excited, amused, taking the hard luck and the good luck together — the kicks and the halfpence, as the saying is — the picturesque common lot that holds so many possibilities for the deserving or perhaps for the lucky. Yes. One goes on. And the time, too, goes on — till one perceives ahead a shadow-line warning one that the region of early youth, too, must be left behind. (XVII, 3)

The young captain has glimpsed this final shadow line and experiences a terrible reluctance to cross it. The joys of youth are still too fresh in his memory for him to wish to accept a role in which every experience, every action will be tempered by an awareness of responsibility. And, he reasons, why accept responsibility, why form another senseless link in mankind's chain of being when everything is so "stupid and overrated" (XVII, 23).

The young captain rebels against the newly apprehended fact that he is a man and that all men are mortal. He wishes to prevent the world from grinding him down, for a while, at least, by not accepting the responsibilities of the seaman's craft. To this youth, the world is one vast gray prison. He throws up a good job, ostensibly to return home, but in reality because he has been overcome by the "green sickness" of youth. The Eastern sun which would warm young Marlow is almost a curse to the narrator of *The Shadow Line*:

I walked in the sunshine, disregarding it, and in the shade of the big trees on the esplanade without enjoying it. The heat of the tropical East descended through the leafy boughs, enveloping my thinly-clad body, clinging to my rebellious discontent, as if to rob it of its freedom. (XVII, 8)

The Officers' Home to which he goes to await a ship for England has few guests: "It was as still as a tomb" (XVII, 9), and the filthy clutter of the chief steward's room echoes the state of the young mate's mind:

It was a strange room to find in the tropics. Twilight and stuffiness reigned in there. The fellow had hung enormously ample, dusty, cheap lace curtains over his windows, which were shut. Piles of cardboard boxes, such as milliners and dressmakers use in Europe, cumbered the corners; and by some means he had procured for himself the sort of furniture that might have come out of a respectable parlour in the East End of London – a horsehair sofa, arm-chairs of the same. I glimpsed grimy antimacassars scattered over that horrid upholstery, which was awe-inspiring, insomuch that one could not guess what mysterious accident, need, or fancy had collected it there. (XVII, 9)

At the Officer's Home the young narrator meets Captain Giles, and his response to this old man evidences that though the rational part of his being has for the time blotted the beauty and meaning out of his life, his spiritual being is still responsive:[6]

Captain Giles was at the head of the table. I exchanged a few words

<hr>

[6] Walter Wright points out that as the young man "has not violated his instinctive nature, he can be restored" (p. 46).

of greeting with him and sat down on his left. Stout and pale, with a great shiny dome of a bald forehead and prominent brown eyes, he might have been anything but a seaman. You would not have been surprised to learn that he was an architect. To me (I know how absurd it is) he looked like a church-warden. (XVII, 11–12)

Giles is, indeed, an architect – in this case the architect of the young narrator's career. He is, in fact, more than a church-warden, for his functions in the temple of the seaman's craft go beyond the mere protection of church property. He is a wily spiritual guide for the young mate's soul. He is, the narrator informs us, "an expert in – how shall I say it? – in intricate navigation" (XVII, 12).

Giles is the incarnation of the ship officer's tradition. In his attempts to make the narrator cross the shadowline, he does not attempt to appeal to his mind, but rather directs his pointed questions to the young man's instincts as a mariner. The old man realizes that the "perfect love of the work" is still very much present in the young man, and that it can save him from a life of disenchantment. To trick the young mate into accepting a position of responsibility – a command of a ship whose captain has died at sea – Captain Giles concocts a ludicrous comic-opera plot. The narrator is completely fooled, and accepts the command. The reader knows Giles has probably already indicated to the Harbor Master that the young man would accept, and has perhaps asked the official for sufficient time to lead him into such an acceptance.

1. The drama created by the image and symbol in the first two chapters

The symbolic relationship between Giles and the young narrator is highly important in the first two chapters of the novel. Time and again in this section, the disenchanted mate misjudges Giles. At first he sees the old man as no more than a moralist who criticizes him for quitting a good berth. A bit later, when Giles is musing aloud as a part of the plan which he has created to get the mate back into the world of ships, the young man pities his old mentor:

And he began to speculate. It was not for this – and it could not be for that. As to that other thing it was unthinkable. The fatuousness of all this made me stare. If the man had not been somehow a sympathetic personality I would have resented it like an insult. As it was, I felt only sorry for him. Something remarkably earnest in his gaze prevented me from laughing in his face. Neither did I yawn at him. I just stared. (XVII, 20)

To the mate, Giles is a "tactless idiot", and his actions partake of "perfect stupidity" (XVII, 22). He is "hopeless Giles", and the entire world is "stupid and overrated even as Captain Giles" (XVII, 23). Giles is the embodiment of the tradition of the sea with its very few simple ideas of moral courage and responsibility. The young man's failure to understand Giles' benevolent plotting is, then, evidence of the failure of the conscious part of his being to understand the code of the master-mariner. But that part of the young mate's being which is not dependent on wisdom responds to Captain Giles: "Captain Giles... began to haul at his gorgeous gold chain till at last the watch came up from the deep pocket like solid truth from a well" (XVII, 27). Before he can cross the shadow-line, the young mate's conscious rapport with Giles must coincide with that of his unconscious. The narrator has shrunk from his responsibilities and fancies that he is a free man, but paradoxically he cannot be free until he discovers that he must bind himself to his fellow man and to the obligations of the seaman's craft. D. H. Lawrence's ideas about the conflict of the rational self with the unconscious seem to apply particularly well to the young narrator's situation in *The Shadow Line:*

Men are not free when they are doing just what they like. The moment you can do just what you like, there is nothing you care about doing. Men are only free when they are doing what the deepest self likes. And there is getting down to the deepest self! It takes some diving.

Because the deepest self is way down, and the conscious self is an obstinate monkey. But of one thing we may be sure. If one wants to be free, one has to give up the illusion of doing what one likes, and seek what IT wishes done.[7]

When the young mate goes to the Harbor-Master's office to accept the position as captain, he moves as if in a dream. He sees Captain Ellis, the Harbor-Master, as a symbolic figure, a deputy-Neptune whose pen is his trident. The despair which overwhelmed the young man before he was chosen for a command is completely forgotten: "It seemed as if all of a sudden a pair of wings had grown on my shoulders. I merely skimmed along the polished floor" (XVII, 33). The Harbor-Master instructs his private launch be made ready to ferry the young man out to the ship which will transport him to Bankok and his command. The Harbor-Master's assistant, Mr. R., informs the young man that the last person to enjoy the use of the launch was a Duke. This bit of information adds to the dream-like quality of the narrator's experience: "I floated down the staircase. I floated out of the official and imposing portal. I went on floating along" (XVII, 35). In his elation he imagines himself as a character in a fairy-tale:

And first I wondered at my state of mind. Why was I not more surprised? Why? Here I was, invested with a command in the twinkling of an eye, not in the common course of human affairs, but more as if by enchantment. I ought to have been lost in astonishment. But I wasn't. I was very much like people in fairy tales. Nothing ever astonishes them. When a fully appointed gala coach is produced out of a pumpkin to take her to a ball, Cinderella does not exclaim. She gets in quietly and drives away to her high fortune. Captain Ellis, (a fierce sort of fairy) had produced a command out of a drawer almost as unexpectedly as in a fairy tale. (XVII, 39–40)

And his ship is "an enchanted princess" whose call has come to him "from the clouds" (XVII, 40).

The dream and fairy tale imagery is highly important in this first secton of *The Shadow Line* for two reasons. The young captain's buoyant emotional state as he receives the command is best described as an unreal experience, for Conrad wishes the

[7] D. H. Lawrence, *Studies in Classic American Literature* (Garden City, N. Y., 1953), p. 17.

narrator's second victory over the forces which would sicken his heart and keep him from kinship with mankind to be the important one, the real one. And, as the personages in a fairy tale have little control over the elements of their ultimate success or failure, Conrad wishes to show that his young hero's first, less important salvation, like his second, is less a matter of the conscious exercise of will than an unconscious identification with the seaman's tradition which allows him to take advantage of the vagaries of chance.

The last four chapters of *The Shadow Line* echo the circumstances and enlarge upon the theme of the first two.[8] The young

---

[8] Albert Guerard, in *Conrad the Novelist* (Cambridge, Mass., 1958), p. 30, wishing to make *The Shadow Line* conform to the pattern and theme of "The Secret Sharer", writes of the first two chapters: *"The Shadow Line,* while written in part in the pure unpretentious prose of 'The Secret Sharer', is distinctly less perfect. It gets underway very slowly and uncertainly. To make the two stories truly analogous we need only cut out the first two chapters of *The Shadow Line:* need only begin with the two untested narrator-captains on board for the first time, communing with themselves. Conrad apparently conceived of *The Shadow Line* as dealing with the passage from ignorant and untested confidence through a major trial to the very different confidence of mature self-command. So conceived the story ought logically to have reflected, in its first pages, a naive and buoyant confidence. What it really presents is a neurotic immobilization onshore, for which the opportunity of a first command is expected to provide a cure." Robert Haugh, in *Joseph Conrad: Discovery in Design* (Norman, Okla., 1957), p. 84, calls the prelude to command in *The Shadow Line* "mean and petty" and suggests that the reader not familiar with Conrad will have difficulty wading through these first chapters. Frederick Karl, in *A Reader's Guide to Joseph Conrad* (New York, 1960), p. 273, writes: "The frame of the story, a simple first person narrative by the omniscient author, takes one-quarter of the book, but it subsequently proves of minor importance compared with the ordeal of the young Captain on his command, the *Melita.*" Ian Watt, in "Story and Idea in *The Shadow Line*", *Critical Quarterly*, II (Summer, 1960), 133–148, however astutely observes that the young captain's irritability in the first chapters is a necessary part of the total design of the novel. Walter Wright perceives that the seeming tediousness of the actions in the first chapters is but a subtle disguise for the dramatic psychological conflict which Conrad presents here: "If one is hurrying to reach the outward action of the tale, the long disquisition, about one-third of the story's length, on the youth's hesitations before the spiderlike cunning of Giles finally captures him, is a tedious preamble to action. But the action in which Conrad was interested was the war between the two forces – the deep-

mate, now nominally a captain, sinks again into the black pit of despair, and again he conquers the forces working against his acceptance of responsibility. The second time he conquers the "green sickness of youth", however, his victory is more complete, and he fully understands its nature, thus permanently exorcising the spirit of his youthful despair.

Once on board his command, the young captain senses, as he looks at himself in the saloon's mirror, that he has taken his place in that chain "which binds men to each other, which binds together all humanity – the dead to the living and the living to the unborn" (XXIII, xii):

It struck me that this quietly staring man whom I was watching, both as if he were myself and somebody else, was not exactly a lonely figure. He had his place in a line of men whom he did not know, of whom he had never heard; but who were fashioned by the same influences, whose souls in relation to their humble life's work had no secrets for him. (XVII, 53)

Suddenly the captain perceives another reflection in the mirror. The ghastly, pugnacious face of the first mate, Mr. Burns, disturbs the captain's reverie and foreshadows the struggle which is later to take place between the two officers.

Burns tells the young captain about the last captain of the ship, an old man who went mad and wished at the last to take his ship and all hands with him in death. The young captain then perceives that taking one's place in the tradition of the sea entails something more than merely stepping on board a ship as her captain. The task is not that simple, and vastly more dangerous:

That man had been in all essentials but his age just such another man as myself. Yet the end of his life was a complete act of treason, the betrayal of a tradition which seemed to me as imperative as any guide on earth could be. It appeared that even at sea a man could

---

rooted, inarticulate, confused impulses to stay and accept, on the one hand, and the intellectual expression of logic and conscious will on the other" (Wright, p. 46). Clearly, Conrad intends to create in the first few chapters of *The Shadow Line* the same mood of youthful disillusionment which Melville did so well in *Redburn*.

become the victim of evil spirits. I felt on my face the breath of unknown powers that shape our destinies. (XVII, 62)

The young captain must defeat the spirit of his malevolent predecessor which still hangs over the ship.

Burns, shortly after pugnaciously informing his new commander that he feels he should have been appointed captain, falls ill and appears to become the receptacle for the malicious spirit of the former captain. The first mate lies below raving about the curse which the old captain put on the ship. Burns believes that the latitude 8° 20′ at which the captain has been buried represents a line which the becalmed ship cannot pass. The narrator, of course, recognizes Burns's mad superstition for what it is, but he is, in some inexplicable way, worried by it: "I felt the inexpugnable strength of common sense being insidiously menaced by this gruesome, by this insane, delusion" (XVII, 82).

2. Symbolism of the voyage and the return

The spirit of the dead captain is on board in yet another sense, as the narrator discovers when he goes to the medicine cabinet to get quinine for his sick crew. When warned by a doctor friend before he starts the voyage that the crew would perhaps become even more sick than they are as the ship lies in port, the captain self-confidently asserted: "I had a good provision of quinine. I should put my trust in that, and administer it steadily, when the ship's health would certainly improve" (XVII, 80). But once the ship is under way, the young captain discovers that his predecessor has sold the quinine to finance his pernicious shore activities. Clearly, no material thing can save the captain and his ship's crew from the destructive element.

The captain is obsessed with the guilt he feels for not examining the quinine stores before getting underway. The responsibility of his command nearly overwhelms him. He writes in his diary:

I am shrinking from it. From the mere vision. My first command. **Now I understand** that strange sense of insecurity in my past. I always suspected that I might be no good. And here is proof positive. I am shirking it. I am no good. (XVII, 107)

The ship floats in a dead calm, and when a fresh breeze does come up one morning it drives her off course:

About sunrise we got for an hour an inexplicable, steady breeze, right in our teeth. There was no sense in it. It fitted neither the season of the year nor with the secular experience of seamen as recorded in books, nor with the aspect of the sky. Only purposeful malevolence could account for it. (XVII, 87)

She is a ship of the dead becalmed on a sea which is alternately hot and fiery, and black and still.[9] The men are living skeletons, unable to perform their work. The captain, who seems to bear a charm against the fever which is ravaging his ship, is spiritually ill, sickened by the weight of his sins and the sense of his unworthiness (XVII, 109). His ship has entered a Hell-like place comparable to the one Marlow's ship enters in "Heart of Darkness":

The impenetrable blackness beset the ship so close that it seemed that by thrusting one's hand over the side one could touch some unearthly substance. There was in it an effect of inconceivable terror and of inexpressible mystery. The few stars overhead shed a dim light upon the ship alone, with no gleams of any kind upon the water, in detached shafts piercing an atmosphere which had turned to soot. It was something I had never seen before, giving no hint of the direction from which any change would come, the closing in of a menace from all sides. (XVII, 108)

Only Ransome among the crew is untouched by the fever. He is normally the cook, for his bad heart makes it impossible for him to carry out the strenuous duties of an able-bodied seaman. With his weak heart which prevents him from a complete identification with the art of the seaman's craft, he fulfils a highly symbolic function, for his physical defect is the exact equivalent of the captain's spiritual defect. The captain, too, in a different sense than Ransome, has a "weak heart", – a too strong sense

---

[9]   F. R. Leavis, *The Great Tradition* (New York, 1948), p. 188, referring to the lyric qualities of the numerous images which make the *Melita* seem to be an enchanted ship doomed to sail forever on a Stygian sea, calls *The Shadow Line* a "prose Ancient Mariner".

of his own incapability which keeps him from immersing himself completely in the work of the ship. After having helped the captain bring the ship through the combined perils of her crew's fever and the dead calm, Ransome, echoing the narrator's actions at the beginning of the story, asks for his discharge. As the captain hears his cook's request he sees that the man's physical handicap has doomed him to be a slave, rather than a master of life:

And I saw under the worth and the comeliness of the man the humble reality of things. Life was a boon to him – this precarious hard life, and he was thoroughly alarmed about himself. (XVII, 129)

How much the hero of *The Shadow Line* has accomplished in coming to terms with the external evil represented by the becalmed sea and the internal evil represented by his lack of self-confidence is symbolically demonstrated in the figure of the forlorn Ransome, fated to carry forever within his breast a weakness which will not let him fully commit himself to the adventure of living.

The narrator was brought out of the depths of his first period of despair by a responsible job claiming him for its own as if by magic, and when his ship seems fated to stand on the burning sea till she is charred to a cinder, a rain squall comes up and as if by magic drives her swiftly on her course. In what amounts to a ritual baptism, the captain is immersed in the waters which accompany the saving wind:

Suddenly – how am I to convey it? Well, suddenly the darkness turned into water. This is the only suitable figure. A heavy shower, a downpour, comes along, making a noise. You hear its approach on the sea, in the air, too, I verily believe. But this was different. With no preliminary whisper or rustle, without a splash, and even without the ghost of impact, I became instantaneously soaked to the skin. (XVII, 114)

Like his first salvation, his second is not primarily the result of the conscious effort of his will, but rather is caused by a mysterious compounding of his unconscious devotion to duty – "The seaman's instinct alone survived whole in my moral dissolution"

(XVII, 109) – and the elemental forces of nature which bestow upon mankind as much good as evil.

As he returns to report to Captain Giles, the young captain understands that the homely virtues which the old man spouts possess a profound meaning. He sees, as Giles tells him, that a man should indeed "stand up to his bad luck, to his mistakes, to his conscience, and all that sort of thing" (XVII, 132). For the first time, the young captain sees the true Captain Giles, Captain Giles the preternatural seer:

It was as if a ponderous curtain had rolled up disclosing an unexpected Captain Giles. But it was only for a moment, just the time to let him add, "Precious little rest in life for anybody. Better not think of it." (XVII, 132)

The hero of *The Shadow Line* can no longer rejoice in the glad animal movements of childhood, for he has passed through that period of his existence when the harsh, grating noise of the universe oppressed him. He mourns not for youth's "aching joys" and "dizzy raptures", for he has discovered, through his trial at sea, the logic of being which is inherent in the assumption of responsibility.

VII. *NOSTROMO*

"There is something in a treasure that fastens upon
a man's mind".

In the "Author's Note" to *Nostromo*, Conrad calls the novel his
"most anxiously meditated" (IX, vii). In his prefatory note to
The Secret Agent, he refers to his South-American epic as his
"largest canvas" (XIII, ix), and Richard Curle reports that
Conrad thought of *Nostromo* as his principal achievement.[1]
Many critics agree that *Nostromo* is Conrad's largest and finest
achievement, but there is a curious lack of agreement as to the
meaning and the method of the novel. All commentators, of
course, agree that the novel is magnificently complex, and that
its vision of life is brooding, even pessimistic. Critical agreement,
however, is not so evident in regard to other essential elements
in *Nostromo*.

Frederick Karl, while calling *Nostromo* Conrad's "broadest
and most profound" novel, finds in it a "lack of staying power":
"Conrad watched with dismay as the novel grew, and then
rather than rework his material to suit greater length, he un-
naturally clipped short the ending."[2] Albert Guerard, however,
would have the novel much shorter:

Nostromo is in fact a great but radically defective novel, and its
greatest defect is that it is at least two hundred pages too long. This
is not a matter of generalized diffuseness. The two hundred or more
pages in excess come in the last two hundred and sixty.[3]

---

[1] Richard Curle, *The Last Twelve Years of Joseph Conrad* (London, 1928), p. 94.
[2] Frederick Karl, *A Reader's Guide to Joseph Conrad* (New York, 1960), p. 153.
[3] Albert Guerard, *Conrad the Novelist* (Cambridge, Mass., 1958), p. 203.

Robert Penn Warren sees *Nostromo* as a "complex of personal stories",[4] but H. T. Webster says "Nostromo is much more the tale of a country and an economic process than of individuals."[5] Robert Haugh, speaking for a host of critics who find little significance in the novel's title and who, thus, would seem to be engaged in argument with Conrad, writes: "The simple and magnificent Nostromo is but a grace note in the fortunes of Sulaco." [6]

Close attention to the symbolic and archetypal patterns of Nostromo cannot, of course, provide an answer to all of the perplexing critical problems which surround the novel, but such an approach can serve to illustrate some of the important structural relationships essential to understanding it. The presentation of theme through symbol, symbolic characters, and symbolic relationships between characters, though perhaps not quite so obvious in *Nostromo* as in many other of Conrad's novels and tales, is, nevertheless, the framework upon which the novel is constructed. An analysis of the various complex patterns of image and symbol which Conrad employs in *Nostromo* reveals that, though the novel's "canvas" is large, there is an exquisite attention to detail. Such an analysis also indicates that the novel's center of interest is not perhaps so elusive as it would seem on the surface; that is, in spite of the complex time scheme and numerous characters which *Nostromo* contains, the story belongs essentially to the magnificent Capataz de Cargadores, and he is its tragic hero. Also, though *Nostromo* by no means presents an optimistic world view, there is an affirmation, albeit ironical, in the closing scene of the novel, which would seem to mitigate somewhat the bitter defeat which nearly all the important characters in the novel experience.

[4] Robert Penn Warren, Introduction to the Modern Library edition of *Nostromo* (New York, 1951). Reprinted in *The Art of Joseph Conrad, A Critical Symposium,* ed. R. W. Stallman (East Lansing, Michigan, 1960), p. 220.
[5] H. T. Webster, "Joseph Conrad: A Reinterpretation of Five Novels", *College English,* VII (December, 1945), 130.
[6] Robert Haugh, *Joseph Conrad: Discovery in Design* (Norman, Okla., 1957), p. 149.

A. MYTHIC TONE OF OPENING FRAME

The first chapter of the novel, which contains a description
of the geography of Sulaco's harbor and the tale of an ill-fated
treasure expedition, establishes the novel's mythic tone, and subtly
foreshadows various of its thematic elements. The Golfo Placido,
a place of prevailing calm, isolates the luxuriant beauty of
Sulaco from the fresh ocean breezes just as many of the city's
inhabitants are to be isolated from the adventure of life by their
moral inertia:

Some harbours of the earth are made difficult of access by the
treachery of sunken rocks and the tempests of their shores. Sulaco
had found an inviolable sanctuary from the temptations of a trading
world in the solemn hush of the deep Golfo Placido as if within an
enormous semi-circular and unroofed temple open to the ocean, with
its walls of lofty mountains hung with the mourning draperies of
cloud. (IX, 3)

Ships bound for Sulaco enter another world as they negotiate
the mouth of the Golfo Placido, an isolated place where the
strong ocean breezes cannot reach. The few breezes which do
violate the calm of the gulf are capricious, and it sometimes
takes a sailing ship more than thirty hours to reach Sulaco once
it has entered the gulf. The natural calm and weird cloud for-
mations of the Golfo Placido are forbidding enough during the
day; at night this strange body of water becomes even more
frightening, for at dusk it is transformed into a microcosmic hell:

At night the body of clouds advancing higher up the sky smothers
the whole quiet gulf below with an impenetrable darkness, in which
the sound of the falling showers can be heard beginning and ceasing
abruptly – now here, now there. Indeed, these cloudy nights are
proverbial with the seamen along the whole west coast of a great
continent. Sky, land, and sea disappear together out of the world
when the Placido – as the saying is – goes to sleep under its black
poncho. The few stars left below the seaward frown of the vault
shine feebly as into the mouth of a black cavern. In its vastness your
ship floats unseen under your feet, her sails flutter invisible above
your head. The eye of God Himself – they add with grim profanity

-- could not find out what work a man's hand is doing in there; and you would be free to call the devil to your aid with impunity if even his malice were not defeated by such a blind darkness. (IX, 6–7)

Across this gulf Nostromo and Martin Decoud are to make their desperate journey with the treasure of the San Tomé mine, and each is fated to lose his soul on this dark body of water where a man cannot even invoke the name of the devil.

The Azuera peninsula forms one of the arms of land which enclose the gulf. It is a sterile strip of land: "Utterly waterless, for the rainfall runs off at once on all sides into the sea, it has not soil enough – it is said – to grow a single blade of grass, as if it were blighted by a curse" (IX, 4). The Azuera peninsula, like the Golfo Placido, is a strange and mysterious place, for the Indians of Costaguana believe that on this barren stretch of land lie enormous heaps of treasure guarded only by an obscure curse. The legends which surround the forbidden treasure of Azuera tell of two gringos and a native who risked the evils of the curse in an attempt to obtain the shining gold:

The sailors, the Indian, and the stolen burro were never seen again. As to the mozo, a Sulaco man – his wife paid for some masses, and the poor four-footed beast, being without sin, had probably been permitted to die; but the two gringos, spectral and alive, are believed to be dwelling to this day amongst the rocks, under the fatal spell of their success. Their souls cannot tear themselves away from their bodies mounting guard over the discovered treasure. They are now rich and hungry and thirsty – a strange theory of tenacious gringo ghosts suffering in their starved and parched flesh of defiant heretics, where a Christian would have renounced and been released. (IX, 5)

There is another forbidden treasure in Costaguana – the silver of the San Tomé mine – and all those who seek this treasure are imprisoned by it body and soul, as the spectres of the gringo adventurers are imprisoned on the Azuera peninsula.

Charles Gould, Nostromo, in fact all of Sulaco is to some extent corrupted by the treasure of the San Tomé mine, and all who are thus corrupted are "rich and hungry and thirsty" like the two gringos. When the Occidental Province bows down before the "material interests" represented by the Gould mine, the Sulacans indeed become rich, but they hunger and thirst after the spiritual elements which alone can give their lives meaning. The association of treasure with barrenness which is established in the legend of the Azuera gold is also significant in the total pattern of the novel, for all those who are touched by the "material interests" of the Gould concession are rendered spiritually sterile. It is also significant that Charles Gould and Nostromo, the two individuals who are most deeply involved with the silver, seem to be rendered physically sterile also. The marriage of Charles and Emilia Gould is conspicuously barren, and Nostromo is kept from enjoying the love of either Linda or Giselle Viola by the silver which he has stolen.

In the second chapter of *Nostromo,* with the introduction of "Fussy Joe" Mitchell, Conrad begins to describe the pathetic comic-opera nature of Costaguana politics – frequent revolutions, deposed dictators fleeing from rebellious armies, mobs more intent on a day's drunkenness than a stable government. But even in this overview of the realities of Costaguanan life, Conrad subtly maintains the mythic undertones which he established in chapter one. The simple listing of the names of the ships owned by Captain Mitchell's firm, the Oceanic Steam Navigation Company, merges myth with reality: "Their names, the names of all mythology, became the household words of a coast that had never been ruled by the Gods of Olympus. *Juno* ... *Saturn* ... *Ganymede* ... *Cerberus*" (IX, 10).

B. CHARLES GOULD AS KNIGHT-SAVIOUR

In the absence of Olympian or any other kind of gods in the small coastal republic of Costaguana, one man, Charles Gould, establishes himself as a sort of deity, though this is never his intention. He is not, like Gentleman Brown, an egoistic renegade, for his intention as he assumes control of the San Tomé mine is to make it a rallying point for the forces of justice and enlightenment. He hopes to make Costaguana a model republic, peopled by a happy, well fed, enlightened citizenry. He is less sentimental than Conrad's most famous man of noble ideals, Kurtz, and thus does not fall into the more grotesque postures of the man-god; yet as surely as Kurtz is corrupted by ivory and the superstitious natives of the Congo, Charles Gould is corrupted by the silver of the San Tomé mine and the political instability of Costaguana. At the last, the mine consumes his soul, and he considers human life a small enough sacrifice for the maintenance of stable "material interests".

The comments of the disillusioned Dr. Monygham concerning Gould's extreme self-confidence and the monstrous thing the San Tomé mine is fated to become reveal something of the nature of the illusion which has imprisoned the idealistic young Costaguanerian. The comments of Dr. Monygham, however, must be considered in their dramatic context. That is, the doctor, who betrayed his comrades-in-arms when tortured by the infamous Guzman Bento, has so little confidence in himself that he naturally assumes the worst of others. In addition, Monygham idealizes Gould's wife Emilia and feels that Gould is not worthy of her. Other characters also comment on Charles Gould's actions and character, but Conrad's method of revealing Gould's soul is much subtler and more effectual than the device of direct comment by other characters. By presenting Gould as an archetypal knight isolated by his armor from human passions, and by associating him with images of stone, Conrad demonstrates the flaw which exists in the young man's character and the terribly inhuman being which this flaw, combined with the treacherous influence of the San Tomé mine, makes of him.

Charles Gould is a third generation Costaguanerian, but it is significant that, though he is an accomplished horseman, his riding style is not that of Costaguana:

The only representative of the third generation in a continent possessing its own style of horsemanship went on looking thoroughly English even on horseback. This is not said of him in the mocking spirit of the Llaneros – men of the great plains – who think that no one in the world knows how to sit a horse but themselves. Charles Gould, to use the suitably lofty phrase, rode like a centaur. Riding for him was not a special form of exercise; it was a natural faculty, as walking straight is to all men sound of mind and limb; but, all the same, when cantering beside the rutty ox-cart track to the mine he looked in his English clothes and with his imported saddlery as though he had come this moment to Costaguana at his easy swift *pasotrote,* straight out of some green meadow at the other side of the world. (IX, 48)

As Gould does not ride in the Costaguanerian style, so he cannot sympathize with the oppressed natives of his country in anything but an abstract sense. As a knight-saviour, he is "prepared to stoop for his weapons" (IX, 85) in his noble struggle to liberate Costaguana from the grip of its corrupt politicians, but will not admit that by bribing the government officials he is furthering the very political instability which he so hates. By not bowing and scraping before these corrupt officials, by pointedly not addressing them by their official titles, he hopes to remain aloof from the evil which they represent, but in guarding against one type of evil he is subtly infected by another.

Charles Gould's bearing and his beautiful riding equipment are a symbolic manifestation of his role as the knight-saviour of Costaguana. The Casa Gould each day echoes with the sound of Gould's spurs as he strides forth to the mountain to struggle with the curse which hangs over the San Tomé mine. He possesses no magic sword, but his room is furnished with the shining accoutrements of the modern knight:

One tall, broad bookcase, with glass doors, was full of books; but in the other, without shelves, and lined with red baize, were arranged firearms: Winchester carbines, revolvers, a couple of shot-guns, and even two pairs of double-barrelled holster pistols. Between them, by itself, upon a strip of scarlet velvet, hung an old cavalry sabre, once the property of Don Enrique Gould, the hero of the Occidental Province, presented by Don José Avellanos, the hereditary friend of the family. (IX, 69)

His wife, even though she senses that Gould's association with the mine will destroy his love for her, is struck by his princely appearance as he rides off to the mountain: "With his riding breeches, leather leggings (an article of apparel never before seen in Costaguana), a Norfolk coat of grey flannel, and those great flaming moustaches, he suggested an officer of cavalry turned gentleman farmer" (IX, 71). He is, indeed, much more than a gentleman farmer. He is, as the natives call him, "The King of Sulaco".

Martin Decoud, the young skeptic who is drawn into participating in the political wars of Costaguana by his love for the beautiful Antonia Avellanos, disparages Gould's romantic idealism in a conversation with Emilia Gould:

> I have been watching El Rey de Sulaco since I came here on a fool's errand, and perhaps impelled by some treason of fate lurking behind the unaccountable turns of a man's life. But I don't matter, I am not a sentimentalist, I cannot endow my personal desires with a shining robe of silk and jewels. Life is not for me a moral romance derived from the tradition of a pretty fairy tale. No, Mrs. Gould; I am practical. I am not afraid of my motives. (IX, 218)

Decoud's comments, of course, must, like Monygham's, be considered in their dramatic context, and it is evident that Decoud's profound skepticism colors his impression of his fellows. Yet, it is extremely significant that his indictment of Gould echoes the imagery of Gould as knight which Conrad has presented earlier in the narrative.

When the Monterist revolution which threatens to capture the "material interests" of the San Tomé mine seems assured of success, Gould, in musing on the cruel futility of things, indicates his romantic conception of his relation to the mine, for he imagines this relation to be that of a knight to his sword:

> He had gone forth into the senseless fray as his poor uncle, whose sword hung on the wall of his study, had gone forth – in the defence of the commonest decencies of organized society. Only his weapon was the wealth of the mine, more far-reaching and subtle than an honest blade of steel fitted into a simple brass guard. More dangerous to the wielder, too, this weapon of wealth, double-edged with the cupidity and misery of mankind, steeped in all the vices of self-indulgence as in a concoction of poisonous roots, tainting the very cause for which it is drawn, always ready to turn awkwardly in the hand. There was nothing for it now but to go on using it. (IX, 365)

"El Rey de Sulaco" finds life to be a corrupt and illogical affair, but never does he take off his shining armor, throw away his sword and deal with the problems of Costaguana with his bare hands. He will indeed "stoop for his weapons", but he has an aversion to soiling his fingers. Lord Jim, when he sees the *Patna*'s officers, feels that he has nothing in common with them, that nothing they do can affect him. Gould, like Jim before he accepts his guilt, pursues his dream without realizing that he can be touched by the corruption which he sees surrounding him. He does not possess the "ironic eye" (IX, 378), the double vision which permits a man such as Stein to fuse the dualistic nature of human existence into a scheme which will allow the dream to be pursued without ignoring the dreamer's frailty. The Monterist revolution, the defection of the Sulaco politicos, the loss of the lighter full of silver, offend Gould's dignity. He curses them and the fact that the necessities of the revolution force him to sacrifice his aloofness from Costaguana politics. Were he carefully to examine his own motives, were he to identify the destructive element in himself with that in the external world and thus recognize his common bond with all Costaguanerians, the peons at the mine, the powdered women whom he abhors, and even the corrupt politicians and army officers, he might well save himself and his countrymen from the curse of the San Tomé mine.

Of course, the problem of self-discovery which confronts Charles Gould is by no means as clear-cut as that which faces Lord Jim. It is, however, Gould's failure to discover the realities of his own nature and to compensate for them which is partially responsible for his tragedy. He cannot see that his preoccupation with the material interests of the San Tomé mine robs him of the humane qualities which would make the wealth of the mine a force for justice rather than merely another element in the corrupt design of Costaguana politics. The reader attentive to Conrad's subtle association of Gould with images of stone, however, can recognize the evil inherent in the young idealist's concentration on things material. Early in the novel, as he describes the daily ride of El Rey de Sulaco from the Casa Gould to the mine, Conrad meaningfully juxtaposes the old ruler of Sulaco with the new:

The big equestrian statue of Charles IV at the entrance of the

Alameda, towering white against the trees, was only known to the folk from the country and to the beggars of the town that slept on the steps around the pedestal, as the Horse of Stone. The other Carlos, turning off to the left with a rapid clatter of hoofs on the disjointed pavement – Don Carlos Gould, in his English clothes, looked as incongruous, but much more at home than the kingly cavalier reining in his steed on the pedestal above the sleeping leperos, with his marble arm raised towards the marble rim of a plumed hat. (IX, 48–49)

In the next paragraph Gould's breast is described as "slate coloured" (IX, 49).

Stone imagery also plays a significant symbolic role in several of the scenes which describe Charles Gould's courting of his wife Emilia. The young Charles is sent to Europe for his education. There he decides upon the profession of mining engineer and, to further his education, visits mines in nearly all the countries on the continent. In an artful foreshadowing of the tragic figure whom Gould is to become, Conrad describes the young man's assigning of human feelings to the mines which he visits:

He visited mines in Germany, in Spain, in Cornwall. Abandoned workings had for him strong fascination. Their desolation appealed to him like the sight of human misery, whose causes are varied and profound. They might have been worthless, but also they might have been misunderstood. (IX, 59)

While visiting mines in Italy, Charles meets Emilia, but even her charm cannot completely destroy his preoccupation with "material interests":

The two young people had met in Lucca. After that meeting Charles Gould visited no mines, though they went together in a carriage, once, to see some marble quarries, where the work resembled mining in so far that it also was the tearing of the raw material of treasure from the earth. (IX, 60)

Soon afterward, when Charles tells Emilia of the death of his father, he loses himself completely in the contemplation of the material world, in this case a marble urn:

"It has killed him!" ... She was too startled to say anything; he was contemplating with a penetrating and motionless stare the cracked marble urn as though he had resolved to fix its shape for ever in his memory.... He caught hold of her hand, raised it to his lips, and at that she dropped her parasol to pat him on the cheek, murmured "Poor boy", and began to dry her eyes under the downward curve of her hat-brim, very small in her simple, white frock, almost like a lost child crying in the degraded grandeur of the noble hall, while he stood by her, again perfectly motionless in the contemplation of the marble urn. (IX, 62)

Charles Gould indeed pins his faith to "material interests", so much so that he refuses to participate in the joy and pain of human existence. His decline from the young visionary who courts Emilia and speaks of justice in the abstract to the benevolent but disillusioned dictator of the peons of the San Tomé mine is slow, but possesses a tragic inevitability. Gould's tragedy is not caused by one calamitous mistake in judgment, but rather by a series of small compromises with the evils forced upon him by the exigencies of Costaguanan politics. Yet, as corrupt and confusing as the Costaguana governmental scene is, it is Gould's failure to take a penetrating look at his own motives and emotions which make him the slave of the San Tomé mine. Were he to recognize that he is sacrificing his human emotions at the altar of abstract justice by the "roundabout logic of emotions" (IX, 85), there is the possibility that he could reverse his course of action. However, Conrad does not present this possibility, for in creating the character of Charles Gould he wishes to demonstrate the tragedy of self-recognition not attained.

The horror of what Charles Gould's faith in material interests has made of him and his country Conrad evokes with a variety of devices. As the mine strengthens its grip on Gould's soul, it is significant that he becomes increasingly aloof from his wife and small circle of friends. Never a man to indulge in meaningless convention, as the narrative progresses he speaks less and less, frequently making his decisions with the nod of his head and showing his pleasure or displeasure by a slight alteration of his facial expression:

His silences, backed by the power of speech, had as many shades of significance as uttered words in the way of assent, of doubt, of negation – even of simple comment. Some seemed to say plainly, "Think it over"; others meant clearly "Go ahead", a simple, low "I see", with an affirmative nod, at the end of a patient listening half-hour was the equivalent of a verbal contract, which men had learned to trust implicitly. (IX, 203)

In short, he comes to resemble the equestrian statue of Charles IV, an immobile figure to be talked about, rather than to. The most important decision which he makes, the decision to support a separationist revolution, is not discussed with his wife or advisors (IX, 378). Self-confident and consumed by the fixed idea of justice, he keeps his decision secret until he is ready to effect it.

The peons who work at the San Tomé mine enjoy a certain freedom from harassment by the minor officials in the city of Sulaco, for their uniform of green and white distinguishes them as Gould's workers. Yet in exchange for this freedom, they have entered into another type of slavery which, though it does not cause them physical suffering, robs them of their capability to think and act as individuals. The mayor of the San Tomé village stands as a symbol of the grotesque effect which the Gould Concession's abstract justice has on the Costaguanan natives, just as the absurdly uniformed negro guard of the chain gang in "Heart of Darkness" is a symbol of what the ideals of nineteenth century Belgian colonialism have made of the Congo natives:

The grave alcalde himself, in a white waistcloth and flowered chintz gown with sleeves, open wide upon his naked stout person with an effect of a gaudy bathing robe, stood by, wearing a rough beaver hat at the back of his head, and grasping a tall staff with a silver knob in his hand. These insignia of his dignity had been conferred upon him by the Administration of the mine, the fountain of honour, of prosperity, and peace. (IX, 397)

To demonstrate further the unalloyed essence of the degradation which Gould's "material interests" entail, Conrad creates one of the symbolic minor characters which he handles so well. There is no doubt of the moral and physical cowardice, and the wretched materialism of the Esmeralda hide merchant, Senor Hirsch. He has come to Sulaco to profit from the upheaval which the Costaguana revolution has caused. When chased by a bloodthirsty mob, he is so overcome by fear that he flees to the harbor of Sulaco and hides himself like a frightened rat on one of the untended boats. Later he is captured by the rebel general Sotillo, tortured and killed. Hirsch is, as Paul Wiley notes, one of the many characters in *Nostromo* who attest to the insufficiency of the human being faced by the insidious evils of materialism.[7] It would seem, however, that Hirsch plays an additional role, for though he has an exceedingly minor part in the events which lead to the Occidental Province's seceding from the Republic of Costaguana, he is significantly related to the power behind the secession, Charles Gould. Hirsch's weeping over his inability to transport ox-hides out of the Occidental Province is a degraded form of Gould's feelings for the deserted mines which he saw in Europe:

There were incipient tears in his mute anger at the thought of the innumerable ox-hides going to waste upon the dreamy expanse of the Campo .... There were hides there, rotting, with no profit to anybody – rotting where they had been dropped by men called away to attend the urgent necessities of political revolutions. The practical, mercantile soul of Senor Hirsch rebelled against all that foolishness, while he was taking a respectful but disconcerted leave of the might and majesty of the San Tomé mine in the person of Charles Gould. He could not restrain a heart-broken murmur, wrung out of his very aching heart, as it were. (IX, 203–204)

When Hirsch is certain that he will be able to do no business in hides, he vents his frustration on the Costaguana politicos: "Evidently this was no time for extending a modest man's business. He enveloped in a swift mental malediction the whole country, with all its inhabitants, partisans of Ribiera and Montero alike" (IX, 203). When the San Tomé mine is threatened by Monterist forces, Charles Gould's thoughts on business and politics seem to echo those of the despicable Hirsch: "He might have known, he said to himself, leaning over the balustrade of the corredor, that Ribierism could never come to anything .... It exasperated him. He had persuaded himself that, apart from higher considerations, the backing up of Don José's hopes of

[7]   Paul Wiley, *Conrad's Measure of Man* (Madison, Wis., 1954), p. 100.

reform was good business" (IX, 365). And when Gould in his desperate fight to save the mine subordinates human life to "material interests", what is he but a sort of "hide merchant"?

Near the end of the narrative, Captain Mitchell reports the success of Charles Gould's separationist counter-revolution to a visitor who knows nothing about Costaguana's recent history. After detailing the role which each of the leading critizens of Sulaco played in the revolution, Mitchell mentions the statue of Charles IV, which no longer stands in the city square:

"The equestrian statue that used to stand on the pedestal over there has been removed. It was an anachronism", Captain Mitchell commented, obscurely. "There is some talk of replacing it by a marble shaft commemorative of Separation, with angels of peace at the four corners, and bronze Justice holding an even balance, all gilt, on the top. Cavaliere Parrochetti was asked to make a design, which you can see framed under glass in the Municipal Sala." (IX, 482)

If the identification of Charles Gould with the stone statue of the king is accepted, the grotesque victory column is, then, a symbol of what his "material interests" have made of him and his country.

Conrad's characterization of Gould is so masterfully done that *Nostromo* often seems to be his story. It is his story, however, only in the sense that he is the primary exemplification of the public, political theme of the novel – an exemplification of Conrad's belief that material progress is incapable of securing the happiness of mankind. Conrad is very careful to insure that the reader does not overly sympathize with Gould's private dilemma, for as the narrative progresses, though the actions of Gould become more and more important to Costaguana's fate, the scenes in which he appears become proportionally fewer. Even when he is courting Emilia he is so aloof as to evoke little sympathy. His corruption by the silver of the mine, though perhaps more horrible than that of Nostromo, is not quite so interesting because he is notably less human. Gould is, indeed, "one of us", but not to the degree which Nostromo is. Late in the narrative when a servant reports to Emilia Gould: "The master remains to sleep at the mountain tonight" (IX, 519),

Charles Gould has long since ceased to function as a human being.

Nostromo is fully as much a novel about "how to be" as is *Lord Jim,* and though it lacks an affirmation comparable to Jim's dying vision, it perhaps contains a broader investigation of man's search to discover a meaning and direction in life. Whereas the center of the quest for life's meaning in *Lord Jim* obviously centers in Jim, in *Nostromo,* though it can be demonstrated that the individual histories of all the main characters ultimately converge in that of the magnificent Capataz de Cargadores, the individual consciousness of not one, but four seekers for life's meaning is examined in detail. Of the four exceptional men in *Nostromo* – Gould, Decoud, Monygham, and Nostromo – not one escapes the curse of the silver; but in depicting their struggle, Conrad demonstrates something of the magnificent courage of the human spirit.

C. DECOUD AND MONYGHAM AS TWO ASPECTS OF NIHILISM

Martin Decoud, who obviously plays a role minor to that of either Charles Gould or Nostromo, cannot idealize his motives as they can. He is a skeptic, a Parisian dandy to whom the political upheavals of his native land are offensive because of their extreme illogic:

Of his own country he used to say to his French associates: "Imagine an atmosphere of opera-bouffe in which all the comic business of stage statesman, brigands, etc., etc., all their farcical stealing, intriguing, and stabbing is done in dead earnest. It is screamingly funny, the blood flows all the time, and the actors believe themselves to be influencing the fate of the universe. Of course, government in general, any government anywhere, is a thing of exquisite comicality to a discerning mind; but really we Spanish-Americans do overstep the bounds. No man of ordinary intelligence can take part in the intrigues of *une farce macabre.*" (IX, 152)

While still living in Paris he is appointed a member of a com-

mittee of Sulacans who wish to procure a shipment of small arms
to equip the army of the Occidental Province to withstand the
corrupt pressures of General Montera, the War Minister. Decoud
accepts the position with a spirit of levity and actually accompanies the shipment of arms back to Costaguana: "The whole
burlesque business, he thought, was worth following up to the
end" (IX, 155). Once in Costaguana he is quick in his observation that Charles Gould lives in a fairy-tale, but though he
can recognize the fairy-tale, Decoud cannot prevent himself from
being drawn into it. Charles Gould is fascinated by the treasure
of the San Tomé Mine, Martin Decoud by the beautiful Antonia
Avellanos. Gould carries his sword of "material interests" aloft
into the revolutionary fray; Decoud's magic weapon is his love
for Antonia, and he undertakes various quests in order to gain
the hand of his fair maiden. He becomes the editor of the anti-
Montera newspaper, *Porvenir,* formulates the plan for the separation of the Occidental Province from the state of Costaguana,
and volunteers to help Nostromo spirit a large shipment of San
Tomé silver away from the approaching Monterist forces. It
is in this last desperate affair that Martin Decoud loses his soul.

Even if Conrad had not established the Golfo Placido as a
sort of underworld in the opening frame of the novel, on the
night when Decoud and Nostromo sail into it with the lighter-load
of silver it is an infernal region. The great silence of the gulf
turns Decoud's skepticism inward, and this man who believes
himself to be "not a patriot, but a lover" (IX, 176), who has
no illusions save "the supreme illusion of lover" (IX, 189), who
when speaking of his love for Antonia says he shall cling to his
aspirations to the end (IX, 193), begins to doubt the reality
of the sensational world in which he has placed his trust:

He didn't even know at times whether he were asleep or awake. Like
a man lost in slumber, he heard nothing, he saw nothing. Even his
hand held before his face did not exist for his eyes. The change from
the agitation, the passions and the dangers, from the sights and sounds
of the shore, was so complete that it would have resembled death had
it not been for the survival of his thoughts. In this foretaste of eternal
peace they floated vivid and light, like unearthly clear dreams of
earthly things that may haunt the souls freed by death from the

misty atmosphere of regrets and hopes. Decoud shook himself, shuddered a bit, though the air that drifted past him was warm. He had the strangest sensation of his soul having just returned into his body from the circumambient darkness in which land, sea, sky, the mountains, and the rocks were as if they had not been. (IX, 262)

Decoud is a hero who has descended into the underworld to struggle with the dark powers, but he has not taken with him either the sense of his own destiny or the magic charm which traditionally saves the mythic hero.

In the impenetrable darkness of the Golfo Placido, the lighter carrying Gould, Nostromo, and the silver collides with the steamer carrying the troops of Sotillo, a Monterist who hopes to be the first to have his chance at the treasure which Decoud and Nostromo are carrying away. Nostromo guides the crippled lighter to the largest of the three small islands in the gulf, the Great Isabel, and there leaves Decoud with the treasure. Decoud, while waiting for Nostromo's return, becomes more and more depressed by his feeling of solitude. He who had said that he would cling to his aspiration to the end, "the spoiled darling of the family, the lover of Antonia and journalist of Sulaco, was not fit to grapple with himself single-handed" (IX, 497). After a time, Decoud's love for Antonia – his only touchstone with the external world – begins to fail him:

Decoud lost all belief in the reality of his action past and to come. On the fifth day an immense melancholy descended upon him palpably. He resolved not to give himself up to these people in Sulaco, who had beset him, unreal and terrible, like jibbering and obscene spectres. He saw himself struggling feebly in their midst, and Antonia, gigantic and lovely like an allegorical statue, looking on with scornful eyes at his weakness. (IX, 497–498)

Unlike the traditional mythic hero, he cannot ignore the monsters which fly at him out of the dark hell of his own solitude. Decoud's love for Antonia is clearly not sufficiently strong to allow him to defeat the illogic and farcical cruelty of life which he experiences on the dark Golfo Placido.

Driven frantic by his solitude, Decoud cannot, of course, rationally examine his sense of isolation, but his crazed mind

creates an image which indicates that his subconscious recognizes
the frail tenuity of his connection with life. He envisions the
frightening silence of the gulf as a tense thin cord to which he
hangs in desperation: "He imagined it snapping with a report
as of a pistol – a sharp full crack. And that would be the end
of him . . . . 'I wonder whether I would hear it snap before I
fell', he asked himself" (IX, 499). On the tenth day he can
stand the solitude no longer. Taking four ingots from the hoard
of San Tomé silver, he rows out into the gulf. The image of
Decoud rowing away from the Great Isabel, suicide not yet his
clear intention, is a lyric symbol of his inability to discover the
joy of life:

Taking up the cars slowly, he pulled away from the cliff of the Great
Isabel, that stood behind warm with sunshine, as if with the heat of
life, bathed in a rich light from head to foot as if in a radiance of
hope and joy. He pulled straight towards the setting sun. (IX, 500)

In an excess of self-mutilation Decoud puts the four silver
ingots in his pockets so that he will be sure to sink, leans over
the gunwale of the boat, and shoots himself. Thus, the knight
who has forsaken "material interests", but who has erected his
passions into duties, has also failed to defeat the curse which
hangs over the San Tomé mine and all of Costaguana.

Conrad so brilliantly portrays the character of Martin Decoud,
the dilettante in life, that his story, like Gould's, of itself seems
sufficient to form the basis of a novel. But Decoud's figure in
the vast canvas which is *Nostromo,* when ranged alongside the
others of major importance, is revealed as a symbol of what all
of them might become were they to believe that their own sensations were sufficient reason for being.

In *Lord Jim* Conrad created minor characters by way of
symbolic comment on the psychology of Jim's failure and guilt.
In *Nostromo* he creates several major characters who offer
perspectives from which other major characters may be viewed.
We better understand Nostromo's corruption when we have seen
Gould's. We better understand Decoud's skepticism when we see
Monygham's cynicism. We better understand Monygham's com-

plete lack of self-confidence when we contrast it with Nostromo's magnificent trust in his own capabilities. In short, each major character offers a symbolic comment on every other major character.

Dr. Monygham possesses none of Gould's faith in "material interests", nor can he, like Decoud, erect his passions into duties. Having failed to stand up under the torture of President-Dictator Guzman Bento, Monygham has completely lost faith in the nobility of the human spirit. To him the world is a dark place where the human animal carries on his miserable struggle to no end. Most of all, Monygham cannot believe in himself. When one of the engineers imported to build the railway to Sulaco remarks that Charles Gould's calmness must indicate he is extremely sure of himself, Monygham replies: "If that's all he is sure of, then he is sure of nothing. . . . It is the last thing a man ought to be sure of" (IX, 310). The doctor's lack of faith in himself is exceeded only by his lack of faith in Charles Gould. Naturally the cynical Monygham is quick to discern the evil inherent in the San Tomé mine:

"There is no peace and no rest in the development of material interests. They have their law, and their justice. But it is founded on expediency, and is inhuman; it is without rectitude, without the continuity and the force that can be found only in a moral principle. Mrs. Gould, the time approaches when all that the Gould Concession stands for shall weigh as heavily upon the people as the barbarism, cruelty, and misrule of a few years back." (IX, 511)

Since Monygham is not fooled by the rationalized emotions of Gould, Decoud, or Nostromo, and since he is seemingly "honest" with himself, it is perhaps natural that many readers of *Nostromo*, with Albert Guerard, would accept Monygham's cynical outlook as the one Conrad wished to express in the novel.[8] Certainly much of the pessimism which *Nostromo* leaves with the reader is a result of Dr. Monygham's piercing distrust in himself and others, yet to offer Monygham's values as those of either the novel or its creator is to overlook certain essentials

[8] Guerard writes: "The horizon offered by the book itself seems to me, simply, Dr. Monygham's dark one" (p. 198).

of Conrad's philosophy and art. Of course, one could easily look to other works by Conrad and see that though he sometimes sympathizes with the cynic, he never allows him or his values to triumph. Such an extrinsic approach to the problem of what Dr. Monygham represents is not, however, necessary. Immediately after Monygham has questioned the worth and intelligence of man's having confidence in himself, Conrad gives us a view of the doctor's face – a face which does not image forth the light of truth:

The candle, half-consumed and burning dimly with a long wick, lighted up from below his inclined face, whose expression affected by the drawn-in cicatrices in the cheeks, had something vaguely unnatural, an exaggerated remorseful bitterness. As he sat there he had the air of meditating upon sinister things. (IX, 310)

Monygham hugs his guilt in a spasm of self-abuse, not recognizing that man need not be a flawless being for life to be worthwhile. Like Jim, Monygham lies to himself. He has "made himself an ideal conception of his disgrace", a conception which takes "no account of physiological facts or reasonable arguments" (IX, 375). Of an eminently loyal and courageous nature, Monygham has experienced under torture a "pain which makes truth, honour, self-respect, and life itself matters of little moment" (IX, 373). Feeling himself no longer worthy of these ideals since he has betrayed his comrades, he sublimates the desire for them which he cannot stifle into an exaggerated admiration for Emilia Gould. But Monygham's admiration for Gould's wife does not destroy or even mitigate his cynicism. He fawns in front of her in a selfish indulgence of his desire for punishment, sentimentally imagining the purity of his love for her, desiring to kiss the hem of her skirt. He thinks of her not as a human being but as woman idealized, and his feelings for her do not restore his self-respect, but allow him to disguise his callous use of Nostromo as a virtuous act performed for his lady.

The ugly nature of Monygham's cynicism is subtly but unmistakably revealed in the image which identifies Monygham as a vulture impatiently waiting to feast on the soul of the vain

Nostromo. When Sotillo threatens to ravage the city of Sulaco
in an attempt to find the silver with which Decoud and
Nostromo have escaped, Monygham devises a plan which will
save the city for a time sufficient for Gould to complete his
preparations for defence of the mine. Monygham is to pretend
to be a traitor, telling Sotillo he knows where the treasure is
hidden and keeping him occupied with the search for it until
it is too late to overwhelm the mine. He goes to the Custom
House, Sotillo's headquarters, to begin his dangerous deception.
Against the setting sun he sets out on his dangerous errand, his
crippled ankles making his gait grotesque: "The doctor, holding
a straight course for the Custom House, appeared lonely, hop-
ping amongst the dark bushes like a tall bird with a broken
wing" (IX, 411). Immediately after this image of Monygham,
the narrative shifts to Nostromo, awakening after his swim from
the Great Isabel to the Costaguana shore. He is being watched
by a vulture:

The first thing upon which Nostromo's eyes fell on waking was this
patient watcher for the signs of death and corruption. When the man
got up the vulture hopped away in great, sidelong, fluttering jumps.
He lingered for a while, morose and reluctant, before he rose, circling
noiselessly with a sinister droop of beak and claws. (IX, 413)

The vulture flies away, and Nostromo lifts his eyes to the sky
and says: "I am not dead yet" (IX, 413). Upon arriving in
Sulaco, Nostromo goes to the Custom House and there meets
Monygham. Monygham sees Nostromo can be useful: "He did
not think of him humanely, as of a fellow creature just escaped
from the jaws of death. The Capataz for him was the only
possible messenger to Cayta" (IX, 432). As the doctor "with
Machiavellian subtlety" (IX, 432) pursues his scheme to use
Nostromo, he mentions Decoud's supposed death. Nostromo's
reply is an echo of his words to the vulture: "There is no need
to talk of dead men. But I am not dead yet" (IX, 433). Like
a vulture, Monygham uses the corruption of others to feed his
own ego, and he is a symbol of the arrogant depravity of the
declared pessimist.

D. NOSTROMO AS BOATSWAIN

Nostromo, the fourth seeker after the truth of life, unites the various private histories of the novel. He stands as a symbol of the "crushing, paralyzing sense of human littleness" (IX, 433) which Monygham is so ready to confirm, yet from his defeat emanates a qualified hope in that he nearly defeats the curse which hangs over the San Tomé silver. In any case, Nostromo achieves a victory over the cynicism of which Monygham is a symbol.

The novel is named after the magnificent Capataz de Cargadores; he is more vibrantly alive than any other figure in the book, and the narrative ends with his death. Yet, many critics, sensitive to the magnificent artistry which Conrad exercised in creating Charles and Emilia Gould, Decoud, and Monygham, wish to make Nostromo into a minor character whose fate is less complicated and less interesting than that of the other important characters.[9] Such a view, however, overlooks the sig-

[9] Ernst Bendz, *Joseph Conrad: An Appreciation* (Gothenburg, Sweden, 1923), p. 64, who decided that Conrad must have been a bit unsure of the conception of *Nostromo* since its composition took him two years, wrote: "Another, and perhaps weightier, objection might be formulated thus: there is no really leading character in the book, no *hero*, in fact, in the sense of a personage kept continually to the foreground, and dominating his entourage either through the influence of his actions or by virtue of his intrinsic qualities. Gian' Battista, – 'Nostromo', – does neither. In a great number of the events he plays no part at all, or an invisible one. As one critic has finely observed: – 'We believe in Nostromo, but we are told about him – we have not met him.' The reader of novels is not in favour of heroes acting too persistently behind the curtain. As a protagonist in the story, Nostromo is on a level with, rather than above, half a dozen others, one of whom at least – Don Carlos Gould, 'the Idealist-creator of Material Interests' – might have been worked up into as great a character of romance and as effective a centerfigure." Conrad read Bendz's pamphlet and wrote a letter of appreciation in which he mentions the criticism of Nostromo: "I will take the liberty to point out that Nostromo has never been intended for the hero of the Tale of the Seaboard. Silver is the pivot of the moral and material events, affecting the lives of everybody in the tale. That this was my deliberate purpose there can be no doubt. I struck the first note of my intention in the unusual form which I gave to the title of the First Part, by calling it 'The Silver of the Mine', and by telling the story of the enchanted treasure of Azuera, which, strictly

nificance of Nostromo's name, his highly important role before
and during the Separationist revolution, and the symbols and
symbolic action in the last two chapters of the novel.

"Nostromo" is Captain Mitchell's elision of the Italian words
nostro and *uomo* – "our man". The name by which the wealthy
Sulacans refer to the Capataz de Cargadores is a symbol of their
casual treatment of him as a man, and though Nostromo's
corruption by the silver stems primarily from his vain self-ap-
proval, his justifiable rage at being referred to almost contemp-
tuously as "our man" is also a factor in his corruption. That
Nostromo resents his role as a sort of privileged lackey is most
evident when he speaks to Monygham in the Custom House:
"Is it that the 'hombres finos' – the gentlemen – need not think
as long as there is a man of the people ready to risk his body
and soul? Or, perhaps, we have no souls – like dogs?" (IX, 435).
Much earlier there is a hint that "Nostromo" offends the magnificent Capataz de Cargadores. When Decoud asks after the
Capataz in the Viola household, Linda refers to him as Gian'
Battista:

---

speaking, has nothing to do with the rest of the novel. Te word 'silver'
occurs almost at the very beginning of the story proper, and I took care
to introduce it in the very last paragraph, which would perhaps have
been better without the phrase which contains that key-word. Some of
my critics have perceived my intention; the last of them being Miss
Ruth Stauffer in her little study of my Romantic-Realism, published in
Boston in 1922" (G. Jean-Aubry, ed., *Joseph Conrad: Life and Letters,*
Garden City, New York, 1927, II, 296). Those who read this comment by Conrad as license to depreciate Nostromo's role in the novel
should, however, be rather cautious. Conrad was not the sort to angrily
disagree with a critic. Characteristically, as in the case of the Bendz
letter, he would offer some modification of a too boldly stated view.
Miss Stauffer's mention of the silver in *Nostromo* is slight (Ruth Stauffer,
Joseph Conrad: His Romantic-Realism, Boston, 1922, p. 39), and the
role of the silver in Nostromo is so obvious that for Conrad to point it
out to Bendz seems a rather cunning criticism of Bendz's perception.
Did Conrad subtly indicate to Bendz that he had missed some essentials
in *Nostromo?* Even if the silver is the pivot of the action and Nostromo
not, strictly speaking, the hero, his story may be the one which brings
the themes of the novel into their sharpest focus. The jungle of "Heart
of Darkness" is the "pivot of the action", but this does not preclude
Marlow's being the hero of that story.

"You mean Nostromo?' said Decoud.

"The English call him so, but that is no name either for man or beast", said the girl, passing her hand gently over her sister's hair.

"But he lets people call him so", remarked Decoud.

"Not in this house", retorted the child. (IX, 232)

There is, then, a conflict between Nostromo's name and his self-conception which mirrors his inner conflict.

Mitchell's mispronunciation of *nostro uomo* significantly forms the Italian word for boatswain. Nostromo was, in fact, boatswain on the Italian ship which brought him to Sulaco, and he carries over this function to his shore activities. The boatswain on a merchant ship is perhaps the most indispensable member of the ship's crew. He is the highest ranking of the ship's men and, as such, is responsible for all the housekeeping activities of the ship and for maintaining discipline among the crew. It would be, perhaps, no exaggeration to say that a ship could more easily do without a captain than a boatswain, for without a reliable boatswain, the orders of the ship's officers are only so many words. As a boatswain is indispensable to the ship's captain, Nostromo is indispensable to the Europeans of Sulaco. He saves Ribiera, the Gould-backed President-Dictator, from a mob and sees him safely on board a ship. He is a body-guard for the wealthy Englishman who visits the country for a few days to invest in a railroading enterprise. His well-organized force of "cargadores" is a sort of proletarian counterpart of the great force for order which the San Tomé mine represents. Nostromo, at the head of his Cargadores, is, as Decoud remarks, the "active usher-in of the material implements for our progress" (IX, 191). If a riot occurs, the Europeans can count Nostromo and his men on their side. He "seems to have a particular talent for being on the spot whenever there is something picturesque to be done" (IX, 224). When the Monterist revolution is at its peak, he takes the lighter-load of freshly minted San Tomé silver out of Sulaco, thus preventing Sotillo and Montera from securing the wealth which they need to keep their revolutionary armies together. When Sulaco is beleaguered by the combined forces of Sotillo and Montera, Nostromo goes through the Monterist lines surrounding Cayta to inform the loyal General Barrios that he must return to defend Sulaco. Were Nostromo to fail in any of his tasks, especially the last two, the orderly "material interests" of Charles Gould would collapse in a chaos of civil disorder. Nostromo is, then, a sort of boatswain, a guiding force without which the government of the Occidental Province would founder.

Early in the novel Conrad describes the pride Captain Mitchell takes in having discovered the talents of Nostromo. Mitchell admires his foreman much as one would a magnificent horse or a well-constructed ship:

> Captain Mitchell plumed himself upon his eye for men – but he was not selfish – and in the innocence of his pride was already developing that mania for "lending you my Capataz de Cargadores" which was to bring Nostromo into personal contact, sooner or later, with every European in Sulaco, as a sort of universal factotum – a prodigy of efficiency in his own sphere of life. (IX, 44)

Nostromo is, however, not merely an efficient work animal. He possesses a high intelligence and a sensitive soul, which, coupled with the intricate moral decision he is required to make, render his story perhaps more profound and complicated than those of Gould, Decoud and Monygham. He is a "universal factotum" in a moral as well as a physical sense, for in his story are united all the various threads of moral failure which run through the novel. Gould places his faith in "material interests", Decoud in idealized sensual love; Monygham's ruling passion is his distrust of himself. Before Nostromo dies he has fallen prey to each of these destructive passions, yet he manages to salvage something from these failures which the other three cannot.

The Europeans, by believing Nostromo to be incorruptible because of his immense vanity, demonstrate their naively cruel attitude toward the Capataz, for why should he, a man of the people, be less corruptible than his wealthy masters. That Nostromo is vain, however, there can be no doubt. He thinks of each job undertaken as a chance for further adulation. Both the Europeans and the third person narrator speak of Nostromo's vanity, but the most effectual revelation of his self-regard and

its potentially destructive power is the scene in which he casts
off a mistress with whom he has become bored. The girl accuses
Nostromo of neglecting her. He swears, with a clever wink at
the crowd which surrounds him, that he loves her as much as
ever. She asks him for a gift to prove his love. He refuses, and
she seethes in anger. He kisses her cavalierly, lifts her to the
saddle beside him and calls for a knife:

"A knife!" he demanded at large, holding her firmly by the shoulder.
Twenty blades flashed out together in the circle. A young man in
holiday attire, bounding in, thrust one in Nostromo's hand and
bounded back into the ranks, very proud of himself. Nostromo had not
even looked at him.
"Stand on my foot", he commanded the girl, who, suddenly subdued,
rose lightly, and when he had her up, encircling her waist, her face
near to his, he pressed the knife into her little hand.
"No, Morenita! You shall not put me to shame", he said. "You
shall have your present; and so that everyone should know who is
your lover to-day, you may cut all the silver buttons off my coat."
There were shouts of laughter and applause at this witty freak,
while the girl passed the keen blade, and the impassive rider jingled
in his palm the increasing hoard of silver buttons. He eased her to
the ground with both her hands full. (IX, 129–130)

More dear to Nostromo than the wealth represented by his
silver buttons is the adulation of the crowd, and the girl of the
streets slashing away at the buttons on Nostromo's breast is an
unforgettable image of the lengths to which this proud man
will go to protect his precious reputation.

Nostromo is not, however, a simple peon whose soul can be
satisfied by the admiring glances of the crowd and his own
magnificent self-confidence. He desires recognition from Sulaco's
European community and is resentful when he does not receive
it. When Decoud condescendingly compliments him on his
saving of President-Dictator Ribeira from the angry mob,
Nostromo replies: "And how much do I get for that señor" (IX,
226). In an attempt to draw attention to himself he frequently
stops members of the prosperous Sulacan families on the street
and cadges smokes from them. Nostromo's sense of his own
worth is grossly exaggerated, of course, but this does not excuse

the Europeans from treating him as if he were a clever pet with no soul.

Nostromo's resentment reaches its peak in the scene in which he meets Dr. Monygham in the Custom House. The Capataz has deposited the treasure on the Great Isabel and is still intent on saving it from the Monterist forces. When he sees Monygham's shadow on the Custom House wall, he shrinks back into the darkness, fearful that if his presence is discovered by the rebel forces the treasure will be endangered. When the Capataz recognizes Monygham, he steps out of the shadows, but the crippled doctor, intent on his assumed role of traitor, notices him but slightly. The Capataz is enraged:

> It angered him to be disarmed and skulking and in danger because of the accursed treasure, which was of so little account to the people who had tied it round his neck. He could not shake off the worry of it. To Nostromo the doctor represented all these people.... And he had never even asked after it. Not a word of inquiry about the most desperate undertaking of his life. (IX, 426)

When Monygham finds that Sotillo has moved his headquarters from the Custom House, he deigns to talk to Nostromo of the desperate adventure on the Golfo Placido. The previous night Monygham has heard Hirsch tell Sotillo that the lighter full of treasure was sunk in the collision on the gulf. Sotillo and Monygham both believe Hirsch's mistaken supposition, and when Monygham reports this story to Nostromo, the latter, wishing to protect the treasure, does not contradict him. Monygham then tells Nostromo that he wishes Sotillo had gotten hold of the treasure, for he is sure that in that case the rebel general would have immediately made off with the loot and not have bothered even to land his troops at Sulaco. "I could almost wish you had shouted and shown a light", says Monygham (IX, 434). Nostromo is immediately overcome by the feeling that he has been used as a mere tool:

> This unexpected utterance astounded the Capataz by its character of cold-blooded atrocity. It was as much as to say, "I wish you had shown yourself a coward; I wish you had had your throat cut for your pains." Naturally he referred it to himself, whereas it related

only to the silver, being uttered simply and with many mental reservations. Surprise and rage rendered him speechless, and the doctor pursued, practically unheard by Nostromo, whose stirred blood was beating violently in his ears. (IX, 434)

Though he does not until later decide that he "must grow rich very slowly" (IX, 503), it is during the conversation with Monygham that Nostromo changes from the poor trustworthy Capataz de Cargadores into the rich, deceitful Captain Fidanza. Monygham continues his discourse on how he would have solved the problem of Sotillo's aggression, and ends his egoistic, cynical comments with a remark on Charles Gould's general unworthiness. Nostromo overcomes his rage to reply to Monygham, but he is no longer the "incorruptible":

The Capataz had mastered the fury that was like a tempest in his ears in time to hear the name of Don Carlos. He seemed to have come out of it a changed man – a man who spoke thoughtfully in a soft and even voice. (IX, 434)

Nostromo stares fixedly at the corpse of Hirsch and feels he also is dead:

And the Capataz, listening as if in a dream, felt himself of as little account as the indistinct, motionless shape of the dead man whom he saw upright under the beam, with his air of listening also, disregarded, forgotten, like a terrible example of neglect. (IX, 435)

Nostromo in the Custom House, like Decoud on the Great Isabel, loses his sense of individuality. Each decides to punish himself for his stupidity, Decoud by killing himself, Nostromo by obliterating his incorruptibility, that part of himself which he deems most precious. Near the end of their conversation, Monygham addresses Nostromo as "Capataz". Nostromo replies: "What Capataz? ... The Capataz is undone, destroyed. There is no Capataz. Oh, no! You will find the Capataz no more" (IX, 436).

Nostromo accepts the errand of informing Barrios that he must return to Sulaco. As the steamer carrying Barrios's troops and Nostromo back to Sulaco enters the Golfo Placido, Nostromo sees the lighter's boat floating abandoned. He leaps from the rail of Sotillo's ship, climbs into the boat, and rows

to the Great Isabel. There he finds Decoud has disappeared
and has taken four ingots of silver with him. Nostromo is now
in a position analogous to Jim's on the *Patna*. Faced by the
weakness of others, Nostromo betrays himself. The silver is
unimportant to the "hombres finos"; one of them appointed to
help him in spiriting the treasure away has stolen some of it.
Nostromo has been placed in an extremely difficult situation,
for if he returns the silver he may be accused of stealing the
four ingots and murdering Decoud. Robbed of his self-respect,
Nostromo pins his faith to the "material interests" represented
by the lighter load of silver; he decides he "must grow rich
very slowly" (IX, 503). By not returning the silver, Nostromo
echoes the failures of Gould and Monygham. He loses faith in
himself when he learns he has been used as a tool, that neither
the silver which he nearly died to save, nor he himself is of
any great consequence to the "hombres finos" of Sulaco. Like
Gould, he trusts in "material interests" when he decides to keep
the silver. Like Monygham, he has lost faith in himself and will
be forced to idealize his sense of guilt in order to maintain his
sanity.

Because Nostromo carries the vital message to Barrios, the
Monterist forces are defeated and Sulaco leads the Occidental
Province in a successful secession from the republic of
Costaguana. The prosperous port has so much shipping that a
lighthouse is needed to mark the Great Isabel. Nostromo, now
Captain Fidanza, returning from one of his silver-selling voyages,
learns that plans are underway to erect the lighthouse, and in
a brilliant stroke of politicking, he manages to have his old
friend Giorgio Viola appointed as keeper. Viola's older daughter
Linda has long been intended for Nostromo, and he knows that
courting visits to the Great Isabel will offer him an admirable
pretext for "growing rich very slowly".

E. SYMBOLISM IN CLOSING FRAME

The lighthouse of the Great Isabel is one of the most powerfully
drawn symbols in Nostromo, for in association with old Viola's

two daughters, Linda and Giselle, it perfectly demonstrates
Nostromo's failure to recognize his guilt. When Nostromo first
ponders the difficulties which the lighthouse will cause him he
thinks:

> It was dark. Not every man had such a darkness. And they were
> going to put a light there. A light! He saw it shining upon disgrace,
> Perhaps somebody had already.... (IX, 525)

Like Jim, he magnifies his disgrace while it is the guilt alone
which matters.

Nostromo asks for the hand of Linda, Viola's beautiful older
daughter, who, by her tending of the beacon of the lighthouse
for her senile father, is identified with the light of truth which
would reveal Nostromo's guilt. But Nostromo will not permit
his fault to be discovered either by himself or the world at
large, which would hold him in contempt for it. While still
engaged to Linda, he carries on a clandestine affair with her
sister, Giselle. However, Nostromo does not love Giselle. He is
attracted to her because of an unrecognized sense of his guilt.
The imagery of Nostromo's last meeting with Viola's younger
daughter symbolically illustrates his desperate flight from the
truth. One sister represents light and fidelity; the other, darkness
and shame. As Nostromo approaches Giselle's window, she opens
her arms to him:

> "Come nearer! Listen! Do not give me up, Giovanni! Never, never!...
> I will be patient!..."
> Her form drooped consolingly over the low casement towards the
> slave of the unlawful treasure. The light in the room went out, and
> weighted with silver, the magnificent Capataz clasped her round her
> white neck in the darkness of the gulf as a drowning man clutches
> at a straw. (IX, 545)

Soon after he starts his affair with Giselle, Nostromo is mistaken
by old Viola for a trespasser and is mortally wounded by him.
Emilia Gould, the good fairy of this tale in which the evil curse
is not defeated, "having thrown over her dress a grey cloak
with a deep hood" (IX, 558), comes to hear Nostromo's last
words:

Mrs. Gould's face, very white within the shadow of the hood, bent over him with an invincible and dreary sadness. And the low sobs of Giselle Viola, kneeling at the end of the bed, her gold hair with coppery gleams loose and scattered over the Capataz's feet, hardly troubled the silence of the room. (IX, 558)

And Nostromo makes his confession:

"Ha! Old Giorgio – the guardian of thine honour! Fancy the Vecchio coming upon me so light of foot, so steady of aim. I myself could have done no better. But the price of a charge of powder might have been saved. The bonour was safe.... Señora, she would have followed to the end of the world Nostromo the thief.... I have said the word. The spell is broken!" (IX, 558)

In calling himself a thief, of course, Nostromo does not really acknowledge his guilt. He still harbors the feeling that he has been shamefully used and that his theft of the silver was justified. But by bringing Nostromo to the threshold of discovery, Conrad ironically demonstrates the truth of the values which he has decided his hero shall not discover. Nostromo says: "I die betrayed – betrayed by –" (IX, 559). Conrad adds: "But he did not say by whom or by what he was dying betrayed" (IX, 559). Nostromo does not know in what or whom his betrayal consists, but Conrad's ironic tone at this point makes the reader aware that the magnificent Capataz dies betrayed by himself.

In his last spasm of egoism, Nostromo wishes to confess the hiding place of the treasure to Mrs. Gould, the "good fairy, weary with a long career of well-doing, touched by the withering suspicion of the uselessness of her labors, the powerlessness of her magic" (IX, 520). Nostromo, almost maliciously, says to her:

"You have been always good to the poor. But there is something accursed in wealth. Señora, shall I tell you where the treasure is! To you alone.... Shining! Incorruptible!" (IX, 560)

But Mrs. Gould refuses to hear anything about the stolen silver, and when she comes out of the dying man's room to confront Monygham, "excited to the highest pitch, his eyes shining with eagerness" (IX, 560), odious in his confident cynicism, she simply says: "He told me nothing". For Mrs. Gould to admit Nostromo's moral failure, for her to knowingly transmit the curse of the forbidden treasure, would indeed have been "altogether too dark". Mrs. Gould's "lie" at the end of *Nostromo* is much like Marlow's at the end of "Heart of Darkness". Both are "white" lies designed to restore those very few simple ideas without which mankind will be defeated by the destructive element.

Thus, though all those who struggle with the treasure in *Nostromo* – even Mrs. Gould, who is bereft of a husband by it – are defeated, Conrad, by his creation of symbolic character and action, has afforded his readers an emotional experience too profound for mere discursive artistry. And, though he has assiduously avoided drawing a moral in *Nostromo,* the novel represents the reality of human experience – a mine from which one cannot help but recover at least a small fragment of knowledge about "how to be".

VIII. *THE SECRET AGENT*

"What one feels so hopelessly barren about declared pessimism
is simply its arrogance".

Most Conrad critics would agree that H. T. Webster's description of *The Secret Agent* as "a good Hitchcock Thriller"[1] is
obviously mistaken. Substantial critical agreement ends, however,
with agreement to disagree with Webster, for there exists no
general critical accord as to the meaning and intent of *The
Secret Agent*. Leo Gurko sees *The Secret Agent* as a novel
without a hero.[2] In his excellent article on *The Secret Agent*,
Robert Stallman suggests that Time is the hero of this difficult
novel, that Conrad intends Time to be *the* Secret Agent.[3] Lois
Michel sees the novel as a statement of qualified optimism;[4]
Frederick Karl would seem to read the novel as essentially
pessimistic, describing it as the story of Winnie's decline and fall.[5]

Though Conrad, in what seems an almost malicious intent
to mislead his readers, subtitled *The Secret Agent* "A Simple
Tale", he is perhaps not quite as perverse in concealing the
meaning of this story of moral and political anarchy as has
been suggested by past commentators. In the "Author's Note",
in an attempt to defend himself against the charge of creating
in *The Secret Agent* gratuitous images of ugliness and despair,

[1] H. T. Webster, "Joseph Conrad: A Reinterpretation of Five Novels",
College English, VII (December, 1945), 125–134.
[2] Leo Gurko, *"The Secret Agent*: Conrad's Vision of Megapolis",
Modern Fiction Studies, IV (Winter, 1958), 307–318.
[3] R. W. Stallman, "Time and *The Secret Agent"*, *Joseph Conrad: A
Critical Symposium* (Ann Arbor, Mich., 1960), pp. 234–254.
[4] Lois A. Michel. "The Absurd Predicament in Conrad's Political
Novels", *College English*. XXIII (November, 1961), 131–136.
[5] Frederick Karl, *A Reader's Guide to Joseph Conrad* (New York,
1960).

Conrad indicated that he felt it should be only too obvious that the novel's "squalor and sordidness ... lie simply in the outward circumstances of the setting" (XIII, viii), and that the tale contains an "inspiring indignation" and an "underlying pity" which temper the perhaps more obvious contempt. Other clues as to the ultimate meaning of *The Secret Agent* may be sought in the "Author's Note" in Conrad's references to Winnie Verloc. In speaking of the inception of the novel, Conrad says:

Slowly the dawning conviction of Mrs. Verloc's maternal passion grew up to a flame between me and that background, tingeing it with its secret ardour and receiving from it in exchange some of its own sombre colouring. At last the story of Winnie Verloc stood out complete from the days of her childhood to the end, unproportioned as yet, with everything still on the first plan, as it were; but ready now to be dealt with. (XIII, xii)

In the next paragraph of the Note, Conrad refers to the other characters in the novel as subsidiary to Winnie, as "personages whom the absolute necessity of the case – Mrs. Verloc's case – brings out in front of the London background" (XIII, xiii). One could hardly ask for a clearer statement of the author's intent, and an examination of various of the patterns of image and symbol in *The Secret Agent* would seem to indicate that Conrad fulfilled his intent. Above the ugliness, disorder, and decay of the city of London, Conrad raises the figure of Winnie Verloc. She certainly is not a tragic figure of the proportions of Jim, or even Almayer, for that matter, but inherent in Winnie's story is a simple dignity that can be dissipated but never completely destroyed by Verloc, the Professor, and the whole crowd of anarchists and police.

A. CITY IMAGERY

To Winnie, who is the embodiment of uncalculating natural passion, the symbolic presence of the great brooding city of London forms a sharp contrast. The London of *The Secret Agent* is the London of the Romantic poets, the city of Blake, where natural instincts are debased, where "the youthful harlot's curse / Blasts the new-born infant's tear". The sun which shines on Conrad's London is a bloodshot sun, and nature is forced so far out of joint by the city that "neither wall, nor tree, nor beast, nor man cast a shadow" (XIII, 11). Verloc, walking in the eerie glow of this sun which casts no shadows, seems to take on a certain aspect of rustiness (XIII, 12). Significantly enough, "Mr. Verloc was not in the least conscious of having got rusty" (XIII, 12). Verloc, who identifies with the perverted soul of the great city, is unstirred by the spectacle of "rusty" men, of men turned into base, selfish, insecure machines. He sees only the town's material wealth, and during his walk to the foreign Embassy early in the novel, the presence of the city overwhelms him. As he approvingly eyes the opulence in evidence on the London streets, he forgets his role as an anarchist *agent provocateur*; in fact, his musings lead him to the conclusion that people of great material wealth have to be protected against "the shallow enviousness of unhygienic labor" (XIII, 12). Verloc, who lives on a "sordid street seldom touched by the sun" (XIII, 39), is a creature of material interests alone; there is "a veil between Mr. Verloc and the appearances of the world of senses" (XIII, 174).

The business in which Verloc engages as a front for his activities as "secret agent" represents yet another comment on the city's perversions of man's natural passions. Dealers in pornographic literature, or what Conrad calls "shady wares", can exist only in situations in which man's sexual instincts are so restricted by materialistic moral conventions that these instincts seek release through voyeurism rather than through natural sexual intercourse. Only in the city, where brick walls imprison and slimy gutters degrade man's natural sexuality, could Verloc successfully sell one of his "faded, yellow dancing girls... as though she had been alive and young" (XIII, 5). Conrad, of course, does not suggest, either in *The Secret Agent* or elsewhere, that man's natural passions should be unrestrained by any sort of logical control, but it is one of the basic assumptions of his philosophy that man sinks nowhere so low as when he slips into the black abyss of material interests.

Certainly, one may argue that Verloc and the rest of Conrad's anarchists are so intellectually and morally weak that the city subjugates them rather too easily. Verloc would certainly not be much of a man even if he were not caught up in the evil materialism of the city. Michaelis who preaches cold reason and "could not tell whether the sun still shone on the earth or not" (XIII, 120), Yundt, with his worn-out terrorist passion, Ossipon with his beliefs in the pseudo-scientific doctrines of Lombroso – all would be jealous, self-seeking whiners outside the confines of the dark city. Yet, it is certain that these strange fish would be less grotesque were they not inhabitants of Conrad's London, that "slimy aquarium from which the water had been run off" (XIII, 147).

Even the more respectable members of Conrad's metropolitan society do not escape the deadly tentacles of material interests. The Assistant Commissioner for the Special Crime Department, when he first questions Chief Inspector Heat, appears in a setting which symbolically indicates the awful perversions with which the material objects of the great city threaten unsuspecting man:

At headquarters the Chief Inspector was admitted at once to the Assistant Commissioner's private room. He found him, pen in hand, bent over a great table bestrewn with papers, as if worshipping an enormous double inkstand of bronze and crystal. Speaking tubes resembling snakes were tied by the heads to the back of the Assistant Commissioner's wooden armchair, and their gaping mouths seemed ready to bite his elbows. (XII, 97)

The Assistant Commissioner, who found life as a colonial police officer much to his liking because in such a post he could exercise his natural capabilities for rather more adventurous police work, now recognizes himself as "a square peg forced into a round hole" (XIII, 114). But the Assistant Commissioner's recognition of the unfitness of the role which he is playing does not lead to complete self-recognition. He still becomes involved in the solution of the Greenwich Observatory bombing, and he becomes involved not because of any ideal notion of the mission of the police in the affair, but because he wishes to protect Michaelis, who is the favorite in the salon of a great lady who is in turn a close friend of the Assistant Commissioner's wife. To material interests, to the interests of a wife whom he obviously does not love but who has good connections, the Assistant Commissioner sacrifices his natural abilities.

Chief Inspector Heat is also a tool of the material interests of the great city. He can comprehend only the criminal who works at his job as though it were a sort of secure, unionized, eight-to-five task. Heat admires the decorum of the ordinary burglar, but "the general idea of the absurdity of things human" (XIII, 91) exasperates the Chief Inspector. Any act, criminal or not, which is committed for other than material reasons defies the understanding of the Chief Inspector. The triangular bit of Stevie's overcoat which Heat carries away from the hospital where Stevie's shattered body lies rather confuses him, for it contains a clearly lettered address, 32 Brett Street, Verloc's house. Heat can understand neither why Verloc should be involved in the observatory bombing, nor why anyone concerned in such a desperate affair should handicap himself by clearly marking his clothing. The label in Stevie's overcoat, of course, has been sewn in by Winnie as insurance against Stevie's becoming utterly lost on those rare occasions when he is allowed to venture into the city alone. The address label is a symbol of the love which Winnie feels for her brother, and Heat, who understands only the operations of the quasi-logical realm of the materialistic city, cannot explain the label. As he remarks to the Assistant Commissioner: "It's simply unaccountable. It can't be explained by what I know" (XIII, 133). It also seems significant that Heat makes this admission of ignorance "with the frankness of a man whose reputation is established as if on a rock" (XIII, 133), for Heat's reputation indeed rests upon assumptions which are as harsh and bloodless as a rock.

Only Winnie, who feels "profoundly that things do not stand much looking into" (XIII, 177), is able to break the materialistic spell which binds all the characters of the novel save Stevie. In the dark canvas which is *The Secret Agent,* she is the only figure who dwells, albeit briefly and imperfectly, in the light of human love. As Brett Street is a place of complete darkness except for an almost insignificant bit of nature which the city cannot kill: "only a fruiterer's stall at the corner made a violent blaze of light and color" (XIII, 150), so the London of *The Secret Agent* would perhaps be altogether too dark without the brief violent blaze of light and color which Winnie creates in her tragic struggle with the materialistic forces of the city. Certainly Winnie has made her sacrifices to the god of materialism, for she has forsaken a handsome, vital young suitor, a man whom she perhaps really loved, in order to obtain a secure place for Stevie in Verloc's household. Winnie's sacrifice, however, is not made for the sake of a reputation, for a fixed idea, or for things material, and it seems much more instinctive, much less calculating than the sacrifice which her mother makes when she commits herself to a charity home.

The family unit which Winnie's self-sacrifice creates is certainly a rather strange one, consisting as it does of Verloc and Winnie, who feel little love for one another, Winnie's aged and sick mother, and Stevie, Winnie's mentally retarded brother. But in a world out of joint, in a world where Verloc's shop door is closed during the day and open at night, where anarchists fatten up in prison and where police officers protect criminals, in Winnie's family unit, based upon her profound love for her brother, exists the only set of human relationships bearing any resemblance to natural order.

B. SYMBOLIC RELATIONSHIP BETWEEN WINNIE AND STEVIE

Only Winnie and Stevie are capable of acting on natural impulse, and it is significant that they are the only characters in the novel who perform any sort of deed in rebellion against the monstrous society of the city. All the other characters in the novel are imprisoned by materialism and partake of Yundt's "worn-out passion" (XIII, 43) and of Verloc's "fanatical inertness" (XIII, 12). Anarchists and police alike operate in accordance with Michaelis's doctrine of cold reason and fail to realize that man is not essentially a rational creature. The most carefully laid plans of Heat, the Assistant Commissioner, and most especially of Verloc, are upset by Winnie's simple act of love, by her sewing the address label in Stevie's overcoat.

Stevie himself, whose mentality has not developed sufficiently to be capable of rational thought, is certainly a meaningful symbolic figure, and his function in Conrad's plea against what man makes of man in the city is perhaps best seen during the cab ride which Stevie, Winnie, and their mother take to the charity home. The cab which appears to take them on their journey is a particularly disreputable one. Both the cab driver and his horse show the effects of the city. The cab driver, significantly enough, is not a whole man; he is partly mechanical, as a "hooked iron contrivance protuding from the left sleeve" (XIII, 156) of his coat attests. The horse is a grotesque parody of what a horse would be in its natural state:

The little stiff tail seemed to have been fitted in for a heartless joke; and at the other end the thin, flat neck, like a plank covered with old horse-hide, drooped to the ground under the weight of an enormous bony head. The ears hung at different angles, negligently; and the macabre figure of that mute dweller on the earth steamed straight up from ribs and backbone in the muggy stillness of the air. (XIII, 166)

Stevie is confused and enraged by the cab driver's treatment of his horse. "Don't whip. You mustn't", says Stevie, but the cab driver does whip, "not because his soul was cruel and his heart evil, but because he had to earn his fare" (XIII, 157). Stevie cannot understand that the cab driver's cruelty to his horse, like all the other forms of cruelty in the city, is a function of materialism. Stevie can, however, because he is unrestricted by the specious reason of the city, sympathize with pain and suffering other than his own. The pseudo-rational characters of *The Secret Agent* speak largely selfish nonsense. It remains for Stevie, whose rudimentary reasoning powers are a function of the world of sensations, to utter some of the most meaningful words in the narrative: "Bad world for poor people" (XIII, 171). And Stevie, who is a symbol of those natural feelings which are of no material worth in the city, is killed by Verloc, the agent of the evil, confused logic of civilization.

Stevie's death does not, however, signal the death of the world of instinct, love, and natural sympathy in *The Secret Agent*. Winnie's murder of Verloc is an instinctive act of natural passion. Surely, like Stevie's desire to take the cab driver and his horse to bed, Winnie's act is natural sympathy gone wild, but it does serve to affirm that the natural, irrational facet of the human being is a force which must be reckoned with. Conrad does not, of course, suggest that the natural impulses of mankind are altogether noble or that man's passions need no rational control. After Stevie gives his unreasoning sympathy to the driver and his infirm horse, he as unreasoningly turns vicious: "The anguish of immoderate compassion was succeeded by the pain of an innocent and pitiless rage" (XIII, 169). Winnie's murder of Verloc is a further indication of the evil inherent in unrestrained passion. It is evident, however, that Stevie and Winnie in their acts of passion are closer to the true dignity of human nature than are the anarchists and the police in their acts of misguided reason. In killing her husband, Winnie lashes out against an intolerable system, and though she herself perishes, there is a triumphant quality in her struggle. She has, in at least a qualified sense, vanquished the most powerful of material interests – fear of death.

C. THE PROFESSOR AS DEATH SYMBOL

Death takes a tangible form in *The Secret Agent* in the symbolic figure of the Professor. He is significantly "indifferent to rain or sun in a sinister detachment from the aspects of sky and earth" (XIII, 96), and avoids arrest, though the police know of his anarchist activities, by a very simple device. He carries on his person sufficient high explosives to destroy not only himself, but any police officers who attempt to arrest him. Says the Professor: "I depend on death, which knows no restraint and cannot be attacked" (XIII, 68). But the Professor and the death which he represents are attacked, attacked by Winnie's love for Stevie.

Heat, Ossipon, Verloc, all those who identify with the materialistic soul of the great city are terrified by death in the form of the Professor. Only Winnie, who is capable of viewing life in other than material terms, overcomes fear of death. Her victory is, of course, not sudden and certain, for shortly after killing Verloc, she too almost succumbs to the logic of selfishness. When she tells Ossipon of Stevie's death, and also of her contemplated suicide, she cries out: "Oh Tom! How could I fear to die after he was taken from me so cruelly! How could I! How could I be such a coward!" (XIII, 298). Later, after Ossipon has cruelly deserted her, Winnie presumably overcomes her fear of death as she leaps from the cross-channel boat. Certainly, there is some truth in the newspaper account which describes Winnie's suicide as an "act of madness or despair" (XIII, 307). What on its surface seems an "act of madness and despair" is, however, an act of selflessness, an act which is the result of the city's abnegation of love. In Winnie's suicide and grief for her brother exists "as often happens in the lament of poor humanity rich in suffering but indigent in words, the truth – the very cry of truth ... in a worn and artificial shape picked up somewhere among the phrases of sham and sentiment" (XIII, 298).

In the last chapter of *The Secret Agent,* the Professor preaches to Ossipon: "All passion is lost now. The world is mediocre, limp, without force" (XIII, 309). The Professor is, however, mistaken. Passion does still exist in the world as long as in the breast of otherwise insignificant creatures such as Winnie Verloc dwells the Secret Agent – love.

IX. *UNDER WESTERN EYES*

"... political institutions are incapable of securing
the happiness of mankind".

Under Western Eyes is not Conrad's greatest tragedy. It is
overshadowed by *Lord Jim, Nostromo,* and *Victory,* and has
consequently been neglected by Conrad critics, but it deserves
analysis both for what it reveals about the human dilemma and
for what it indicates concerning Conrad's symbolic method of
writing. One could almost wish that Conrad had not chosen
such a timely political theme for the novel, or that he had not
exhibited such a prophetic vision in his handling of pre-revo-
lutionary Russian politics, for the accurate political predictions
and the characterization of Russian revolutionaries which *Under Western Eyes* contains sometimes obscure the fact that the
novel's main interest centers not in a political process, but in
the anguished discovery which an individual makes. But to wish
Conrad had not been true to his subject matter is to damn
Under Western Eyes for its excellence. Conrad's adept handling
of the political theme in the novel, while offering a possible
stumbling block for those readers unable to keep pace with the
genius of Conrad's art, constitutes an admirable background
against which is cast Razumov's personal tragedy.

One must to some extent agree with Robert Haugh that in
Under Western Eyes "the realization of truth is an intellectual
perception, lacking the vivid image, the depth of stress pattern"[1]
present in some of Conrad's greater works. That is, image and
symbol are less evident and less integral to the design of this

---

[1] Robert Haugh, *Joseph Conrad: Discovery in Design* (Norman, Okla.,
1957), p. 135.

novel than to most of Conrad's fiction. Yet, without an awareness of the method and the meaning of the various symbols which Conrad does employ in *Under Western Eyes,* the truths which he wishes to reveal in the novel can be easily missed.

A. RAZUMOV AS "ONE OF US"

Razumov himself is a symbolic character in that in fulfilling his function as a tragic hero he demonstrates both the courage of the human heart and the complex relationship between conscious and unconscious guilt. Razumov is, as clearly as Lord Jim, "one of us", and it is significant that though this phrase is not so essential in *Under Western Eyes* as it is in *Lord Jim,* it does occur several times in the former novel. Like Jim, Razumov is "as lonely in the world as a man swimming in the deep sea" (XXII, 10), and he must learn to keep himself afloat in this sea by the exertions of his hands and feet. He, too, must learn to submit to the destructive element.

Razumov's physical appearance establishes him as a possessor of that nobility of form commonly associated with the tragic hero, and at the same time would seem to indicate that his character is not yet fully formed:

Mr. Razumov was a tall, well-proportioned young man, quite unusually dark for a Russian from the Central Provinces. His good looks would have been unquestionable if it had not been for a peculiar lack of firmness in the features. It was as if a face modelled vigorously in wax (with some approach even to a classical correctness of type) had been held close to a fire till all sharpness of line had been lost in the softening of the material. But even thus he was sufficiently good-looking. His manner, too, was good. (XXII, 5)

As there is a certain lack of firmness in his facial features, so in discussion he is "easily swayed by argument and authority" (XXII, 5). In short, Razumov is a young man who can comprehend neither his own mind nor that of others, a man who would live by his intellect, not realizing that even the most rational decisions made by man have far-reaching emotional implications.

Significantly, related to Razumov's role as an archetypal hero is the fact that his parentage is obscure. Some of his acquaintances speculate that he is the son of an archpriest, but "his outward appearance accorded badly with such humble origin" (XXII, 6). Razumov enjoys the protection of the distinguished Prince K–, and this lends credence to the story that the young student is the Prince's son by an archpriest's daughter. The latter theory is, of course, the correct one, but even though the Prince is established as Razumov's father, the relationship between these two is clearly not one which affords the young man any help in making the most crucial decision of his life. Not until he is a student at the University does Razumov meet his father, and this first meeting is only a brief encounter in the office of the attorney who acts as Razumov's legal guardian. Prince K– is as remote from his son as is Lord Jim's pious father from him. The Prince, a gouty old invalid, afraid that his wife may discover his youthful philanderings, gives his son a modest allowance, is ready out of self-interest to help Razumov betray Haldin, and protects Razumov to some extent from abuse by the police; yet, the old man never officially recognizes his son, and Razumov, practically speaking, is without a family.

Razumov's lack of family ties serves two purposes. It makes him more acceptable as a symbolic character, since the archetypal hero typically has an obscure parentage, and it makes his moral dilemma much more difficult. If Razumov were the acknowledged son of a nobleman, or were he, on the other hand, of peasant stock, his resolution to betray Haldin would clearly be less complex. In either of these hypothetical situations, his relation to the moral principle upon which he makes his decision would be more recognizable both to Razumov himself and to the reader. As it is, we must realize that "the peculiar circumstances of Razumov's parentage, or rather his lack of parentage, should be taken into the account of his thoughts" (XXII, 26), and that the isolation in which he makes his decison regarding Haldin paradoxically renders this decision more universal.

The narrowest interpretation of Razumov as a symbolic

character would perhaps emphasize Conrad's statement that the young man's "closest parentage was defined in the statement that he was a Russian. Whatever good he expected from life would be given to or withheld from his hopes by that connexion alone" (XXII, 11). Razumov himself, in a conversation with Peter Ivanovitch, recognizes that Russia constitutes the only family which he has and that he is consequently bound to her by indissoluble bonds:

"The very patronymic you are so civil as to use when addressing me I have no legal right to – but what of that? I don't wish to claim it. I have no father. So much the better. But I will tell you what: my mother's grandfather was a peasant – a serf. See how much I am one of *you*. I don't want any one to claim me. But Russia *can't* disown me. She cannot!" Razumov struck his breast with his fist. "I am *it*!" (XXII, 208)

But Razumov's story is not really limited by its Russian setting any more than *Lord Jim* is limited by being set in the Malayan archipelago. As Conrad says in the "Author's Note" to *Under Western Eyes*, the story contains a "general truth which underlies its action, together with my honest convictions as to the moral complexion of certain facts more or less known to the whole world" (XXII, vii).

The name Conrad chose for his young Russian hero also universalizes the themes presented in the novel, for as Leo Gurko notes: " 'Razumov' in both Polish and Russian means 'understand' ".[2] And, what Razumov must understand transcends things Russian. Trapped between the evil of autocracy and the evil of anarchy, he must realize that in the final analysis it is not subscription to one political theory or another which enables man to master the dark powers in the universe. He must acknowledge that his betrayal of Haldin represents something more than a disputation of Haldin's revolutionary views; that it is, in fact, an attempt to revoke the invisible bond which ties one man to another. Finally, he must realize that the human being cannot "bear a steady view of moral solitude without going

[2] Leo Gurko, "*Under Western Eyes:* Conrad and the Question of 'Where To?' ", *College English*, XXI (May, 1960), 448.

mad" (XXII, 39), and that the man who blames his actions on the situation in which he finds himself rather than on his own moral inertia is merely disguising his egoism.

There is nothing singularly Russian about Razumov's attempt to establish his intellect as the sole criterion by which to judge his actions. Many Frenchmen and Englishmen, many Poles and many Swiss would say, with Razumov: "If I must suffer let me at least suffer for my convictions, not for a crime my reason – my cool superior reason – rejects" (XXII, 35). But Conrad demonstrates that there is more to a crime, more to any human action, than the "cool superior" force of the intellect can detect. Over and against the beautifully conceived intellectual scheme which Razumov conceives to obfuscate his egoism, Conrad projects image and symbolic action which demonstrate the truth of the language teacher's contention that "words... are the great foe of reality" (XXII, 3). Had we only Razumov's words by which to judge the morality of his actions, it would be difficult to detect his falsity. It is, after all, only common sense that he should refuse to risk his future for a "sanguinary fanatic" (XXII, 34) such as Haldin. Yet, words and common sense cannot hide the young rationalist's guilt. As Razumov imagines the consequences which may result from his association with Haldin, he thinks not of the implications of political theory, but of himself dying, poor and neglected:

Others had fathers, mothers, brothers, relations, connexions, to move heaven and earth on their behalf – he had no one. The very officials that sentenced him some morning would forget his existence before sunset. He saw his youth pass away from him in misery and half starvation – his strength give way, his mind become an abject thing. He saw himself creeping, broken down and shabby, about the streets – dying unattended in some filthy hole of a room, or on the sordid bed of a Government hospital. (XXII, 21)

Returning from his encounter with Ziemianitch, who has promised to help Haldin escape, Razumov decides to betray the young assassin to the police. But his decision, in accordance with the civil law of the state, obviously leaves him with an unrecognized sense of guilt. Immersed in self-pity and self-justification, Razumov hardly notices what part of the city he is in. With a crash, two sledges collide near the curb of the street on which he is walking. He does not notice the accident at all, but the abusive shout of one of the sledge drivers to his fellow awakens Razumov's guilt. At the bellow, "Oh, thou vile wretch" (XXII, 36), Razumov's thoughts abruptly shift to Haldin:

Suddenly on the snow, stretched on his back right across his path, he saw Haldin, solid, distinct, real, with his inverted hands over his eyes, clad in a brown close-fitting coat and long boots. He was lying out of the way a little, as though he had selected that place on purpose. The snow round him was untrodden. (XXII, 37)

When Lord Jim comes out of the courtroom after his trial, one of the spectators trips over a native dog and shouts: "You miserable cur". Jim, of course, applies this remark to himself and threatens to fight the man who he mistakenly thinks has insulted him. Like Jim, Razumov reads his guilt in words not at all intended for him.

B. SYMBOLIC COMMENTS ON RAZUMOV'S CHARACTER

Razumov does not, of course, consciously recognize his guilt until shortly before he makes his confession to Natalia. Each time he seems to be on the verge of discovering the true nature of his betrayal of Haldin, Razumov strengthens his egoistic resolution by repeating the cynical code of autocracy which his intellect has betrayed him into following. His conscious mind will not permit him to recognize that in betraying Haldin he has violated the solidarity of mankind, a moral bond without which all of the political credos which have ever been written represent only so many hollow words. Razumov's subconscious, however, presses him to recognize his guilt, and Conrad renders the conflict between his young hero's cynical intellect and his intuitive moral sense singularly dramatic by creating a significant symbolic relationship between Haldin and Razumov.

Haldin is, in fact, Razumov's "secret sharer". As Leggatt

climbs out of the night ocean into the life of the young captain in "The Secret Sharer", so Haldin, on an impulse, seeks out Razumov's apartment as a hiding place. Leggatt, of course, has never set eyes on his protector before he grasps the ladder hanging over the ship's side, and though Haldin and Razumov have met and even held brief discussions before the fateful day of Mr. de P–'s assassination, they are by no means intimate friends. Razumov is taken as unawares by Haldin's appearance as the young captain is by Leggatt's. Both Leggatt and Haldin have committed murder, and each asks that his secret sharer accept complicity in the crime. Perhaps the most important resemblance between Leggatt and Haldin, however, is the fact that each saves the soul of the protector he has sought out. Even though Razumov betrays Haldin to the police, even though Razumov would deny his bond with his secret sharer, the phantom of the betrayed man haunts his betrayer and forces him to recognize at the last that a solitary and fearful existence is more horrible than poverty and death.

When Razumov first discovers Haldin in his apartment, Haldin addresses him as "brother": "Yes, brother. Some day you shall help to build" (XXII, 19). Of course, Haldin calls Razumov his "brother" since he mistakenly supposes that his acquaintance shares his revolutionary sympathies. Yet, there is a more profound brotherhood between Haldin and Razumov than either one of them realizes. Haldin, in fact, represents Razumov's fear of a complete commitment to life. Razumov, too, has the desire to correct social injustice, but his secret fears, his half-formed ambitions, his mistrust of himself trick him into putting his faith in an enlightened dictator:

Everything was not for the best. Despotic bureaucracy ... abuses ... corruption ... and so on. Capable men were wanted. Enlightened intelligences. Devoted hearts. But absolute power should be preserved – the tool ready for the man – for the great autocrat of the future. Razumov believed in him. The logic of history made him unavoidable. (XXII, 35)

Razumov persuades himself that he is "sacrificing his personal longings of liberalism – rejecting the attractive error for the stern Russian truth" (XXII, 36). Yet, ratiocination cannot destroy Razumov's instinctive sympathy with Haldin.

Twice more before he sends Razumov on the abortive mission to Ziemianitch, Haldin calls his betrayer "brother", and, caught up in the passions of his visionary politics, lectures him on the nobility of rebellion:

"Men like me leave no posterity, but their souls are not lost. No man's soul is ever lost. It works for itself – or else where would be the sense of self-sacrifice, of martyrdom, of conviction, of faith – the labours of the soul? What will become of my soul when I die in the way I must die – soon – very soon perhaps? It shall not perish. Don't make a mistake, Razumov. This is not murder – it is war, war. My spirit shall go on warring in some Russian body until all falsehood is swept out of the world. The modern civilization is false, but a new revelation shall come out of Russia. Ha! you say nothing. You are a sceptic. I respect your philosophical scepticism, Razumov, but don't touch the soul. The Russian soul that lives in all of us. It has a future. It has a mission, I tell you, or else why should I have been moved to do this – reckless – like a butcher – in the middle of all these innocent people – scattering death – I! I!... I wouldn't hurt a fly!" (XXII, 22)

Haldin's statement is a blend of naiveté and destructive sentimentalism, yet in the dramatic situation it represents the truth of human solidarity which Razumov refuses to recognize. Haldin believes his soul will not perish because it is infused with high-sounding revolutionary liberalism. He is never to recognize, as Razumov will, that man's soul is immortal in spite of the temporal limitations of political belief; man's soul lives on because he is a spiritual rather than a political being.

1. *Haldin's phantom*

The first time Razumov's imagination manifests his subconscious guilt by projecting Haldin as a phantom, Razumov is on the way back from the inn where he has seen Ziemianitch. When Razumov arrives at his apartment where Haldin awaits him, he is so agitated by the conflict between his intellectual cynicism and his half-recognized intuitive identification with P–'s assassin, that the real Haldin appears to him as a phantom. As Razumov enters the dark room, he cannot see Haldin but can hear him breathing – a subtle image of the state of Razumov's soul. When the lamp is lit, Haldin appears, lying on the bed staring at the ceiling:

In the distant corner of the large room far away from the lamp, which was small and provided with a very thick china shade, Haldin appeared like a dark and elongated shape – rigid with the immobility of death. This body seemed to have less substance than its own phantom walked over by Razumov in the street white with snow. It was more alarming in its shadowy, persistent reality than the distinct but vanishing illusion. (XXII, 55)

Razumov is repulsed by Haldin's exaggerated visionary poses, and when the murderer who would not hurt a fly speaks as if he were a Messiah – "the oppressors of thought which quickens the world, the destroyers of souls which aspire to perfection of human dignity, they shall be haunted. As to the destroyers of my mere body, I have forgiven them beforehand (XXII, 58) –, Razumov congratulates himself on his decision to betray him: "The fellow's mad... It was a particularly impudent form of lunacy – and when it got loose in the sphere of public life of a country, it was obviously the duty of every good citizen..." (XXII, 59). But Razumov, though he can dispute Haldin's politics, cannot dissolve the bonds of human brotherhood. After Haldin has left the apartment, not suspecting that Razumov has betrayed him, Razumov's conscience torments him. His subconscious identification with Haldin is so great, in fact, that he must torture himself to match the physical torture which he knows Haldin will experience: "His mind hovered on the borders of delirium. He heard himself suddenly saying, 'I confess', as a person might do on the rack. 'I am on the rack', he thought. He felt ready to swoon" (XXII, 65). The night he betrays Haldin, even though his secret sharer is no longer in the room, Razumov cannot bear to sleep on the bed on which Haldin has lain. Instead he sleeps on a hard, uncomfortable horsehair sofa, his subconscious mind imaging forth in his dreams the solitude to which his betrayal of Haldin has doomed him: "Several times that night he woke up shivering from a dream of walking through drifts of snow in a Russia where he was as completely alone as any betrayed autocrat could be; an immense, wintry Russia" (XXII, 66).

So powerful is Razumov's unrecognized guilt that Haldin's phantom becomes almost an old friend. The spectre of the assassin appears regularly to Razumov, and it is a manifestation of the disintegration of Razumov's spiritual and intellectual being that he accepts Haldin's ghost as a real phenomenon, forcing it to disappear by advancing toward it menacingly as if to strangle it. In Geneva, where Razumov goes to spy on a cell of revolutionaries, Haldin's ghost does not leave him. Razumov becomes, symbolically, the dead Haldin, for he is accepted by Haldin's family and his revolutionary friends in lieu of the man who has been executed by the Tsarist police. Natalia Haldin calls Razumov "brother", as did Victor Haldin before her, and Peter Ivanovitch, the arch-priest of the revolution, accepts Razumov as a "brother" in the cause of rebellion.

Even while Razumov conceives an "ideal conception of his disgrace", he cannot dissolve the phantom presence of Victor Haldin:

In all the months which had passed over his head he had become hardened to the experience. The consciousness was no longer accompanied by the blank dismay and the blind anger of the early days. He had argued himself into new beliefs; and he had made for himself a mental atmosphere of gloomy and sardonic reverie, a sort of murky medium through which the event appeared like a featureless shadow having vaguely the shape of a man; a shape extremely familiar, yet utterly inexpressive, except for its air of discreet waiting in the dusk. It was not alarming. (XXII, 246)

But paradoxically, as it becomes more and more certain that Razumov's betrayal of Haldin will not be detected, Haldin's phantom becomes more powerful. Finally, when Peter Ivanovitch's circle of revolutionaries mistakenly decides that it is Ziemianitch who has betrayed their comrade, when Razumov is completely free of suspicion, the ghost of the betrayed man nearly drives him out of his mind. As Razumov sits in his room, secure in the knowledge that his shameful act will never be discovered, Haldin's ghost materializes in a shape that cannot be obliterated by a cleverly turned autocratic slogan or a menacing gesture:

Calm, resolved, steady in his great purpose ... he happened to glance towards the bed. He rushed at it, enraged, with a mental scream: "It's you, crazy fanatic, who stand in the way!" He flung the pillow on the floor violently, tore the blankets aside.... Nothing there. (XXII, 302)

All the powers of Razumov's intellect, all the force of his self-seeking cannot dispel his unconscious apprehension of the solidarity of mankind and the evil which his betrayal of Haldin represents.

2. Ziemianitch representative of Razumov's subconscious

The conflict within Razumov's soul is, however, mirrored not only in his symbolic relationship with Haldin. In Ziemianitch, the sledge driver, and Mikulin, the Tsarist official, are also seen symbolic manifestations of elements in Razumov's character. Haldin, before the assassination of Minister de P–, has made arrangements for escape with Ziemianitch. Haldin sends Razumov to contact Ziemianitch so that the latter can set the escape plans in motion. The very fact that Razumov accepts Haldin's errand indicates the conflict between the young isolationist's conscious and unconscious motives, but a clearer demonstration of Razumov's unconscious desire to help Haldin is evident in his encounter with Ziemianitch, for the imagery in this section of the narrative is that of the subconsious mind.

The section of the city in which Ziemianitch lives seems to be another world, disconnected from the real world of St. Petersburg, and Razumov, as he hastens on his desperate errand, seems to the people he passes to be a disembodied spirit, "looming up black in the snowflakes close by, then vanishing all at once – without footfalls" (XXII, 26). The inn where Razumov seeks Ziemianitch is peopled by phantoms even more grotesque than the spectre of Haldin which Razumov has already seen – "an elderly woman tied up in ragged shawls", "a wild-haired youth in tarred boots and a pink shirt" who grins foolishly, uncovering his pale gums, "the owner of the vile den, a bony short man in a dirty cloth captan coming down to his heels", "bleary unwashed faces", "a mild-eyed ragged tramp", "a horrible, nondescript, shaggy being with a black face like the muzzle of a bear", "a wet and bedraggled creature, a sort of sexless and shivering scarecrow" (XXII, 28). These creatures of the St. Petersburg underworld also inhabit the depths of Razumov's being. They are the destructive element present in the soul of every man, the filth of the human race which Razumov, because of his intellectually justified isolation, believes cannot touch him.

Further into the lair of human misery and filth, further into his own subconscious mind, Razumov must travel to meet Ziemianitch, Ziemianitch who "would drive Satan himself to his own abode":

> Razumov crossed a quadrangle of deep snow enclosed between high walls with innumerable windows. Here and there a dim yellow light hung within the four-square mass of darkness. The house was an enormous slum, a hive of human vermin, a monumental abode of misery towering on the verge of starvation and despair. In a corner the ground sloped sharply down, and Razumov followed the light of the lantern through a small doorway into a long cavernous place like a neglected subterranean byre. (XXII, 28–29)

Ziemianitch is drunk and cannot be aroused, and Razumov in his egoistic fury beats the sledge driver's prostrate body:

> Razumov belaboured Ziemianitch with an insatiable fury, in great volleys of sounding thwacks. Except for the violent movements of Razumov nothing stirred, neither the beaten man nor the spoke-like shadows on the walls. And only the sound of blows was heard. It was a weird scene. (XXII, 30)

Ziemianitch is too drunk to be awakened, and Razumov decides to get rid of Haldin in another way – to betray him to the police.

The Ziemianitch episode is dramatically sound, of course, for it results in Razumov's betrayal of Haldin, which eventually leads him to his discovery of the solidarity of mankind. The Razumov – Ziemianitch encounter also gives the reader deep insight into the various conflicts which rage in the depths of Razumov's being. Ziemianitch at the same time represents Razumov's unrecognized sympathy with the people who suffer under Tsarist oppression and his instinctive desire to help Haldin escape because he is a fellow human being. Significantly, Razumov cannot awaken Ziemianitch; that is, Razumov cannot awaken his subconscious sympathies for the "bright Russian soul" and must fall back on the powers of his intellect in an attempt to justify his isolation.

Like so many Conradian heroes before him, Razumov feels that he has been shamefully tried, and blames his inability to cope with a complicated moral problem not on himself, but on the situation. Because he cannot yet recognize that all men are bound to one another and that he is in fact involved in the fate of both Haldin and Ziemianitch, Razumov himself thinks of these two men as symbols of the forces which are conspiring against him:

Razumov was glad he had beaten that brute – the "bright soul" of the other. Here they were: the people and the enthusiast. Between the two he was done for. Between the drunkenness of the peasant incapable of action and the dream-intoxication of the idealist incapable of perceiving the reason of things, and the true character of men. It was a sort of terrible childishness. But children had their masters. "Ah! the stick, the stick, the stern hand", thought Razumov, longing for power to hurt and destroy. (XXII, 31)

Razumov does hurt and destroy, for disguising his selfish motives under a cloak of rationality, he sends Haldin to certain death. Haldin, in describing the political necessity of the assassination of Minister de P–, told Razumov that the killing was not murder, but an act of war, and Razumov echoes Haldin's distorted self-justification when he calls an act of betrayal an act of honor. No cost is too great, thinks Razumov, to maintain his isolation from the turmoil of Russian politics. Of course, when Razumov falls in love with Natalia Haldin, he discovers the hollowness of his skepticism; but earlier, before leaving St.

Petersburg, he has met a living example of his sterile view of life in the person of Councillor Mikulin.

3. *Mikulin*

Mikulin is obviously an older Razumov, a man who has assiduously avoided emotional ties of any kind. Unmarried, with few friends, he lives in a luxurious apartment and is an "enlightened patron of the art of female dancing" (XXII, 305). Like Razumov, he calls himself a "thinking man", and cold logic dictates that he shall perform his work for the state without becoming emotionally involved. Mikulin, too, recognizes the evils of autocracy, but he is so cynical about life and about the human capability for self-government that he accepts the Tsarist system as the best of many possibilities. He is loyal to the Tsarist government most of all, however, because it is a veneer which separates him from life. Through Mikulin, then, Conrad demonstrates the horrid desiccation of skepticism. It is also significant in an analysis of Razumov's spiritual growth to note that Mikulin's rationalism did not, after all, isolate him from the chaos of life. Several years after his interviews with Razumov, Mikulin is executed by the same government which he served loyally for his entire life.

4. *The language teacher*

Another, perhaps subtler, metaphorical comment on the nature of Razumov's character is seen in the teacher of languages who narrates a good portion of *Under Western Eyes*. The language teacher resembles Mikulin and Razumov before his self-discovery, in that he is a "thinking man", a rationalist who can only dimly perceive the emotions and passions which sway the human heart.[3] The language teacher is also unaware of the invisible

[3] Douglas Hewitt writes of the language teacher: "There is a certain fussiness about him but there is no indication that his incomprehension

and indissoluble spiritual ties which link all mankind, for he mistakenly assumes that Razumov's story will be almost incomprehensible to the "Western" reader. Razumov is unlike the young men in the West of Europe:

This is not a story of the West of Europe. Nations it may be have fashioned their Governments, but the Governments have paid them back in the same coin. It is unthinkable that any young Englishman should find himself in Razumov's situation. This being so it would be a vain enterprise to imagine what he would think. The only safe surmise to make is that he would not think as Mr. Razumov thought at this crisis of his fate. (XXII, 25)

Remarking on the fact of Razumov's keeping a diary, the language teacher shows himself to be incredibly naive concerning the psychology of confession: "Being myself a quiet individual I take it that what all men are really after is some form or perhaps only some formula of peace... What sort of peace Kirylo Sidorovitch Razumov expected to find in the writing up of his record it passeth my understanding to guess" (XXII, 5). Russia is not like the rest of Europe and "Western ears... are not attuned to certain tones of cynicism and cruelty, of moral negation, and even of moral distress already silenced at our end of Europe" (XXII, 163). In the language teacher's opinion, Razumov's notions of "honour and shame are remote from the ideas of the Western world" (XXII, 293). The more the language teacher protests that Razumov's story could have happened only in Russia, however, the more it is evident that it is, in fact, a universal story and that Razumov is faced with the age-old conflict between his

---

is a personal inadequacy, because there is no deeper knowledge against which to measure it. There is no view *sub specie aeternitatis* to compare with the view under western eyes. There can be no doubt that Conrad is in general agreement with his judgments" (Douglas Hewitt, *Joseph Conrad: A Reassessment,* Cambridge, 1952, p. 81). If there is, indeed, no "deeper knowledge" in *Under Western Eyes,* the novel is no more than a nihilistic tract. It would seem more in keeping with Conrad's other fiction and with the textual evidence of *Under Western Eyes* to agree with Walter Wright that Razumov does discover something better, that "before death he has managed to triumph over his destiny" (Walter Wright, *Romance and Tragedy in Joseph Conrad,* Lincoln, Nebr., 1949, p. 101).

intellect, which would isolate him from mankind, and his emotions, which would force him to recognize the fact of human solidarity. The old teacher's remarks in regard to the strangeness of Razumov's story also aid in establishing the ironic rhythm which is such a necessary part of tragedy. The language teacher's failure to detect the truth in Razumov's confession echoes the failure of Razumov himself to discover the truth of those very few simple ideas which bind man to his fellow.

The "Western eyes" of the old teacher are clearly symbolic of the failure of rationalism to know the full implications of the tragic nature of man's existence. When Razumov confesses to Haldin's sister, he says that he must do "one thing more" before his soul can rest. This "one thing more", of course, is to confess to Ivanovitch's revolutionaries, but the language teacher, imprisoned by his rationalism, cannot understand Razumov's compulsion: "Natalia Haldin might have guessed what was the 'one thing more' which remained for him to do; but this my Western eyes had failed to see" (XXII, 377). Neither can Conrad's learned grammarian understand why the revolutionists forgive Razumov after his confession to them. He cannot perceive that Razumov has at the last professed to a faith greater than the intellect can comprehend, that Razumov, as Sophia Antonovna says, has "discovered that his bitterest railings, the worst wickedness, the devil work of his hate and pride, could never cover up the ignominy of the existence before him", that there is, in fact, "character in such a discovery" (XXII, 380).

The language teacher senses that a curse hangs over the Russian character in general and Razumov and his friends in particular. When he mentions the curse, Razumov remarks that "the great problem ... is to understand thoroughly the nature of the curse" (XXII, 194). Such a discovery should be easy, remarks the language teacher, but it is obvious that he is terribly wrong. The curse which hangs over Razumov is, in fact, a very complicated one, and to defeat it, he must do more than merely change his political viewpoint.[4] In fact, Razumov writes

---

[4] Frederick Karl sees Razumov as converted to Haldin's views: "Razumov ... almost at once recognizes that Haldin is sincere and that

in his diary that it is love for Haldin's sister, not a sympathy with revolutionism which has forced him to confess. He writes of the light which shone from her soul which uncovered the falsehood dwelling in his, but, he cautions: "Don't be deceived, Natalia Victorovna, I am not converted" (XXII, 361). Revolutionary policies are as repugnant to Razumov after he has come into intimate contact with their most prominent representatives as they were on the night Haldin walked into his room. When Razumov meets Peter Ivanovitch and his circle of admirers, he sees that their ideals are only cleverly disguised forms of bitter egoism; and, their blindness helps him to see his own.

Admittedly, the inhabitants of the Chateau Borel are caricatures, but it would be a difficult task to prove that the soul of the fanatical revolutionary does not readily lend itself to caricature. In any case, *Under Western Eyes* is not so much the story of a political process as the complicated and profound presentation of the effect of a betrayal on the soul of an individual.[5] Thus, it is not the revolutionary circle as representative of political unrest which matters so much as Razumov's reading in it his own weaknesses. Conrad's young intellectual, before he comes to the Chateau Borel, has already reasoned that revolutionism is not politically sound. It remains for him to see beyond what Peter Ivanovitch's followers profess to stand for into the nihilism which they indeed represent.

---

the police and the General are despicable – he senses that Haldin's sympathies should have been his" (Frederick Karl, *A Reader's Guide to Joseph Conrad,* New York, 1960, p. 217). Such a view, it seems, does not take full account of Razumov's unambiguous statement, "I am not converted" (XXII, 361).

[5] Irving Howe, in "Order and Anarchy: The Political Novels", *Kenyon Review,* XV (Autumn, 1953), 520, writes: "Conrad has failed to accept the challenge of his own book: to confront the revolutionists in their strength and not merely in their weakness, to pit Razumov against men of serious if wrong-headed commitment rather than merely against 'apes of a sinister jungle', as in his preface he so fatally calls them." It seems obvious, however, that Razumov's primary struggle is not with his political adversaries, but with himself. Lord Jim could outsmart the scurvy crew of the *Patna* or beat them in a first-fight; it is the destructive element within himself which he must master.

C. THE CHATEAU BOREL AND ITS INHABITANTS AS SYMBOLS OF THE EVILS OF NIHILISM

The Chateau Borel, the center of Russian revolutionary activities in Geneva, seems to Razumov to be a deserted prison:

The bars of the central way and wrought-iron arch between the dark weather-stained stone piers were very rusty; and, though fresh tracks of wheels ran under it, the gate looked as if it had not been opened for a very long time. But close against the lodge, built of the same grey stone as the piers (its windows were all boarded up), there was a small side entrance. The bars of that were rusty too; it stood ajar and looked as though it had not been closed for a long time. In fact, Razumov, trying to push it open a little wider, discovered it was immovable. (XXII, 203)

The huge house is inhabited, but the souls of its tenants are as sterile as the stone of the two discolored urns which stand before its front door, as unclean as its grimy, weatherstained walls, and as bare and dark as its dusty parlor.

In this circle of hell reserved for the egoists, Razumov meets Peter Ivanovitch, "the noble arch-priest of the Revolution (XXII, 210), "Europe's greatest feminist" (XXII, 205). Ivanovitch is notable among the revolutionists because he has managed a particularly daring escape from a Tsarist prison; he is a feminist because two women on separate occasions during his escape risked their lives to aid him. Yet, for all his admiration for woman in the abstract, he is terribly cruel to his hapless stenographer, Tekla, forcing her to sit immobile for hours while he attempts to unravel the flimsy chain of his thoughts. Tekla reports that on some bitterly cold days when she sits for five or six hours at a stretch taking Ivanovitch's dictation, she has to set her teeth to keep them from chattering in the chill air: "Perhaps if I had let my teeth rattle Peter Ivanovitch might have noticed my distress, but I don't think it would have had any practical effect. He's very miserly in such matters" (XXII, 149). Like Kurtz who so volubly spoke of justice and love in the abstract, but killed and enslaved his native followers, Ivanovitch cannot live up to the practical demands of his noble feminist pronouncements.

Peter Ivanovitch's politics are of only subsidiary interest, and there is no direct logical attack on them in *Under Western Eyes*. Revolutionary or Tsarist, Ivanovitch is a blind, selfish man who represents an evil greater than that which can be encompassed in political theory, and to demonstrate the egoistic benightedness of this revolutionary leader, Conrad employs a subtle bit of imagery. Ivanovitch wears spectacles which contain smoked blue glasses, and in each scene in which he appears they are described in some detail. Their color is remarkable; it is incongruent for such a large, powerfully built man to wear such strange glasses, and the glasses reflect like two tiny mirrors, hiding Ivanovitch's eyes from the world. When Natalia and the language teacher, in search of Razumov, enter a hotel room where the Geneva Commune has gathered, the language teacher remarks on the uncommon effect of Ivanovitch's glasses: "He suggested a monk or a prophet, a robust figure of some desert-dweller, something Asiatic; and the dark glasses in conjunction with this costume made him more mysterious than ever in the subdued light" (XXII, 329). Ivanovitch dominates the group, "alone, standing up, with his dark glasses, like an enormous blind teacher" (XXII, 329). Ivanovitch's glasses, then, are a symbol of his inability to see beyond his own selfish interests, and he himself as a symbol of egoism, is repulsive to Razumov and an indirect factor in the young intellectual's discovery of the egoism inherent in his betrayal of Haldin.

Still another indication of Ivanovitch's egoism and the relative unimportance of his political belief to the main themes of *Under Western Eyes* is to be seen in his relationship with Madame de S–. Ivanovitch uses her money to further the revolutionary activities of the Geneva Commune, but it is clear that he associates himself with her primarily because she supports him in high style. And, with Madame de S–, Ivanovitch enjoys the added bonus of having his self importance increased by the old lady's title and old-line wealth. In the introduction to *Under Western Eyes*, Conrad calls this pair "the apes of a sinister jungle" (XXII, ix), and the jungle which they inhabit is clearly the oldest and most elemental one, coeval with man's desire to make his own self-interest the sole arbiter of his conduct.

Through the symbolic figure of Madame de S–, Conrad subtly identifies egoism with the negation of life. When Razumov first meets Madame de S– she requests that he draw his chair very close to hers so that they may talk more easily. What Razumov sees when he looks at the old lady's face horrifies him:

He sat down. At close quarters the rouged cheekbones, the wrinkles, the fine lines on each side of the vivid lips, astounded him. He was being received graciously, with a smile which made him think of a grinning skull. (XXII, 215)

And that she is serving her own selfish interests in supporting Ivanovitch's anti-Tsarist activities is made evident by her crazed outburst in which it is not the oppressors of the Russian peasantry against whom she rails, but the "thieves" who have spoiled her family estates. Madame de S–'s solution to the internal problems of the Russian government is quite simple:

"As to extirpating", she croaked at the attentive Razumov, "there is only one class in Russia which must be extirpated. Only one. And that class consists of only one family. You understand me? That one family must be extirpated." (XXII, 222)

This "ancient, painted mummy", this "galvanized corpse" and her burly feminist companion are unmistakable symbols of the evils of that form of egoism which leads to personal and political nihilism; and within the dramatic framework of the novel, Razumov's repulsion for them forces him further toward his self-discovery.

D. RAZUMOV'S IDENTIFICATION WITH ROUSSEAU AS SYMBOLIC INDICATION OF THE FAILURE OF RATIONALISM

Razumov's self-discovery, of course, represents a conversion, but not a conversion from Royalist to revolutionary sympathies. His conversion is from nihilistic egoism to belief in the solidarity of mankind. When Razumov first thinks of betraying Haldin, he justifies it on the grounds that he can in no way be called to account for his "brother":

"Betray. A great world. What is betrayal. They talk of a man betraying his country, his friends, his sweetheart. There must be a moral bond first. All a man can betray is his conscience. And how is my conscience engaged here; by what bond of common faith, of common conviction, am I obliged to let that fanatical idiot drag me down with him? On the contrary – every obligation of true courage is the other way." (XXII, 37)

Yet, even as he justifies his betrayal of Haldin, Razumov cannot escape from the unrecognized sense of his responsibility for him. When he ceases to intellectualize his guilt even for a moment, he is overwhelmed by dread of his moral obligation, much as the young captain in *The Shadow Line* is overcome by a fear of accepting his duties as a member of the seaman's craft. Razumov dreads the knowledge of that part of his being which the intellect cannot satisfy. When he ceases to think, he feels " a suspicious uneasiness, such as we may experience when we enter an unlighted strange place – the irrational feeling that something may jump upon us in the dark – the absurd dread of the unseen" (XXII, 35).

Justifying his shame while it is his guilt alone that matters, he becomes a Tsarist spy and travels to Geneva, there to report back to Mikulin on the activities of Ivanovitch's circle. It is significant that the street on which Razumov spends much of his time while in Geneva, the street on which Natalia Haldin and her mother live, is named the "Boulevard des Philosophes", for the philosophers are to aid Razumov not at all in his search for his identity as a part of the human community. "The Boulevard des Philosophes", "a singularly arid and dusty thoroughfare" (XXII, 115), is as sterile and as deserted as that receptacle of Ivanovitch's destructive philosophy, the Chateau Borel.

The means and the nature of Razumov's discovery of self are perhaps most clearly symbolized, however, in the scene which describes his compulsive behaviour at the foot of an effigy of Rousseau. Mastered by an irrational desire to record his experiences with the members of the Geneva Commune, Razumov flees to an island on the shore of Lake Geneva, thinking that here he will be safe from the prying eyes of the revolutionists he has come to Geneva to betray. The island is, of course, symbolic of Razumov's desire for moral isolation, but it is also highly significant that Razumov writes in the very shadow of "the exiled effigy of the author of the *Social Contract*" (**XXII**, 291) and the *Confessions,* for the confessions which Razumov is soon to make are themselves a form of social contract. And, Razumov is to be driven to confess his guilt not by the urging of his intellect, but by the intuitional longings of his soul, by his "romantic" impulses. When Razumov falls in love with Natalia Haldin, the living symbol of the betrayed Victor Haldin, he realizes that he cannot continue to live his egoistic lie. He first confesses to Natalia, and then seeks out the assembled revolutionary council to confess to them. Nikita, nicknamed Necator, the party's enforcer, exacts on Razumov a cruel, but appropriate vengeance, bursting his eardrums so that he shall never again hear a confession. [6] Deaf, Razumov wanders purposelessly through the streets of Geneva and is run over by a carriage which breaks both of his legs and crushes his side. Razumov has paid for his betrayal of Victor Haldin, but in paying he has attested to the truth of human solidarity and has demonstrated that those who place their faith wholly in the self or the efficacy of political institutions are hopelessly blind to the very few simple ideas which alone can save mankind from self-destruction.

E. IRONIC RHYTHM OF CLOSING FRAME

In the closing frame of the novel, Sophia Antonovna reports to the language teacher that Peter Ivanovitch has deserted his circle of friends and has run off to Russia with a peasant girl.

[6] In regard to Nikita's brutal attack on Razumov, Vernon Young writes: "In the face of this stupefying and almost gratuitous form of cruelty, the reader is justified in demanding the ethical and dramatic necessity for Razumov's extreme punishment" ("Joseph Conrad: Outline for a Reconsideration", *Hudson Review,* II, Spring, 1949, 11). Some would argue that deafness is not too extreme a punishment for sending a man to his death. In any case, the tragic hero's receiving a punishment greater than he deserves is one of the requirements of tragedy. It also intensifies the irony of the conclusion of *Under Western Eyes* that Nikita is, in reality, a Tsarist spy.

Sophia cannot see that Ivanovitch's act is but the culmination of his egoism, and her words of praise for the feminist are the last words of the novel: "Peter Ivanovitch is an inspired man" (XXII, 383).

Thus, *Under Western Eyes* ends on an unmistakably ironic note, but the irony of Ivanovitch's betrayal only adds to the magnificence of Razumov's discovery. And Conrad, who has not dealt in the specifics of political theory in *Under Western Eyes*, but has chosen to demonstrate the realities of human existence symbolically, has made the reader indeed "see" that human happiness is a quality of the heart, rather than an attribute of political institutions.

X. VICTORY

"Woe to the man whose heart has not learned
while young to hope, to love – to put its trust
in life".

In a 1924 letter to Henry S. Canby, Conrad wrote that in *Victory* he had "tried to grasp at more 'life stuff' " than in any of his other works.[1] *Victory*, indeed, contains great amounts of "life stuff", for in this story, perhaps Conrad's most aesthetically perfect representation of the conflict between the forces which would isolate man from his fellow and those which would cause him to accept the joy and pain resulting from recognition of the solidarity of mankind, Conrad reveals the delight, the mystery, the truth of human existence. In *Victory*, as in all his other significant works, Conrad makes symbolism the vehicle of both form and meaning, and to understand either the moral values of the world which Conrad has created in the novel or the essential construction of that world, one must be aware of both the meaning and structural relationships of its symbolic elements.

Victory is frequently called a melodramatic novel, but one must agree with Robert Haugh that the reader who detects melodrama in *Victory* testifies to his own frailties, rather than those of Conrad. As Haugh says:

Many find *Hamlet* to be melodramatic upon first viewing, with much unexplained swordplay and violence; not so upon a perceptive fourth or fifth viewing. The spectator learns to experience the complexities of situation, the relationship of one sequence to another, and the growth of thematic meaning in the dramatic flow. Properly read, Conrad's *Victory*, while nothing so splendid as *Hamlet*, has also literary capacities which elevate it above melodramatic formula fiction.[2]

---

[1] G. Jean-Aubry, ed., *Joseph Conrad: Life and Letters* (Garden City, N. Y., 1927), II, 342.

It can, in fact, be demonstrated, through an explication of the symbolism of *Victory,* that Conrad does not resort to melodramatic devices which would violate the probabilities of character and action as he has created them. Heyst, Lena, Jones, Ricardo, and Pedro are all dead at the end of *Victory,* but their deaths are inevitable in the dramatic pattern of the novel.

A. SYMBOLS DEPICTING THE CONFLICT WITHIN HEYST'S SOUL

1. *Heyst as knight-saviour*

From the flaw in Heyst's character, from his subscription to his father's belief that the world is a bad dog which will bite if given a chance, results the welter of blood at the end of *Victory;* and from the subtle symbolism which the novel contains, comes the reader's awareness of both the enormity of Heyst's error in judgment and the conflict which rages within the soul of this "enchanted" man.[3] Within the breast of Axel Heyst, as in the depths of the volcano which lies some miles north of his island kingdom of Samburan, there is a restless flame which cannot be extinguished. The image of Heyst smoking his nightly cigar as the volcano glows on the horizon is a brilliantly conceived symbol of the dynamic emotional force dormant in Axel Heyst:

His nearest neighbor . . . was an indolent volcano which smoked faintly all day with its head just above the northern horizon, and at night levelled at him, from amongst the clear stars, a dull red glow, ex-

---

[2] Robert Haugh, *Joseph Conrad: Discovery in Design* (Norman, Okla., 1957), p. 103.

[3] Douglas Hewitt, in *Joseph Conrad: A Reassessment* (Cambridge, 1952), p. 106, is unconvinced of the defect in Heyst's character. Hewitt writes: "All sense of there being a flaw in his nature disappears because it is so generally and so vaguely expressed, and because it is swamped by the response of admiration which he receives as a man who is in touch with the beauty and tranquillity of the islands. We feel, rather, that in some subtle way he is superior to the generality of men." Attention either to the symbolism of the novel or Heyst's awareness that he is a "disarmed man" would seem sufficient to illustrate the flaw in his character. One might also suggest that Conrad, with Aristotle, perceived the dramatic possibilities of a hero "superior to the generality of men".

panding and collapsing spasmodically like the end of a gigantic cigar puffed at intermittently in the dark. Axel Heyst was also a smoker; and when he lounged out on his verandah with his cheroot, the last thing before going to bed, he made in the night the same sort of glow and of the same size as that other one so many miles away. (XV, 4)

Before he settled permanently on Samburan, Heyst had been a wanderer, "an impermanent dweller amongst changing scenes", secure in his belief that by wandering from one place to another he could pass through life "without suffering and almost without a single care in the world – invulnerable because elusive" (XV, 90). But while spending a few days in the port of Delli, Heyst meets the unfortunate Morrison who has had his boat impounded by the Portuguese port authorities. Heyst pays Morrison's fine, and Morrison, unable to repay his benefactor in any other way, makes him a partner in his visionary Tropical Belt Coal Company. Morrison dies on a European trip made to gain capital for the coal company; the company fails, and Heyst sees in his futile relationship with Morrison concrete evidence of his father's skeptical philosophy.[4] Heyst vows to isolate himself completely from all human attachments. Speaking to Davidson, he says:

"I suppose I have done a certain amount of harm, since I allowed myself to be tempted into action. It seemed innocent enough, but all action is bound to be harmful. It is devilish. That is why this world is evil upon the whole. But I have done with it! I shall never lift a little finger again. At one time I thought that intelligent observation of the facts was the best way of cheating the time which is allotted to us whether we want it or not; but now I have done with observation, too." (XV, 54)

However, the fact that Heyst did help Morrison, the fact that this man who believes "hard facts" to be the sole reality cannot

---

[4]   The portrait of the elder Heyst hangs in the main room of Heyst's house on Samburan, a symbol of the skepticism which the son cannot escape. Arthur Sherbo, in "Conrad's *Victory* and *Hamlet*", *Notes and Queries,* CXCVIII (November, 1953), 492–493, points out several verbal parallels between *Hamlet* and *Victory* and also notes that both Hamlet and Heyst are markedly influenced by their fathers.

scorn the suffering of a fellow human being, indicates that though the rational part of his being fears involvement, his intuitive self will not permit him to dissolve his ties with humanity. Morrison, in fact, functions solely as a symbol of those impulses which Heyst's intellect will not recognize, and having the Heyst-Morrison episode before him, the reader can better judge the probability and the quality of Heyst's rescue of Lena.

After Morrison has died and the Tropical Belt Coal Company has been liquidated, Heyst becomes so bitter that it is evident that the skeptical philosophy of the father is ill-suited to the emotional make-up of the son. In Heyst's cynicism after the Morrison affair is seen the same type of bitterness as in Hemingway's Frederick Henry at the end of *A Farewell to Arms*. Both men have observed the lack of any comprehensible plan in human affairs, and both are incredibly bitter because, in spite of their disappointment, they cannot quell their instinctual belief that there is, indeed, a beneficent providence which controls the affairs of human beings. Possessing this belief, they understandably feel more bitter toward the cruel workings of fate than the man who has never believed at all.

When Heyst has been living on Samburan for some time, he finds it necessary to travel to Sourabaya to settle some financial affairs of the estate his father has left him. There in the pavilion of Schomberg's hotel he meets Lena, the forlorn waif from the streets of London who is being victimized by the grotesque Zangiacomo and the absurdly lustful Schomberg. Lena is a member of an orchestra, the only distinction of which is the fact that all its members are female. Heyst, who has vowed to be indifferent to all experience, all beauty, and all ugliness, cannot, however, remain indifferent to the frightfully distorted sounds of the Zangiacomo orchestra. As he lies on his bed in Schomberg's hotel, the discordant sounds of the orchestra intrude upon his silence and he is inexplicably drawn to investigate the source of such ugliness. Once in Schomberg's shoddy music hall, Heyst is overwhelmed by the sordidness of the music and those who are producing it:

The uproar in that small, barn-like structure, built of imported pine

boards, and raised clear of the ground, was simply stunning. An
instrumental uproar, screaming, grunting, whining, sobbing, scraping,
squeaking some kind of lively air; while a grand piano, operated upon
by a bony, red-faced woman with bad tempered nostrils, rained hard
notes like hail through the tempest of fiddles. The small platform
was filled with white muslin dresses and crimson sashes slanting
away from shoulders provided with bare arms, which sawed away
without respite. (XV, 68)

There is, for Heyst, however, something fascinating in the noise
which the orchestra is making, something of the horror of life
which he has sworn to avoid, "something cruel, sensual and
repulsive" (XV, 68):

"This is awful!", Heyst murmered to himself... The Zangiacomo
band was not making music; it was simply murdering silence with a
vulgar, ferocious energy. One felt as if witnessing a deed of violence;
and that impression was so strong that it seemed marvellous to see
the people sitting so quietly on their chairs, drinking so calmly out
of their glasses, and giving no signs of distress, anger or fear. Heyst
averted his gaze from the unnatural spectacle of their indifference.
(XV, 68–69)

The sounds of the orchestra are clearly symbolic of the harsh
grating noise of suffering humanity, and Heyst's surprise that the
audience in Schomberg's pavilion can ignore the tortured squeaks
and groans which Zangiacomo's musicians are making is evidence that he unconsciously rejects his father's skeptical philosophy.

Heyst feels a detached pity for all of the coarse, joyless creatures working in Zangiacomo's band, and especially for a young
woman who seems a bit more refined and much more unhappy
than her fellow musicians. Heyst feels he must help her. Again
he violates the dictates of his father's skepticism, and it is highly
significant to an understanding of the conflict between Heyst's intellect and his emotions to note that his offering to aid Lena is a
distinctly impulsive action:

Heyst laid down his half-smoked cigar and compressed his lips. Then
he got up. It was the same sort of impulse which years ago had made
him cross the sandy street of the abominable town of Delli in the
island of Timor and accost Morrison, practically a stranger to him

then, a man in trouble, expressively harassed, dejected, lonely. It was the same impulse. But he did not recognize it. (XV, 71)

As Heyst walks up to the musician's platform to speak to Lena, he is "unchecked by any sort of self-consciousness"[5] (XV, 72).

The archetypal framework which Conrad constructs at this point in the narrative also indicates that though Heyst believes life to be a bad dog he cannot avoid stooping to pet it. Before he meets Lena, Heyst has appeared as a sort of latter-day prince: "In the fulness of his physical development, of a broad, martial presence, with his bald head and long moustaches, he resembled the portraits of Charles XII, of adventurous memory" (XV, 9). When Heyst meets Morrison on the streets of Delli, he bows and speaks to him "in the manner of a prince addressing another prince on a private occasion" (XV, 12). Thus, Heyst's rescue of Lena, during which he assumes the role of the knight and she that of a damsel in distress, has been skillfully foreshadowed.

The bony, red-faced Mrs. Zangiacomo, her purple-bearded husband, and Schomberg, as ridiculous as a sexually excited hippopotamus, are the demon figures from whose presence Heyst must steal his lady, and Mrs. Schomberg fulfills the archetypal role of the "helper". Enraged by Mrs. Zangiacomo's brutal treatment of Lena, Heyst rushes to the platform to offer his assistance to the lonely girl. He tells her he has seen Mrs. Zangiacomo

[5] Walter Wright's comment on Heyst's impulse to aid Lena lends credence to the view that the rational part of Heyst's being is in conflict with his emotional impulses: "Though Conrad does not expatiate on Heyst's psychology, it is evident that his aloofness cannot be violated by those who are not themselves alone. They belong in a world which he has renounced, and their security makes him independent of them. What he does not perceive is that his own solitariness of mind lets him imaginatively enter the minds of others who are similarly isolated and that imaginative creation of their feelings compels him to identify himself with their destiny. Though Conrad does not explain Heyst's action in this direct, expository manner, yet in the indirect narrative of the wanderer, his imagination is revealed as unable to remain bound by facts, even when he has tried intellectually to evade going beyond them to become interested in men's minds. The captain in *The Shadow Line* was a man of ships despite his conscious effort to break with the sea. Heyst is fascinated by the mystery of life, even when he is trying to deny it" (*Romance and Tragedy in Joseph Conrad*, Lincoln, Nebr., 1949, p. 103).

pinch her and Lena remarks, "and suppose she did – what are you going to do about it?" (XV, 73). Heyst replies as a knight would: "What would you wish me to do? Pray command me" (XV, 73). Later, as he discusses Lena's plight with her, he says: "I am not rich enough to buy you out ... even if it were to be done; but I can always steal you" (XV, 81). Steal her he does, spiriting her off in the middle of the night, hotly pursued by Zangiacomo and Schomberg. Safe with Lena on his island retreat, Heyst, albeit a bit ironically, refers to Lena as "princess of Samburan" (XV, 193) and asks her whether he has found favor in her sight. He may smile at his heroic actions, which he believes to be, at best, rather absurd; he may curse his saving of Lena because it makes his heart vulnerable to hundreds of unapprehended dangers. It is clear, however, that when he is confronted by the spectacle of human suffering, his actions are not wholly in accordance with his father's skeptical doctrine. Certainly, the elder Heyst would not recommend to his son that he ignore a fellow human being in distress. A gentleman is obligated to alleviate suffering whenever possible. But the elder Heyst would advise that the gentleman form no emotional ties with those whom he helps. This part of his father's teaching Heyst cannot obey, but his failure to recognize this makes for a singularly painful conflict in his soul, and renders his tragedy practically inevitable.

2. *Lena as phantom presence*

Heyst justifies the contradiction between his skeptical philosophy and his actions by a complicated process of rationalization. The night he meets Lena he paces to and fro in his room:

> ... revolving in his head thoughts absolutely novel, disquieting, and seductive; accustoming his mind to the contemplation of his purpose, in order that by being faced steadily it should appear praiseworthy and wise. For the use of reason is to justify the obscure desires that move our conduct, impulses, passions, prejudices and follies, and also our fears. (XV, 83)

However Heyst may rationalize his saving of Lena, it is clear that this action is an impulsive commitment to the sorrows and joys of life. Lena, in fact, represents all those human commitments which the elder Heyst would have his son deny, and it is significant to a full understanding of Heyst's psychological conflict that Lena, on several occasions, seems to Heyst to be a phantom.[6] The night Heyst meets Lena he is so troubled that he cannot sleep, and he decides to calm himself by taking a walk about the grounds surrounding Schomberg's hotel. As he walks, absorbed in the process of rational self-justification, he is alarmed to discover that he is not alone:

Raising his head, he perceived something white flitting between the trees. It vanished almost at once; but there could be no mistake.... Then he saw the white, phantom-like apparition again; and next moment all his doubts as to the state of her mind were laid at rest, because he felt her clinging to him after the manner of supplicants all the world over. Her whispers were so incoherent that he could not understand anything; but this did not prevent him from being profoundly moved. He had no illusions about her; but his sceptical mind was dominated by the fulness of his heart. (XV, 83)

Lena tells Heyst of Schomberg's advances, and pleads for help. Again she appears to Heyst as a phantom:

What he saw was that, white and spectral, she was putting out her arms to him out of the black shadows like an appealing ghost. He took her hands, and was affected, almost surprised, to find them so warm, so real, so firm, so living in his grasp. He drew her to him, and she dropped her head on his shoulder. (XV, 86)

Much later, when Heyst reports to Lena his conversation with Jones, he is again struck by the ethereal quality of her presence:

The fleeting weight of her body on his knees, the hug round his neck, the whisper in his ear, the kiss on his lips, might have been the unsubstantial sensations of a dream invading the reality of waking life; a sort of charming mirage in the barren aridity of his thoughts. (XV, 319)

[6] Frederick Karl, in *A Reader's Guide to Joseph Conrad* (New York, 1960), p. 261, notes the symbolic significance of Lena's several names: "When Heyst asks Lena her name, she says that she is called Alma, also Magdalen, although she does not know why. As her first name, Alma, implies, she manifests certain soul-like qualities – the soul of Heyst is Lena; and as Magdalen she can be saved by Heyst from whoredom."

Lena clearly represents Heyst's unrecognized identification with the spectacle and mystery of life. She is a phantom dwelling in Heyst's subconscious, a phantom which the elder Heyst's skepticism cannot destroy, and when the younger Heyst ceases his cynical ratiocination for even a moment, he finds that the ogre of life about which his father has warned him is not necessarily a cruel monster which will devour all those unwary enough to draw near it. It can be transformed by the man who ignores "hard facts" into a beautiful creature vibrating with warmth and promise.

B. SYMBOLS OF THE HOLLOWNESS OF HEYST'S SKEPTICISM

Any spiritual identification which Heyst admits with Lena is, until the very end of the novel, very fleeting. He is quick to recall his straying emotions by employing one of his father's aphorisms any time he detects that his will to "look on, make no sound" is seriously weakened. Even after he has seemingly committed himself to assume an important role in Lena's destiny, he is "hurt by the sight of his own life, which ought to have been a masterpiece of aloofness" (XV, 174). He still believes what his father has written, that "of the strategems of life the most cruel is the consolation of love" (XV, 219), and he assiduously cultivates "that form of contempt which is called pity" (XV, 174) in order to keep love from penetrating his heart. The philosophical writings of the elder Heyst contain in them no hint of cruelty, and the son's practice of his father's teachings is completely without malice; yet in Heyst's aloofness there is a selfishness which is inherently evil. Of course, this evil is most forcefully demonstrated in the death of Lena and the suicide of Heyst at the end of the novel, but there is a subtler representation of the sort of depraved being which Heyst's philosophy of detachment may make of him to be seen both in the relationship between Schomberg and his wife, and in the contrasting, but not wholly dissimilar interests which Schomberg and Heyst take in Lena.

1. *Schomberg*

The fat hotel owner and his wife act out a debased form of the
story of Lena and Heyst. Heyst is saved from spiritual ruin by
Lena's sacrificing her life; Schomberg is saved from certain
financial ruin by his wife's sacrificing her self-respect in helping
Heyst and Lena to escape. Heyst is attracted mainly by the sound
of Lena's voice and her seeming refinement, and Schomberg is
attracted by her physical charms, but each in his own way intends to
use Lena – Heyst to indulge himself in that form of contempt called pity, and Schomberg to satisfy his lust. When Heyst discovers
that human attachments frequently compound human suffering,
he decides that life is blighted, an experience with no promise or
joy. When Lena runs off with Heyst, Schomberg is also disillusioned, and he decides, as Heyst later does, that a contest
with Jones and his followers is hardly worth the trouble:

Instead of caring for no one, he felt that he cared for nothing. Life
was a hollow sham; he wasn't going to risk a shot through his lungs
or his liver in order to preserve its integrity. It had no savour –
damn it! (XV, 109)

Heyst and Schomberg, of course, have very little in common intellectually or morally, but Schomberg's despicable self-indulgence provides an insight into Heyst's distrust of life – a selfishness
no less sinister because its basis is rational rather than physical.
When Heyst, describing himself as a man of "universal scorn and
unbelief" (XV, 199), tells Lena about Morrison, he says: "I have
never been so amused as by that episode in which I was suddenly
called to act such an incredible part. For a moment I enjoyed it
greatly. I got him out of his corner, you know" (XV, 199). To
Heyst, the saving of Morrison is clearly no more important than
the act of feeding a stray dog. In his rationality Heyst views human
beings as ciphers, as nameless and insignificant victims of the
"Great Joke" (XV, 198). Lena, however, is aghast at the cruelty
and egoism of Heyst's dealing with Morrison: "You saved a man
for fun – is that what you mean? Just for fun?" (XV, 199). She
easily perceived the evil inherent in Schomberg's lust for her, and

she just as easily perceives that Heyst's gratifying himself by helping Morrison is but a subtly disguised form of cruelty.

Aided by Mrs. Schomberg, whose shawl wrapped around Lena's few belongings becomes a symbol of female sacrifice, just as the knife does which Lena takes from Ricardo, Heyst carries Lena off to Samburan, a place where he believes he "can safely defy the fates" (XV, 57). He thinks he can avoid evil by seeking geographic isolation; he does not yet know that the destructive element can be escaped neither by moral nor physical isolation, that it is an omnipresent element which cannot be avoided, because man carries it in his own breast. Samburan, with its deserted mine, its buildings decaying, and the "gigantic and funereal blackboard sign of the Tropical Belt Coal Company, still emerging from a wild growth of bushes like an inscription stuck above a grave" (XV, 42), images the desolation of Heyst's soul. This desert island is not an Eden alive with the promise of life, but a desolate place where reign death and decay, the negations of life and fruitfulness.

2. Wang

Aside from the natives, who avoid the white man's side of the island, Heyst lives alone on Samburan with his Chinese servant Wang, the only one of the Chinese mine workers who chose to remain after the Tropical Belt Coal Company dissolved. Wang, like "Number One", his name for Heyst, is also "invulnerable because elusive". Why he chose to remain on Samburan while his countrymen left is never fully explained. He has taken a native woman as his wife, but Wang's reason for staying behind seems too complex to be explained by his marriage to the Alfuro woman. In any case the reasons behind Wang's decision are not of primary interest. He is important only in his function as a symbolic character who gives the reader further insight into the essential nature of Heyst's moral isolation. Schomberg, though he has little in common with Heyst, sheds some light on the internal psychology of the enchanted man. Wang, who has much in common with "Number One", further illuminates Heyst's soul.

When Lena has been on the island with Heyst only a few days, she becomes aware of Wang's unnatural presence. During a conversation between Lena and Heyst which Heyst concludes with the words "Nothing can break in on us here" (XV, 223), the outer world, in the form of Wang, does break in on them. As Heyst reaches out to embrace Lena, she draws away: "He had just felt the clasp of her arms round his neck, when, with a slight exclamation 'He's here!' – she disengaged herself and bolted away into her room" (XV, 223). Though Heyst is outraged with Wang, the servant has had good reason to disturb his master. He has come to report that he has sighted a boat in the straits surrounding Samburan, the boat, as it is later revealed, which carries Jones and his devilish crew. Dramatically, then, Wang's interruption represents no violation of probability. Psychologically, Wang's entry at this crucial moment is highly significant, for he is a symbol of Heyst's scorn of life which would keep him from embracing Lena.

Heyst, ever seeking to justify himself, reveals that he stays in the islands because to stay is the easiest course:

He was no longer enchanted, though he was still a captive of the islands. He had no intention to leave them ever. Where could he have gone to, after all these years? Not a single soul belonging to him lived anywhere on earth. Of this fact – not such a remote one, after all – he had only lately become aware. (XV, 66)

Wang, also alone, rationalizes his fears into duties and decides that his easiest course is the abandonment of Heyst to Jones and his partners:

The graves of Wang's ancestors were far away, his parents were dead, his elder brother was a soldier in the yamen of some Mandarin away in Formosa. No one near by had a claim on his veneration or his obedience. He had been for years a labouring, restless vagabond. His only tie in the world was the Alfuro woman, in exchange for whom he had given away some considerable part of his hard-earned substance; and his duty, in reason, could be to no one but himself. (XV, 307)

Like Heyst, who would surround his life with a wall of scorn and indifference, Wang surrounds himself and his Alfuro woman with a flimsy bamboo fence (XV, 225). Both Wang and his master attempt to separate themselves from the human community with barriers which would be laughably absurd were not their psychological significance so tragic.

Afraid of the white men who have intruded upon the quiet decay of Samburan, Wang decides that "Number One" must fend for himself. He steals Heyst's revolver, the only firearm on the island except for Jones's arsenal, and retreats to the village of his wife. When Heyst exhausts every other possibility of dealing with Jones and Ricardo, he decides that he and Lena must also seek refuge in the Alfuro village. As Heyst and Lena struggle up the narrow path to the native village, they encounter a barricade of felled trees which the natives have constructed to isolate themselves from the white man. Heyst's explanation to Lena of this manifestation of the natives' superstition is also a partial explanation of the barrier which he has erected around his own emotions, though he does not, of course, realize it:

"This", Heyst explained in his urbane tone, "is a barrier against the march of civilisation. The poor folk over there did not like it, as it appeared to them in the shape of my company – a great step forward, as some people used to call it with mistaken confidence. The advanced foot has been drawn back, but the barricade remains. . . . It's a very ridiculous thing", Heyst went on; "but then it is the product of honest fear – fear of the unknown, of the incomprehensible. It's pathetic, too, in a way. And I heartily wish, Lena, that we were on the other side of it." (XV, 344)

As Heyst approaches the barricade alone, Lena sees Wang's face appear between the logs:

In a spot facing Heyst a pair of yellow hands parted the leaves, and a face filled the small opening – a face with very noticeable eyes. It was Wang's face, of course, with no suggestion of a body belonging to it, like those cardboard faces at which she remembered gazing as a child in the window of a certain dim shop kept by a mysterious little man in Kingsland Road. Only this face, instead of mere holes, had eyes which blinked. She could see the beating of the eyelids. The hands on each side of the face, keeping the boughs apart, also did not look as if they belonged to any real body. (XV, 345)

Wang seems to have no body because his isolation is, like Heyst's, solely the result of ratiocination. Were he to permit his emotions to take a part in dictating his course of action, he would help "Number One" in his struggle against Jones. However, ruled by his self-interest, which he rationalizes into duty, Wang retreats from a commitment which has the potential of causing him physical and intellectual suffering. After Wang has stolen the revolver, but before he has retreated to the native village, he tells Heyst that he is leaving: "Me no likee. One man, two man, thlee man – no can do! Me go now" (XV, 310). Heyst attempts to dissuade him, at the same time thinking that he and Wang are quite different in their approach to life: "Through his mind flashed the hope that something enlightening might come from that being so unlike himself, taking contact with the world with a simplicity and directness of which his own mind was not capable" (XV, 310). Heyst can perceive Wang's oversimplified approach to life, but he cannot detect his own. Like his father, like another famous skeptical philosopher, Thomas Hobbes, Heyst ignores the beauties of human existence to dwell on the nastiness and brutishness of man's abbreviated life.

C. THE EDEN MYTH

Nasty and brutish Heyst's life might have become had he been left to his own rational devices. Had Jones and his murdering crew never arrived at Samburan, Heyst's destiny might have taken quite another turn. It is conceivable that he would have begun to scorn Lena, who had trapped him into committing himself to an attachment which he could only conceive as meaningless. The scorn could shade into indifference, and Heyst might have resumed his wandering, smug in the egoistic pleasures of his fugitive and cloistered rationality. But to the isolated island of Samburan comes the outside world in the person of "plain Mr. Jones" – the destructive element which, paradoxically, is necessary to make Heyst aware of the dream.

1. *Jones as Satan*

Conrad's characterization of Jones is one of his greatest achievements, for Jones functions not only as the embodied evil of the world, but as a psychological double for Heyst, all the while remaining probable as a flesh and blood human being. Jones as evil incarnate utters, in dramatic situations subtly structured to make his speeches probable, words bearing an archetypal association with the prince of darkness. When Schomberg's launch draws alongside the mailboat which carries Jones, the latter leans over the rail and, exhibiting what seems a preternatural knowledge, calls Schomberg by name. When he registers at the hotel, he informs Schomberg that he is "plain Mr. Jones, a gentleman at large" (XV, 103). His voice is "hollow, . . . distant, uninterested, as though he were speaking from the bottom of a well" (XV, 110). When he speaks to Schomberg to tell him that he is no ordinary gentleman, his voice seems to imply "some sort of menace from beyond the grave" (XV, 112).

Either as a vagabond gambler or a mythic merchant of evil, Mr. Jones is little interested in Schomberg. This gentleman who resembles an "insolent spectre on leave from Hades" (XV, 116) becomes bored unless he is engaged in a contest of wits; thus, his decision to go to Samburan on the basis of Schomberg's rather far-fetched tale of Heyst's hoarded wealth is psychologically probable. Jones actually seems to be more interested in a contest with Heyst than in the treasure.

Out of the sea surrounding Samburan, out of the "flaming abyss of emptiness" (XV, 216) come Jones, Ricardo, and Pedro to test the soul of Axel Heyst. At this point in the narrative there is an intensification of Jones's identity as Satan. The night descends on Samburan as the evil trio land, and they seem to Heyst to be not human beings but symbols of the life which he has attempted to escape:

From the first he was positive that these men were not sailors. They wore the white drill suit of tropical civilisation; but their apparition in a boat Heyst could not connect with anything plausible. The civilisation of the tropics could have had nothing to do with it. It was more like those myths, current in Polynesia, of amazing strangers, who arrive at an island, gods or demons, bringing good or evil to the innocence of the inhabitants – gifts of unknown things, words never heard before. (XV, 228)

When Heyst asks his spectral visitor who he is and where he has come from, Jones simply replies: "I am he who is –" (XV, 317). Jones further identifies himself as a gentleman who "having been ejected ... from his proper social sphere because he had refused to conform to certain usual conventions", is now a rebel "coming and going up and down the earth" (XV, 317). Heyst sees Jones and his crew as "envoys of the outer world" (XV, 329), and Jones, in a later conversation with Heyst, echoes these words:

"I, my dear sir? In one way I am – yes, I am the world itself, come to pay you a visit. In another sense I am an outcast – almost an outlaw. If you prefer a less materialistic view, I am a sort of fate – the retribution that waits its time." (XV, 379)

Jones is, then, a symbol of ultimate evil, "a person to be reckoned with" (XV, 378). He is also subtly identified with the particular evil which rules the soul of Axel Heyst. Both Heyst and Jones are "gentlemen". Jones is a wanderer "going up and down the earth", and Heyst has deliberately become a "waif and stray" (XV, 92). Heyst believes the world to be a bad dog, a factory where wages are paid in counterfeit money (XV, 196). Jones has decided that in order to protect himself he must act "as if the world were still one great, wild jungle without law" (XV, 113). Ricardo must constantly devise new stratagems of evil to keep his gentleman from becoming bored, all the while recognizing that Jones participates in them only "as a sort of sport" (XV, 260). Significantly, Heyst has described his relationship with Morrison as a sort of sport: "I have never been so amused as by that episode... Funny position, wasn't it? The boredom came later" (XV, 199).

Jones is very near the truth when he says to Heyst: "We pursue the same ends ... only perhaps I pursue them with more openness than you – with more simplicity" (XV, 320). Jones has listened to the lies about Heyst which Schomberg has spread, and he believes that Heyst has, indeed, stolen a great deal of money from Morrison. Thus Jones's words, in which he identifies Heyst as a fellow thief, are particularly probable in the dramatic situation. They also carry a significance far beyond what either Jones or Heyst realizes at the moment. That is, Heyst is potentially as evil as Jones in making his scornful individual consciousness the sole arbiter of his action. Jones is a thief and a murderer just for fun; Heyst tampers with the lives of his fellow human beings just for fun.

When Jones, Ricardo, and Pedro land on Samburan, Lena, sensitive to the breach of traditional morality which she has committed in coming to live with Heyst, wonders whether the troubles which the evil trio has brought with it are not a form of punishment. Heyst is amused at her naiveté:

"What? Are our visitors then messengers of morality, avengers of righteousness, agents of Providence? That's certainly an original view. How flattered they would be if they could hear you!" (XV, 354)

But Jones and his followers are indeed "messengers of morality" – not protectors of the marriage code, to be sure, but emissaries of darkness whose complete evil will, paradoxically, save the soul of Axel Heyst.

2. *Heyst and Lena as Adam and Eve*

To make Heyst's redemption clearer on the individual level, and to demonstrate the universal significance of the knowledge which Heyst attains at the last, Conrad subtly employs the myth of the Garden of Eden. He does not, however, force his characters to assume allegorical roles which violate the probabilities of character and action; rather, he shows the characters which he has constructed with assiduous attention to reality, fulfilling their inevitable individual and symbolic roles.

The variety of epithets applied to Heyst early in the story would seem to make him a sort of symbol of all humanity. He is "Hard Facts" (XV, 8) Heyst, "Enchanted Heyst" (XV, 7), "Heyst the

Spider" (XV, 21), "Heyst the Enemy (XV, 24) – alternately, depending upon the observer, a rationalist, a romantic, a materialist, or a criminal – in short, a universal man. As Heyst meditates on the nature of his existence, he reflects: "There must be a lot of the original Adam in me, after all", and he realizes that "this primeval ancestor is not easily suppressed", that "the oldest voice in the world is just the one that never ceases to speak" (XV, 173). The epithet which Wang applies to Heyst also serves to establish the ruler of Samburan as an archetype of the first man. While the Tropical Belt Coal Company was still carrying on mining operations, Heyst was the chief supervising officer, and, as such, was referred to by the Chinese coolies as "Number One". When his countryman have left, Wang continues to refer to Heyst as "Number One", though the title has ceased to have any meaning in a realistic sense. Wang's repetition of this epithet, however, is highly significant symbolically.

Lena, the orphan from the streets of London, becomes the symbol of universal woman – self-sacrificing, and able to perceive the essentials of character and situation by sheer intuiton. As Eve was born out of Adam's lonely thoughts, Lena feels her existence depends upon Heyst. She says to him: "Do you know, it seems to me, somehow, that if you were to stop thinking of me I shouldn't be in the world at all!" (XV, 187). The unique isolation of the island of Samburan also strikes Lena: "Here we are, we two alone, and I can't even tell where we are." "A very well-known spot of the globe", replies Heyst (XV, 188). Near the end of the novel Heyst playfully says to Lena: "I wonder . . . whether you are just a little child, or whether you represent something as old as the world" (XV, 359).

Lena, like her original, offers the fruit of the tree of knowledge to her mate, but in Conrad's retelling of the myth of Eden, the knowledge of good and evil is not a curse; it offers life instead of death. Lena tramples the serpent beneath her foot and redeems Heyst from the living death which has been his existence.

3. Ricardo's knife as a symbol of death

Late the night Jones and Ricardo arrive, Lena awakes with a start to find Heyst rummaging through the drawers of his desk. He is searching for the revolver which Wang has stolen, but he does not reveal this to her. Her remarks at this point carry a powerful double meaning. Frightened by Heyst's stealthy movements, she says in a whisper: "You are looking for something", and twice repeats the question: "What is it you have missed?" (XV, 251) Heyst is need "looking for something" – the joy of life which he has never tasted. This, too, is what he has missed. With Wang's theft of the revolver, Heyst, who has been morally disarmed all his life, becomes physically disarmed, and Lena decides she must provide him with some means to protect himself. She decides she must steal Ricardo's knife and give it to Heyst.

When Heyst finally decides he must confront the villains, he gives Lena a set of complicated instructions to insure her safety. She is to put on a black dress, cover her face with a veil, and hide in the jungle until Heyst gives her the signal to return to the house.[7] When Heyst leaves, however, she does not flee to the jungle, but clothed as if for a wedding with death, waits for Ricardo, hoping to charm his knife from him. She thinks not of her own life but of Heyst's safety: "She saw only her purpose of capturing death – savage, sudden, irresponsible death, prowling round the man who possessed her; death embodied in the knife ready to strike into his heart" (XV, 394).

---

[7]   Albert Guerard, *Conrad the Novelist* (Cambridge, 1958), who believes that "the time has come to drop *Victory* from the Conrad canon" (p. 275), damns the scene in which Heyst gives Lena her instructions as a failure of Conrad's imaginative power, as a lapse in "common sense" (p. 261). Heyst tells Lena: "Wait in the forest till the table is pushed into full view of the doorway, and you see three candles out of four blown out and one relighted – or, should the lights be put out here while you watch them, wait till three candles are lighted and then two put out. At either of these signals run back as hard as you can, for it will mean that I am waiting for you here" (XV, 372). The instructions are, indeed, almost incomprehensibly complicated, but it would be difficult to imagine how Conrad could better demonstrate that Heyst is a man who has "lost the habit of asserting himself", not the "courage

Ricardo has been in the house only a few moments before Lena has the knife: "She had done it! The very sting of death was in her hands; the venom of the viper in her paradise, extracted, safe in her possession – and the viper's head all but lying under her heel." Of course, the knife would be of little help to Heyst against the firearms of Jones and Ricardo. He could make better use of a club fashioned from a tree limb or various other make-shift weapons which he might find lying about the deserted mine. But the value of the knife as an illusion which represents a victory over the forces of evil is inestimable. Heyst is no longer a "disarmed man" when Lena hands the knife to him with the words: "Kill nobody" (XV, 405).

As Heyst rushes into his bedroom after Ricardo has fled, he rips down the curtain which hangs in the doorway (XV, 404), and in so doing he tears away the veil of skepticism which has smothered his moral vision. He is now caught up in the power of Lena's illusion. He has, through her, mastered the sting of death, since he has discovered that life is not a meaningless joke, but an experience which can be made beautiful and significant by the force of the human spirit.

Lena, fatally wounded by Jones, dies, and Heyst, because of what she has come to mean to him both as a person and as the symbol of the illusion whose force he has lately discovered, kills himself. His last words represent his victory. Though he has only briefly experienced the reality of life, he now possesses a full knowledge of its meaning: "Ah, Davidson, woe to the man whose heart has not learned while young to hope, to love – and to put its trust in life!"

Lena is dead. Heyst has killed himself. Wang, in a desperate attempt to insure that the renegades will not come around to the other side of the island and attack the native village, has shot

---

of self-assertion either moral or physical, but the mere way of it, the trick of the thing, the readiness of mind and the turn of the hand that come without reflection" (XV, x). Conrad, with his twenty years of experience in giving and following orders, was well aware that even the simplest of instructions could be misinterpreted. The absurdity of Heyst's directions to Lena is clearly intentional, and Professor Guerard would seem to be criticizing Conrad for one of the excellences of *Victory*.

Pedro, who was guarding the boat. Yet, in spite of this great welter of blood, the ending of *Victory* is not melodramatic. Good has triumphed and evil has consumed itself in perfect consistency with the fictional world which Conrad has created.[8]

In *Victory*, written relatively late in his writing career, as in *Almayer's Folly*, his first novel, Conrad has successfully created a world containing the truth of human experience. And though never faithful to any of the temporary formulas of the writer's craft, he has consistently employed symbols of his own creation, has breathed new life into archetypal patterns, and has revealed something of the mystery surrounding all existence. He has, by the power of the written word, made us hear, feel, see. "That and no more, and it is everything."

[8] Walter Wright explains Heyst's suicide: "The destiny of Heyst is laid down in the beginning, and there is no revolution of personality at the end. In every crisis Heyst has shed the skepticism with which he has tried to cloak himself. After each experience of yielding to natural human impulse he has attempted to wrap the skepticism around him more tightly than before. Does he not shed it now for the last time simply because he knows that not it but the imagination, which has drawn him to others, is the way to truth?" (Wright, *Romance and Tragedy in Joseph Conrad*, p. 106). As for Jones, he does not die of spontaneous combustion like Krook in *Bleak House*. In Conrad's descriptions of Jones as a walking skeleton, a living image of death, there is sufficient evidence that Jones is, in fact, a very sick man. The trip to Samburan nearly killed him, and once there he spends all but a few hours in bed. On the realistic level, he dies because he is a sick man; on the symbolic level he dies because Lena has vanquished the ultimate negation for which he stands.

BIBLIOGRAPHY

BOOKS

Allen, Walter, "Joseph Conrad", *Six Great Novelists* (London, 1955).

Baines, Jocelyn, *Joseph Conrad, A Critical Biography* (Bungay, Suffolk, 1960).

Bancroft, William Wallace, *Joseph Conrad: His Philosophy of Life* (Boston, 1933).

Beach, Joseph Warren, "Impressionism: Conrad", *The Twentieth Century Novel* (New York, 1932).

Bendz, Ernst, *Joseph Conrad: An Appreciation* (Gothenburg, 1923).

Bradbrook, Muriel C., *Joseph Conrad: Poland's English Genius* (Cambridge, 1942).

Butcher, S. H., *Aristotle's Theory of Poetry and Fine Art* (New York, 1951).

Campbell, Joseph, *The Hero with a Thousand Faces* (New York, 1956).

Carlyle, Thomas, "Labour", *Prose of the Victorian Period,* ed. William E. Buckler (Boston, 1958).

Conrad, Jessie, *Joseph Conrad and His Circle* (New York, 1935).

Conrad, Joseph, *Complete Works,* 26 vols. (Garden City, N. Y., 1926).

    III.   *Notes on Life and Letters*
    IV.   *The Mirror of the Sea*
    VI.   *A Personal Record*
    VIII.   *Tales of Unrest*
    IX.   *Nostromo*
    X.   *Within the Tides*
    XI.   *Almayer's Folly*
    XIII.   *The Secret Agent*
    XV.   *Victory*
    XVI.   *Youth: A Narrative, and Two Other Stories*
    XVII.   *The Shadow Line*
    XIX.   *'Twixt Land and Sea*
    XX.   *Typhoon and other Stories*
    XXI.   *Lord Jim*
    XXII.   *Under Western Eyes*
    XXIII.   *The Nigger of the "Narcissus"*
    XXVI.   *Tales of Hearsay*

——, *The Secret Sharer* (New York, 1955) (Signet Edition).

——, *Conrad to a Friend: 150 Selected Letters from Joseph Conrad to Richard Curle*, ed. Richard Curle (London, 1928).

——, *Last Essays* (London, 1926).

——, *Letters from Joseph Conrad: 1895-1924*, ed. Edward Garnett (Indianapolis, Indiana, 1928).

——, *Letters from Joseph Conrad to Marguerite Poradowska, 1890-1920*, ed. John A. Gee and Paul J. Sturm (New Haven, Conn., 1940).

——, *Letters of Joseph Conrad to Richard Curle*, ed. Richard Curle (New York, 1928).

——, *Notes by Joseph Conrad Written in a Set of His First Editions in the Possession of Richard Curle*, ed. Richard Curle (London, 1925).

——, *Conrad's Prefaces*, ed. Edward Garnett (London, 1937).

Crankshaw, Edward, *Joseph Conrad: Some Aspects of the Art of the Novel* (London, 1936).

Curle, Richard, *Joseph Conrad and his Characters* (Fair Lawn, N. J., 1958).

——, *The Last Twelve Years of Joseph Conrad* (London, 1928).

Ford, Ford Madox, *Joseph Conrad: A Personal Remembrance* (Boston, 1924).

Forster, E. M., "Joseph Conrad: A Note", *Abinger Harvest* (New York, 1936).

Gillon, Adam, *The Eternal Solitary: A Study of Joseph Conrad* (New York, 1960).

Gordon, John D., *Joseph Conrad: The Making of a Novelist* (Cambridge, Mass., 1940).

Guerard, Albert J., *Conrad the Novelist* (Cambridge, Mass., 1958).

——, *Joseph Conrad (Direction Series, No. 1)* (New York, 1947).

Harkness, Bruce, *Conrad's "Heart of Darkness" and the Critics* (San Francisco, 1960).

Haugh, Robert, *Joseph Conrad: Discovery in Design* (Norman, Okla., 1957).

Hewitt, Douglas, *Conrad: A Reassessment* (Cambridge, 1952).

Jean-Aubry, Gerard, *Joseph Conrad: Life and Letters*, 2 vols. (Garden City, N. Y., 1927).

——, *The Sea Dreamer*, trans. Helen Sebba (Garden City, N. Y., 1957).

Karl, Frederick, *A Reader's Guide to Joseph Conrad* (New York, 1960).

Lawrence, D. H., *Studies in Classic American Literature* (Garden City, N.Y., 1953).

Leavis, F. R., *The Great Tradition* (New York, 1948).

Megroz, R. L., *Joseph Conrad's Mind and Method* (London, 1931).

Mencken, H. L., "Joseph Conrad", *A Book of Prefaces* (New York, 1917).

Morf, Gustav, *The Polish Heritage of Joseph Conrad* (London, 1930).

Moser, Thomas, *Joseph Conrad, Achievement and Decline* (Cambridge, Mass., 1957).

Retinger, J. H., *Conrad and His Contemporaries* (New York, 1943).

Stallman, Robert, ed., *Joseph Conrad: A Critical Symposium* (Ann Arbor, Mich., 1960).

Stauffer, Ruth, *Joseph Conrad: His Romantic-Realism* (Boston, 1922).

Symons, Arthur, *Notes on Joseph Conrad with Some Unpublished Letters* (London, 1925).

Tindall, William York, "Apology for Marlow", *From Jane Austen to Joseph Conrad* (Minneapolis, Minn., 1959).

Van Ghent, Dorothy, "'On Lord Jim'", *The English Novel: Form and Function* (New York, 1953).

Walpole Hugh, *Joseph Conrad* (New York, 1916).

Warner, Oliver, *Joseph Conrad* (Bristol, 1951).

Wiley, Paul, *Conrad's Measure of Man* (Madison, Wis., 1954).

Wright, Walter, *Romance and Tragedy in Joseph Conrad* (Lincoln, Nebr., 1949).

Zabel, Morton, Introduction to *The Portable Conrad* (New York, 1952).

ARTICLES

Bache, William B., "*Othello* and Conrad's *Chance*", *Notes and Queries,* n.s., II (1955), 478–479.

Benson, Carl, "Conrad's Two Stories of Initiation", *P. M. L. A.,* LXIX (1954), 45-56.

Bojarski, Edmund A., "Joseph Conrad, Alias 'Polish Joe'", *English Studies in Africa,* V (1962), 59–60.

Brown, E. K., "James and Conrad", *Yale Review,* XXXV (1945), 265-285.

Burkhart, Charles, "Conrad the Victorian", *English Literature in Transition* (1880–1920), VI (1963), 1–8.

Collins, Harold R., "Kurtz, the Cannibals and the Second Rate Helmsman", *Western Humanities Review,* VIII (1954), 299-310.

Cook, Albert, "Conrad's Void", *Nineteenth Century Fiction,* XII (1957), 326-330.

Cox, Roger L., "Nostromo as Boatswain", *Modern Language Notes,* LXXIV (1959), 303-306.

Cross, Wilbur, "The Illusions of Joseph Conrad", *Yale Review,* XVII (1928), 464-482.

Cutler, Francis W., "Why Marlow?", *Sewanee Review,* XXVI (1918), 28-38.

Dale, Patricia, "Conrad: A Borrowing from Hazlitt's Father", *Notes and Queries,* X (1963), 146.

Davidson, Donald, "Joseph Conrad's Directed Indirections", *Sewanee Review,* XXXVIII (1925), 163-177.

Davis, Harold E., "Symbolism in *The Nigger of the 'Narcissus'* ", *Twentieth Century Literature,* II (1956), 26-29.

Dean, Leonard F., "Tragic Pattern in Conrad's 'Heart of Darkness'", *College English,* VI (1944), 100-104.

Dowden, Wilfred. "The Light and the Dark; Imagery and Thematic Development in Conrad's 'Heart of Darkness', *Rice Institute Pamphlet,* XLIV (1957), 33–51.

Evans, Robert O., "Conrad's Underworld", *Modern Fiction Studies,* II (1956), 56–62.

——, "Further Comment on 'Heart of Darkness' ", *Modern Fiction Studies,* III (1957), 358-360.

Feder, Lillian, "Marlow's Descent into Hell", *Nineteenth Century Fiction,* IX (1955), 280-292.

Gatch, Katherine, "Conrad's Axel", *Studies in Philology,* XLVIII (1951), 98-106.

Gillon, Adam, "Betrayal and Redemption in Joseph Conrad", *Polish Review,* V (1960), 18-35.

Gleckner, Robert F., "Conrad's 'Lagoon' ", *Explicator,* XVI (1958), Item 33.

Goetsch, Paul, "Joseph Conrad: *The Secret Agent", Die neueren Sprachen,* No. 3, (1963), 97–110.

Gose, Elliot B. Jr., " 'Cruel Devourer of the World's Light': *The Secret Agent", Nineteenth Century Fiction,* XV (1960), 39–51.

Gossman, Ann M., and George W. Whiting, "The Essential Jim", *Nineteenth Century Fiction,* XVI (1961), 75-80.

Graver, Lawrence, "Conrad's 'The Lagoon' ", *Explicator,* XXI (1963), Item 70.

Green, Jesse D., "Diabolism, Pessimism, and Democracy: Notes on Melville and Conrad", *Modern Fiction Studies,* VIII (1962), 287-305.

Greenberg, Robert, "The Presence of Mr. Wang", *Boston University Studies in English,* IV (1960), 129-137.

Gross, Seymour L., "The Devil in Samburan: Jones and Ricardo in *Victory", Nineteenth Century Fiction,* XVI (1961), 81-85.

——, "A Further Note on the Function of the Frame in 'Heart of Darkness' ", *Modern Fiction Studies,* III (1957), 167–170.

——, "Hamlet and Heyst Again", *Notes and Queries,* n.s., VI (1959), 87-88.

Guerard, Albert, "The Nigger of the 'Narcissus' ", *Kenyon Review,* XIX (1957), 205–232.

Gullason, Thomas, "Conrad's 'The Lagoon' ", *Explicator,* XIV (1956), Item 23.

Gurko, Leo, "Death Journey in *The Nigger of the 'Narcissus' ", Nineteenth Century Fiction,* XVI (1961), 75-80.

——, "*The Secret Agent:* Conrad's Vision of Megapolis", *Modern Fiction Studies,* IV (1958), 307-318.

——, "*Under Western Eyes* and the Question of Where To?", *College English,* XXI (1959), 445-452.

Hagan, John, Jr., "The Design of Conrad's *Secret Agent", Journal of English Literary History,* XXII (1955), 148-164.

Harkness, Bruce, "The Epigraph of Conrad's *Chance", Nineteenth Century Fiction,* IX (1954), 209-222.

Haugh, Robert L., "Joseph Conrad and Revolution", *College English,* X (1949), 273-277.

——, "The Structure of *Lord Jim", College English,* XIII (1951), 137-141.

Hertz, Robert, "The Scene of Mr. Verloc's Murder in *The Secret Agent:* A Study of Conrad's Narrative and Dramatic Method", *Personalist,* XLIII (1962), 214-225.

Hoffman, Charles G., "Point of View in 'The Secret Sharer' ", *College English,* XXIII (1962), 651-654.

Holmes, Karen Sue, "Lord Jim, Conrad's Alienated Man", *Descant,* IV (1959), 33-40.

Howe, Irving, "Order and Anarchy: The Political Novels", *Kenyon Review,* XV (1953), 505-521.

——, "The Political Novels II", *Kenyon Review,* XVI (1954), 1-19.

Hunt, Kellog, *"Lord Jim* and *The Return of the Native",* English Journal, XLIX (1959), 447-456.

Karl, Frederick R., "Conrad's Debt to Dickens", *Notes and Queries,* n.s., IV (1956), 398-400.

——, "Conrad's Stein: The Destructive Element", *Twentieth Century Literature,* III (1958), 163-169.

——, "Joseph Conrad and Huck Finn", *Mark Twain Journal,* XI (1960), 21-23.

——, "Joseph Conrad's Literary Theory", *Criticism,* II (1960), 317-335.

——, "The Rise and Fall of *Under Western Eyes",* Nineteenth Century Fiction XIII (1959), 313-327.

Leavis, F. R., "Joseph Conrad", *Sewanee Review,* LXVI (1958), 179-200.

Leiter, Louis, "Echo Structures: Conrad's 'The Secret Sharer' ", *Twentieth Century Literature,* V (1960), 159-175.

Levin, Gerald, "The Skepticism of Marlow", *Twentieth Century Literature,* III (1958), 177-184.

Lordi, R. J., "The Three Emissaries of Evil: Their Psychological Relationship in Conrad's *Victory",* College English, XXIII (1961), 136-140.

Lynskey, Winifred, "Conrad's *Nostromo",* Explicator, XIII (1954), Item 6.

——, "The Role of the Silver in *Nostromo",* Twentieth Century Fiction, II (1955), 16-21.

Marsh, D. R. C., "Moral Judgements in *The Secret Agent",* English Studies in Africa, III (1960), 57–70.

Martin, Sister M., "Conrad's 'Typhoon' ", *Explicator,* XVIII (1960), Item 57.

Masback, Frederick J., "Conrad's Jonahs", *College English,* XXII (1961), 328-333.

Maser, Frederick E., "The Philosophy of Joseph Conrad", *Hibbert Journal,* LVI (1957), 69-78.

McCann, Charles, "Conrad's 'The Lagoon' ", *Explicator,* XVIII (1959), Item 3.

Michel, Lois A., "The Absurd Predicament in Conrad's Political Novels", *College English,* XXIII (1961), 131-136.

Miller, James E., Jr., *"The Nigger of the 'Narcissus':* a Re-examination", *P. M. L. A.,* LXVI (1951), 911-918.

Morris, Robert L., "The Classical Reference in Conrad's Fiction", *College English,* VII (1946), 312-318.

Moyniham, William, "Conrad's 'The End of Tether': A New Reading", *Modern Fiction Studies,* IV (1958), 173-177.

Mudrick, Marvin, "Conrad and the Terms of Modern Criticism", *Hudson Review,* VII (1955), 419-426.

——, "The Originality of Conrad", *The Hudson Review,* XI (1958), 545-553.

Owen, Guy, Jr., "A Note on 'Heart of Darkness' ", *Nineteenth Century Fiction,* XII (1957), 168-169.

——, "Conrad's 'The Lagoon' ", *Explicator,* XVIII, (1960), Item 47.

Phillipson, John S., "Pink Toads: The Working of the Unconscious", *Western Humanities Review,* XIV (1960), 437-438.

Rawson, C. J., "Conrad's 'Heart of Darkness' ", *Notes and Queries,* n.s., VI (1959), 110-111.

Ridley, Florence H., "The Ultimate Meaning of 'Heart of Darkness' ", *Nineteenth Century Fiction,* XVII (1963), 43-53.

Robinson, Arthur, "The Secret Sharer", *Explicator,* XVIII (1960), Item 28.

Sherbo, Arthur, "Conrad's *Victory* and *Hamlet*", *Notes and Queries,* CXCVIII (1953), 492-493.

Sickels, Eleanor, "The Lagoon", *Explicator,* XV (1956), Item 17.

Smith, David R., "Nostromo and the Three Sisters", *Studies in English Literature 1500-1900,* II (1962), 497-508.

Stallman, Robert W., "Conrad and 'The Secret Sharer' ", *Accent,* IX (1949), 131-143.

——, "Conrad Criticism Today", *Sewanee Review,* LXVII (1959), 135-145.

——, "The Structure and Symbolism of Conrad's *Victory*", *Western Review,* XIII (1949), 146–157.

Stein, William Bysshe, "The Lotus Posture and 'Heart of Darkness' ", *Modern Fiction Studies,* II (1956), 235-237.

Thale, Jerome, "Marlow's Quest", *University of Toronto Quarterly,* XXIV (1955), 351-358.

Thompson, Alan, "The Humanism of Joseph Conrad", *Sewanee Review,* XXXVII (1929), 204-220.

Tick, Stanley, "Conrad's 'Heart of Darkness' ", *Explicator,* XXI (1963), Item 67.

Tillyard, E. M. W., "*The Secret Agent* Reconsidered", *Essays in Criticism,* XI (1961), 309–318.

Tomlinson, Maggie, "Conrad's Integrity: *Nostromo, Typhoon, The Shadow Line*", *Melbourne Critical Review,* V (1962), 40-53.

Wagenknecht, Edward, "Pessimism in Hardy and Conrad", *College English,* VI (1944), 100-104.

Warren, Robert Penn, "Nostromo", *Sewanee Review,* LIX (1951), 363-391.

Watt, Ian, "Conrad Criticism and *The Nigger of the 'Narcissus'* ", *Nineteenth Century Fiction,* XII (1958), 257-283.

——, "Story and Idea in Conrad's *The Shadow Line*", *Critical Quarterly,* II (1960), 133-148.

Webster, H. T., "Joseph Conrad: A Reinterpretation of Five Novels", *College English,* VII (1945), 125-134.

Whiting, George W., "Conrad's Devision of 'The Lighthouse' in *Nostromo", P. M. L. A.,* LII (1937), 1183-1190.

——, "Conrad's Revision of *Lord Jim", English Journal,* XXIII (1934), 824-832.

Widmer, Kingley, "Conrad's Pyrrhic Victory", *Twentieth Century Literature,* V (1959), 123–130.

Wilcox, Stewart, "Conrad's Complicated Presentations of Symbolic Imagery in 'Heart of Darkness' ", *Philological Quarterly,* XXXIX (1960), 1-17.

Wills, John Howard, "Conrads' *'The Secret Sharer' ", University of Kansas City Review,* XXVIII (1961), 115-126.

Wilson, Arthur H., "The Complete Narrative of Joseph Conrad", *Susquehenna University Studies,* IV (1951), 229-262.

——, "The Great Theme in Conrad", *Susquehenna University Studies,* V (1953), 51-84.

——, "Joseph Conrad's Children of Pan", *Susquehenna University Studies,* II (1941), 246-248.

Worth, George W., "Conrad's Debt to Maupassant in the Preface to *The Nigger of the 'Narcissus' ", Journal of English and German Philology,* LIV (1955), 700-704.

Wright, Walter F., "The Truth of My Own Sensations", *Modern Fiction Studies,* I (1955), 26-29.

Young, Vernon, "Joseph Conrad: Outline for a Reconsideration", *Hudson Review,* II (1949), 5-19.

——, "Lingard's Folly: The Lost Subject", *Kenyon Review,* XV (1953), 522-539.

——, "Trial by Water: Joseph Conrad's *The Nigger of the 'Narcissus' ", Accent,* XII (1952), 67-81.

Zabel, Morton, "Chance and Recognition", *Sewanee Review,* LIII 1945), 1-22.